PERPETRATION-INDUCED
TRAUMATIC STRESS

PERPETRATION-INDUCED TRAUMATIC STRESS

The Psychological Consequences of Killing

RACHEL M. MACNAIR

Psychological Dimensions to War and Peace
Harvey Langholtz, Series Editor

PRAEGER

Westport, Connecticut
London

Library of Congress Cataloging-in-Publication Data

MacNair, Rachel M.
    Perpetration-induced traumatic stress : the psychological consequences of killing /
Rachel M. MacNair.
        p.   cm.—(Psychological dimensions to war and peace, ISSN: 1540–5265)
    ISBN 0–275–97691–2 (alk. paper)
    1. Post-traumatic stress disorder.   2. Murderers—Psychology.   3.
Homicide—Psychological aspects.   I. Title.   II. Series.
    RC552.P67M393   2002
    616.85'21—dc21   2002025202

British Library Cataloguing in Publication Data is available.

Library of Congress Catalog Card Number: 2002025202
ISBN: 0–275–97691–2
ISSN: 1540–5265

First published in 2002

Praeger Publishers, 88 Post Road West, Westport, CT 06881
An imprint of Greenwood Publishing Group, Inc.
www.praeger.com

Printed in the United States of America

The paper used in this book complies with the
Permanent Paper Standard issued by the National
Information Standards Organization (Z39.48–1984).

10 9 8 7 6 5 4 3 2 1

Contents

Foreword

It is our goal in the series *Psychological Dimensions to War and Peace* to examine war and peace from at least two perspectives: at the national level, we consider the psychological processes that nations go through as they wage war or make peace; and at the individual level, we consider the psychological aspects of war and also its effects on the individual.

Posttraumatic Stress Disorder (PTSD) is a clinically recognized diagnosis and something that is now universally accepted as a predictable reaction to war or other stressful events. It seems axiomatic that the survivor of war or tragedy deserves to be accorded a measure of sympathy, and perhaps a diagnosis of PTSD can be considered a clinical expression of that sympathy for the victim based on what he or she has been through. The *Diagnostic and Statistical Manual of Mental Disorders* (1994) of the American Psychiatric Association and *International Statistical Classification of Diseases and Related Health Problems* (1992) of the World Health Organization both recognize PTSD, and the concept has found its way beyond psychology and into the public dialogue and the popular press.

But it may not at first be so easy to understand why a perpetrator might also suffer from symptoms that are similar to PTSD. After all, wasn't it the perpetrator who brought about the stress-inducing situation in the first place? Why should we feel sympathy for the perpetrator and how can he or she claim to be suffering from anything remotely like PTSD? And even if the perpetrator is suffering, isn't that perhaps some fair justice?

This is the point of Perpetration-Induced Traumatic Stress (PITS), and in *Perpetration-Induced Traumatic Stress: The Psychological Consequences of*

Killing, Rachel MacNair builds a logical argument that PITS should be considered by psychologists as they study the psychology of war and peace. Through analysis of the National Vietnam Veterans Readjustment Study data and an examination of literature and poetry that spans the Trojan War, Shakespeare, and modern warfare, the case is made convincingly that the perpetrator can develop clinical symptoms that are just as clear and just as real as the symptoms we have come to recognize as PTSD.

The case is also made that within a social and cultural context it is sometimes not so apparent who is the perpetrator and who is the victim. For example, in Chapter 9, we see the British veteran of the Anglo-Boer War who is considered a hero by poets and priests but yet is troubled because "they can't stop the eyes of the man I killed from starin' into mine" (Van Wyk Smith, 1978, p. 152). Is it not to be expected that a war veteran would be deeply troubled by such a memory? Why, until now, have psychologists and the general public associated PTSD with the victim only, and why have we not recognized that the act of perpetration, be it voluntary or forced, can also result in symptoms that are similar to PTSD?

MacNair conducts a thorough and dispassionate investigation into aspects of this question; readers may find some of her conclusions disturbing and others comforting. Can a person's professional position and function within society permit or even require them to take the life of another? And how should society view a person who has taken another's life, even in such a socially sanctioned way? It seems reassuring that a police officer is deeply troubled by the fact that he or she has killed someone in the line of duty. As citizens, we would not want a police officer who could dismiss such an act as simply part of the job and we would understand if such an officer subsequently suffered from PTSD-like symptoms. But would this be an example of Perpetration-Induced Traumatic Stress? What of the executioner or the soldier? Does society call on these individuals to take the life of another, and if they feel their perpetration has caused them trauma, is this evidence that PITS is an objectively observable phenomenon? The same questions are posed and examined regarding medical personnel involved in euthanasia or abortions, Nazi officials in the discharge of their duties, researchers whose experiments may harm subjects, and those who kill animals. Does the manifestation of PTSD-like symptoms for these individuals, who were never under any threat to their own lives, demonstrate that PITS is just as real as PTSD?

Nothing here is intended to argue the points of fault, blame, or guilt, nor to claim the mantle of victimhood for those who do not deserve it. The soldier is neither condemned as murderer, nor exalted as hero (although such opinions are examined). On the contrary, if there is a subtle form of vindictiveness that prevents us from acknowledging PITS because of an assumption that it is the perpetrator who is to blame, this bias is not perpetuated here. MacNair does not seek sympathy or forgiveness for the perpetrator, as this is not her purpose. Neither does she attempt to use PITS as a way to demonstrate that the perpetrator has done something wrong or immoral. There are many legal, social, political, and ethical issues that could be examined in light of PITS, but such examinations are left for the reader to consider.

To describe an individual as a "perpetrator" is to condemn them as guilty of wrongdoing, and it therefore seems somehow justified to not even consider the effects of the act of perpetration. In the pages that follow there is an effort to examine in an objective and blame-free way, the question of whether trauma can be the result of an act of perpetration.

Harvey Langholtz
Series Editor

Acknowledgments

I wish to thank Charles Sheridan for his expertise in the study of stress and for his lengthy mentoring of me through the initial stages of this work. James Collins and Jay Hewitt provided extensive help, especially in the area of statistics. Nicole English, with her expertise in computer software, provided indispensable assistance in converting the format of the National Vietnam Veterans Readjustment Study data from the SAS of the 1980s to the SPSS of the 1990s. Cathy Burnett was especially helpful in the study of capital punishment, and Patrick Peebles in the historical study of the Nazis. Peter Singelmann, Neil Bull, and James Galliher also helped with the sociological perspective. David Grossman, as an army officer, has written and presented on the idea of PTSD symptoms resulting from killing and has given valuable advice. He and Joanie Connors, Jean Maria Arrigo, David Lisak, William Chamberlin, and Gladys Frankl all helped bring about the symposium on this topic at the American Psychological Association in 2000, which generated a great deal of lively and helpful discussion.

I also want to thank the innumerable unnamed individuals, including scholars, veterans, and interested friends, who have listened to me discuss the subject and provided a wide variety of new ideas, leads, and perspectives. There were many who thought they were having only a casual conversation, or a chance to learn a little more themselves, but the collection of ideas over the years has made this book possible in a way that could never have happened otherwise.

Chapter 1

Perpetration-Induced Traumatic Stress

ACTIVE PARTICIPATION IN TRAUMA AS A CAUSE OF POSTTRAUMATIC STRESS DISORDER

The origins of the concept of Posttraumatic Stress Disorder (PTSD) are to be found in studies of combat veterans. In World War I, the term "shell shock" was used to describe the phenomenon, and it was essentially thought to be a physical problem. In World War II, it was called "battle fatigue" or "combat fatigue," and it was finally admitted to be psychological in origin. An even older term for it is "soldier's heart." All these terms are imprecise, which reflected the level of understanding people had at the time.

Since it was first officially defined, thousands of articles and many books have come out dealing with various aspects of PTSD. Much of the vast amounts of amassed literature has focused on people who had a trauma inflicted upon them by outside forces. In most cases, they were passive victims. In other cases, they were rescue workers or emergency personnel—people who help such victims. What of those who were active in traumatic circumstances, and helped bring them about? Does a situation that is traumatic enough to cause these symptoms require a lack of control? Does the element of control keep the situation from being a trauma? Alternatively, is it just as bad since the graphic and horrifying nature of the situation is the same, and these are the most important elements? As yet another possibility, the symptoms could actually be *more* severe: active participation accentuates the trauma.

Very little of the literature has considered PTSD symptomatology among perpetrators. Most of this scant literature has analyzed participation in "atrocities" during war, not simply the variable of whether or not a soldier had killed. Situations other than combat have been studied for victim or rescuer causal mechanisms, but not for that of the active perpetrator.

Around the beginning of the twentieth century, Jane Addams noted afteref-fects of having killed. Known for her innovations in social work, the reports from her investigations were anecdotal and primarily aimed at social change advocacy work rather than academic review. While she did publish some work in academic journals, such as the *American Journal of Sociology*, most of her writing is for the popular audience. Among the early builders of sociological theory, she was the only one who addressed and described PTSD directly. Though she did not have the terminology or contemporary concept yet, she was studying World War I at a time when the concept was beginning to form.

After documentation of men who refused to shoot to kill even in the trenches, she talked of insanity among the soldiers in various places, and of their being dazed after participating in attacks. She talks of hearing "from hospital nurses who said that delirious soldiers are again and again possessed by the same hallucination—that they are in the act of pulling their bayonets out of the bodies of men they have killed" (Johnson, 1960, p. 273). This is clearly symptom B(3) from the *DSM-IV* manual (listed also in the *ICD-10*; see the next section on definitions).

One book, *On Killing*, written by Lt. Col. David Grossman, an army psy-chology professor, deals with the subject in the sense Addams had in mind—both in that the psychological consequences of killing are studied, and in the view that more knowledge about this should lead to policy changes in society that would serve as prevention. Grossman (1995) has been in the army all of his adult life and, as such, comes to the question of PTSD as the result of killing in combat from a perspective different from peace activist Jane Addams. He has the advantage of all the conceptual work that has been done on PTSD as a diagnosis and he has the experience of later wars, especially the American war in Vietnam, to make his points. The purpose of his book was to study "the psychological and sociological processes and prices exacted when men kill each other in combat" (Grossman, 1995, p. xxi). Using a few quantitative studies by others to back up various points he makes, his is primarily a qualitative study based on a large number of interviews he conducted with veterans in his capacity as an army psychologist, along with written accounts of wartime experiences and their aftermath.

Grossman looks at the various conditions under which the immediate "psy-chiatric casualties" resulting from combat will be high or low. He debunks the original assumption that "battle fatigue" results from fear of injury or death. For example, the expectation of high civilian psychiatric casualties was behind the Nazi bombing of London, and the British and American bombing of Germany, but these turned out to be counterproductive. Psychiatric casualties were quite low, and the population strengthened its resolve. On the other hand, psychiatric casualties were high in the Nazi concentration camps. Grossman attributes the difference to the "Wind of Hate." Impersonal threats are not as unnerving as face-to-face hatred.

Most importantly, Grossman goes over evidence that the human being has a high resistance to killing. S.L.A. Marshall was an official army historian who did a study by interviewing soldiers after combat to ascertain exactly what they did. He found that only 15–20% of them ever shot their weapons. Even under situations of self-preservation, the resistance to killing is strong. While some have questioned Marshall's methodology, there are pieces of evidence from history that during and before World War II, the rates were similarly low. Given the technology and conditions of the time, there was only a fraction of people killed that would be expected.

Fear does not account for the nonfirers, for they did other combat duties that were amply dangerous. Furthermore, of those who do shoot, there is evidence that the majority intentionally aim high so that they will not actually kill anyone. There is a natural inclination to "posture" in the hope that actual killing can be avoided. Grossman concludes: "Looking another human being in the eye, making an independent decision to kill him, and watching as he dies due to your action combine to form the single most basic, important, primal, and potentially traumatic occurrence of war" (1995, p. 31).

As a result of changes in U.S. Army training techniques, those who did shoot during the war in Vietnam were up to 90–95% of the combatants. The military instituted training that was more realistic and therefore closer to operant conditioning. This worked, but at a price: "this program of desensitization, conditioning, and denial defense mechanisms, combined with subsequent participation in a war, may make it possible to share the guilt of killing without ever having killed" (Grossman, 1995, p. 260). While shooting did not itself mean killing— there were 50,000 bullets expended for every enemy soldier counted as killed— the same training that ensured greater efficiency in the short term also contributed to greater psychological costs in the long run.

In other literature, Green (1990) lists a set of categories for stressors that can cause PTSD, of which the eighth and final one is "causing death or severe harm to another." She notes, without references, that "causing death has been shown to predict worse psychological outcome" (p. 1638). A study of children in Kuwait following the Gulf Crisis (Nader et al., 1993) found that the highest PTSD scores were reported for those children who reported hurting someone else. Most works that suggest killing as a trauma focus on veterans, and will be covered in the next chapter.

The concept that perpetration is itself a form of suffering is not unusual in religious literature. For example, in the *Pastoral Constitution on the Church in the Modern World* put out by the Vatican, a list of different kinds of violence against people is offered with this conclusion: "They poison human society, and they do more to harm those who practice them than to those who suffer from the injury" (*Gaudium et Spes*, 1965, paragraph 22). In nonreligious but still soul-based argument, Socrates in Plato's *Gorgias* has a lengthy discourse on this point, which can be summarized when Socrates says, "You deemed Archelaus happy, because he was a very great criminal and unpunished. I, on the other hand, maintained that he or any other who like him has done wrong and has not been punished, is, and ought to be, the most miserable of all men; and that the doer of injustice is more miserable than the sufferer." The construct of Perpetration-Induced Traumatic Stress (PITS) could be interpreted as a psychological scientific way of operationalizing this view, thereby allowing a test of it as a hypothesis.

DEFINITIONS

One of the definitions of PTSD comes from the American Psychiatric Association and its *Diagnostic and Statistical Manual* (1994), currently in its fourth edition and usually referred to as *DSM-IV*. Another comes from the World Health Organization in its *International Statistical Classification of Diseases and Related Health Problems* (1992), currently in its tenth revision and normally referred to as *ICD-10*.

The symptoms of PTSD for psychiatric diagnosis from *DSM-IV*, Section 309.81, pp. 427–429, are listed below. Notes on variation for young children have been removed.

A. The person has been exposed to a traumatic event in which both of the following were present:
  1. the person experienced, witnessed, or was confronted with an event or events that involved actual or threatened death or serious injury, or a threat to the physical integrity of self or others; and
  2. the person's response involved intense fear, helplessness, or horror.

B. The traumatic event is persistently reexperienced in one (or more) of the following ways:
  1. recurrent and intrusive distressing recollections of the event, including images, thoughts, or perceptions.
  2. recurrent distressing dreams of the event. Note: In children, there may be frightening dreams without recognizable content.
  3. acting or feeling as if the traumatic event were recurring (includes a sense of reliving the experience, illusions, hallucinations, and dissociative flashback episodes, including those that occur on awakening or when intoxicated).
  4. intense psychological distress at exposure to internal or external cues that symbolize or resemble an aspect of the traumatic event.
  5. physiological reactivity on exposure to internal or external cues that symbolize or resemble an aspect of the traumatic event.

C. Persistent avoidance of stimuli associated with the trauma and numbing of general responsiveness (not present before the trauma), as indicated by three (or more) of the following:

    1. efforts to avoid thoughts, feelings, or conversation associated with the trauma

    2. efforts to avoid activities, places, or people that arouse recollections of the trauma

    3. inability to recall an important aspect of the trauma

    4. markedly diminished interest or participation in significant activities

    5. feeling of detachment or estrangement from others

    6. restricted range of affect (e.g., unable to have loving feelings)

    7. sense of a foreshortened future (e.g., does not expect to have a career, marriage, children, or a normal life span)

D. Persistent symptoms of increased arousal (not present before the trauma), as indicated by two (or more) of the following:

    1. difficulty falling or staying asleep

    2. irritability or outbursts of anger

    3. difficulty concentrating

    4. hypervigilance

    5. exaggerated startle response

E. Duration of the disturbance (symptoms in Criteria B, C, and D) is more than one month.

F. The disturbance causes clinically significant distress or impairment in social, occupational, or other important areas of functioning.

Specify if:

Acute: if duration of symptoms is less than three months

Chronic: if duration of symptoms is three months or more

Specify if:

With Delayed Onset: if onset of symptoms is at least six months after the stressor

In short, Criterion A requires a stressor, a trauma as a causal mechanism. The same symptoms from either an imaginary event or an event most people would not regard as traumatic would both be a different disorder. How A(2) fits in with the idea of active perpetration as that etiological stressor will be discussed in more detail in Chapter 8. The definition's Sections B, C, and D are regarded as symptom clusters—intrusion, avoidance and numbing, and arousal, respectively. Criterion E distinguished PTSD from an acute stress reaction, which normally subsides with time and is therefore treated differently. With PTSD, the passage of time has not been sufficient to alleviate the condition.

Criterion F, of course, is intended to specify that this is a diagnosable disorder. This is important for an official definition that can have legal consequences. Some veterans can get compensation. It has been used as a defense in court cases. Some people have been known to acquaint themselves with the symptoms and pretend to have the disorder because of possible legal or other benefits. The psychiatrists are also naturally of a clinical mindset, perceiving extreme cases and isolating a select portion of the population who require treatment.

It is very important to understand that for the purpose of this book, the perspective will be less clinical and more in accord with the presuppositions of social psychology. Posttrauma symptoms are seen on a continuum, with those actually having a full-blown disorder being on the extreme of the continuum. Those with lesser symptoms, or people who have symptoms but are not incapacitated to the level of a disorder, are still of interest. This is in part because the phenomenon of "subclinical" levels is still meaningful. For this reason, the idea of "partial PTSD" shows up in several sources, such as the United States government report of its study of Vietnam veterans on the subject (Kulka et al., 1990) or a study showing that suicide risk is elevated even in partial rather than full-blown PTSD (Marshall et al., 2001). These two sources do use clinical presuppositions, but use the concept of "partial" or "subthreshold" PTSD because they find it necessary in order to understand the actual impact of combat on veterans or the actual impact of trauma on suicidality and impairment in the general population. This approach of a continuum rather than a dichotomy is also important because a great deal of information can be gleaned with the use of the symptoms as a theme—information impossible to get if limited to diagnosed or diagnosable cases.

There are also some important features of the nature of the nightmares to add. One is that they are often eidetic—they are replays of the actual events, as if a videotape of the incident were playing in the head. This is not always the case, but it is especially characteristic of PTSD dreams. The other is that it is not uncommon for such dreams to be accompanied by thrashing around in the bed, having the kind of body movements that accord with feeling the kind of arousal or agitation that occur with such a dream.

The definition in *ICD-10*, F43.1 (p. 344) is in more of a narrative form:

Arises as a delayed or protracted response to a stressful event or situation (of either brief or long duration) of an exceptionally threatening or catastrophic nature, which is likely to cause pervasive distress in almost anyone. Predisposing factors, such as personality traits (e.g., compulsive, asthenic) or previous history of neurotic illness, may lower the threshold for the development of the syndrome or aggravate its course, but they are neither necessary nor sufficient to explain its occurrence. Typical features include episodes of repeated reliving of the trauma in intrusive memories ("flashbacks"), dreams or nightmares, occurring against the persisting background of a sense of "numbness" and emotional blunting, detachment from other people, unresponsiveness to surroundings, anhedonia, and avoidance of activities and situations reminiscent of the trauma. There is usually a state of autonomic hyperarousal with hypervigilance, and enhanced startle reaction, and insomnia. Anxiety and depression are commonly associated with the above symptoms and signs, and suicidal ideation is not infrequent. The onset follows the trauma with a latency period that may range from a few weeks to months. The course is fluctuating but recovery can be expected in the majority of cases. In a small proportion of cases the condition may follow a chronic course over many years, with eventual transition to an enduring personality change.

Anxiety and depression are actually separate phenomena, and as such they are not listed in the *DSM-IV* definition, but they are commonly recognized as associated, as the *ICD-10* says. Those diagnosing must differentiate between PTSD and closely related disorders connected to panic or anxiety, and these can be concurrent conditions. Alcohol and drug abuse are also clearly distinguished but very commonly associated with PTSD. All of these things—anxiety, panic, depression, substance abuse—can also be included in the "psychological consequences" of killing, along with such things as increased paranoia or a sense of disintegration, or dissociation or amnesia at the time of the trauma itself. All will be discussed in this book, but the focus is primarily on PTSD symptoms with perpetration as the causal stressor.

I have coined the term "Perpetration-Induced Traumatic Stress" (PITS) to describe this as a subcategory of PTSD. The term "perpetration-induced" was inspired from the following quotation, in which authors are discussing PTSD as a legal defense in criminal trials: "It must be able to be established . . . that PTSD existed at the time of the violent crime and did not stem from it, as in some perpetrator-induced trauma" (Hall & Hall, 1987, p. 49). This quotation involves an acknowledgment of the phenomenon of traumatic stress from being a perpetrator of crime, but the phrase was used without further analysis.

The word "disorder" has been dropped because the symptomatology is of psychological, sociological, and historical interest even if it does not rise to the level of a disorder. The committee deciding the official definition put the term "post" at the beginning of the title to indicate this as a chronic condition, not an acute one. Acute stress reactions can be expected to subside with time; it is when the same symptoms are chronic that the phenomenon of PTSD is recognized. However, for perpetrators, the condition could be chronic and yet still be ongoing, as with people responsible for years for carrying out executions. Accordingly, the term "post" is not as precise in this context.

This leaves the term as "Perpetration-Induced Traumatic Stress" (PITS). PITS involves any portions of the symptomatology of PTSD, at clinical or subclinical levels, which result from situations that would be traumatic if someone were a victim, but situations for which the person in question was a causal participant.

WHAT PTSD IS NOT

Many people become confused because the term "Posttraumatic Stress Disorder" sounds more comprehensive than it actually is, according to its definition. As mentioned above, posttrauma disorders can include alcohol or drug abuse problems, suicidal thoughts, panic attacks, depression, paranoia, and generalized anxiety. Psychiatrists or psychologists making a diagnosis would distinguish these things from a PTSD diagnosis, though of course they are commonly seen together.

PTSD is not the same as an acute reaction to trauma, which are the negative feelings a person can have right away. These are often remarkably similar to

PTSD symptoms, but over the course of time, they subside. If a person is suffering from these symptoms but mentions that the trauma occurred two weeks previously, he or she can be reassured that there is a good chance the distress is temporary. If the person says the trauma was twenty years ago, then the possibility of PTSD can certainly be considered. It is when symptoms do not subside, when time and normal supportive measures have not been enough, that PTSD might be a possibility.

Acute reactions can be associated with long-term responses, but not always. Not only do some of those with acute reactions find them to subside over time, but there are also those with long-term reactions who did not suffer symptoms at the time of the trauma itself. A delayed reaction is also common, as mentioned in the *DSM-IV* definition.

PTSD is not the same as grief, which also generally subsides over time. Grief is clearly a posttrauma reaction and as such, people who suffer grief sometimes refer to it as PTSD. The symptoms are different, and the treatment is different.

PTSD is not the distortion of time or sense of unreality at the time of the trauma, which is called peritraumatic dissociation. There is reason to believe that such dissociation at the time of the event makes later development of PTSD symptoms more likely, as found in combat veterans and rescue workers (Marmar et al., 1994; Marmar et al., 1996). However, it is not one of the symptoms itself. Feelings of dissociation long after the trauma are also a different but commonly associated phenomenon. Flashbacks are dissociative, as stated in the definition, but feelings involving dissociation or personal disintegration are normally measured separately.

Survivor's guilt, a sense of guilt over having survived a dangerous situation when others did not, was mentioned as a symptom in *DSM-III-R*, but dropped at the time of *DSM-IV*. Other forms of guilt were not mentioned at all. In the case of killing, feelings of guilt can vary widely, from killing that is not socially approved, such as criminal homicide, to killing that is not only approved but also expected, such as soldiers in war. People can feel guilty even under circumstances that involve clear self-defense, but this is a separate problem from PTSD. It may well be associated, and it may have an impact on the course of symptoms. A therapist certainly would wish to deal with it. But severe PTSD can be suffered without any feelings of guilt at all, and guilt can be suffered without any symptoms of PTSD.

PTSD does not involve generally erratic behavior. Though irritable outbursts and flashbacks are among the symptoms, paranoia or unshakable delusions are different. A veteran who is ranting in a way that seems illogical to others is not portraying symptoms of PTSD.

Finally, PTSD is not the same as ordinary stress. Because the word "stress" is in the term, many people confuse it with the kind of stress we are constantly advised to reduce. Excessive, chronic stress can be caused by minor irritants that accumulate too rapidly. Stress can be caused by thoughts rather than events. It can even be caused by imaginary problems. It has some biological differences.

Stress can be dealt with by removing stressors and engaging in stress reduction strategies such as relaxation techniques and aerobic exercise. While these are not useless in treating PTSD, they can only be part of the program; alleviating the symptoms requires different strategies from those commonly employed for stress reduction.

OVERVIEW OF THE BOOK

The first part of the book, Chapters 2 through 7, will look at the psychological consequences of violence against human beings among various groups. Different groups have particular circumstances that can give insight into various aspects of the phenomenon. Conversely, only in looking at the similarities across groups, along with the differences, can a more full understanding of the concept emerge. Accordingly, a review of the literature currently available in these groups is offered.

Chapter 2 examines the most common, well-studied group—combat veterans—who were first noticed for "battle fatigue." The vast majority of studies have not considered or only tangentially considered the role of killing in battle, as opposed to danger or the trauma of seeing friends hurt or killed. Yet this is the first obvious place to consider the role of active participation in traumatic circumstances. The facts of danger and death of others do, of course, confound the findings, along with other contextual and predisposing variables. Throughout all these groups, the idea that a previous trauma of victimization may be strongly associated with, perhaps predisposing toward, the act of perpetration is an ever-present concern. This chapter is by far the heaviest in statistics, because this is the only group that has had systematic quantitative research done with it. Qualitative data—people talking about their experiences—will be the bulk of the evidence for the other groups.

People who carry out executions of condemned prisoners are the group covered in Chapter 3. In this case, it is clearly killing, there is minimal danger to the person carrying it out, there may or may not be some previous personal contact, and the person being executed has been identified by others as guilty. It is a required part of a job, sometimes volunteered for, but often assigned. It is sometimes stigmatized, even by those who approve of the job. These are just a few of the variations to consider, but first the similarities must be found in order to ascertain that there is a common concept. Chapter 4 deals with one group that is extreme in its perpetration: Nazis who were engaged in the graphic carrying out of genocidal activities. Findings can be applicable to other genocides, but the Nazis left the most voluminous documentation from which data can be gathered.

Chapter 5 considers both sides of law enforcement: the police and criminal murderers. While other groups tend to resist the idea that they get posttrauma symptoms from perpetration, police are an exception. Those who have shot someone in the line of duty are commonly admitted to have PTSD symptoms that are worse than those of someone who was shot at. Those convicted of murder, on the other hand, are the most stigmatized group and for the most part lack the component of having their violence be socially sanctioned. They constitute a group in which it would be necessary to uncover evidence of PITS if the concept is indeed applicable in general to the human mind.

Chapter 6 examines a group that is deliberately controversial: those who provide abortions. There are those who claim that this is the ordinary practice of medicine, and an alternative view that this is killing human beings. Can psychology research help provide insight on this question? If we know how the human mind responds to killing, we can research the extent to which this is applicable, partially applicable, or not applicable to this case. Here we are dealing not with the women who procure abortions, about which there is currently much debate, but with the doctors and nurses involved in providing them, a group that receives much less attention.

Those are the groups for which literature reviews can be done. Chapter 7 deals with miscellaneous groups, those for which there are only one or two sources, if any. There are torturers and other people whose violence is highly abusive but less than killing. There is the medical approach of carrying out experiments that are abusive or deadly to those being observed, including human beings and animals. There is also outright killing of animals rather than humans in contexts such as slaughterhouses and blood sports. There are circumstances when people actually ask to be killed, under euthanasia or physician-assisted suicide conditions. Whether or not the concept applies to these specific groups is for future research to determine, but a beginning on any literature for them is offered here. Insight may also be gained by applying the concept of PITS to historical figures and events. This will not allow for the kind of scientific scrutiny and probing which those still living can supply, but historical analysis does allow the study to be expanded to a much larger group of people.

The next two chapters deal with overall implications. Chapter 8 covers psychology and the implications for therapy, for uncovering the causation of the symptoms, and for the definition of PTSD itself. Suggestions are scattered throughout the book that PTSD symptoms can contribute to further violence and that prevention and treatment of PTSD is therefore important to violence prevention efforts; how this fits into psychological observation and theory is explained here. Some initial suggestions for social implications are covered in Chapter 9, with the disciplines of sociology, political science/public policy, and artistic literature including fiction, poetry, and film.

Future research is the topic of the next two chapters. Chapter 10 offers some suggested topics of research that need to be covered. This is a rich subject and here we can only scratch the surface, but at least a few of the items that need further attention are mentioned. These include the context of the perpetration trauma and its aftermath and their meaning to participants. The role of feelings of guilt has received some attention in the scholarly literature, but for this topic it clearly requires more attention. The biological underpinnings of PTSD have quite a robust literature, so the relationship of this to the perpetration-induced form needs examination. Similarly, aspects of personality before and after the trauma have been of interest to those studying victims, and would have differences for those active in causing the trauma that need consideration. The dreams that are a major part of PTSD symptomatology are of particular interest since they do have content, and the content of the dreams that come from memories of killing may vary in some ways from those that come from memories of helplessness. Questions about the effect of PITS on social institutions and the effect of social groups on PITS are numerous. Finally, there is one of the stranger aspects of the phenomenon: the observation that those who participate in killing sometimes actually find that they get a euphoric response to the action. At first, this would seem to contradict the idea that they could be suffering a trauma, but the concept of addiction to trauma—either behavioral or biochemical addiction, or a combination of both—shows that this can actually bolster the case for perpetration as trauma rather than weaken it.

Chapter 11 deals with technical aspects of research peculiar to this particular area. Confounding variables include the possibility that PTSD was already present at the time of perpetrating activity, that there may be a component of stigma even when the violence done is socially approved, and that (especially in current times) many of the practices are controversial and therefore require great care in avoiding bias in researchers and suspicion in research participants. The research methods already developed, from interviews to biological tests to scales, are covered here. The few studies that have looked at PTSD in a prospective way, with data from before the trauma, are discussed. The importance of distinguishing ordinary stress that everyone experiences from posttrauma stress is discussed in more detail, since there are obvious similarities but crucial differences that must be understood to avoid confusion. Finally, questions and problems about placing real individuals who vary so much from one another into categories that may make them seem more similar than they are is addressed, as a philosophical point about mental health diagnoses that has been raised in the scholarly literature.

The concluding chapter covers some final points. Why has this concept not been more widespread previously? What does it mean about how we perceive people who engage in various kinds of killing? What kinds of reactions do different people have when told of the concept? An illustration is offered from a U.S. case that was prominent in the news in the spring of 2001, in which a senator shared with the public his emotional aftermath to having participated in killing civilians as a soldier in Vietnam. Finally, there are some thoughts on what the concept of PITS says about the human mind.

The very idea that the concept of PITS applies not just in one group but that many groups may have this in common has barely, if ever, been addressed in the literature, even though this is common for PTSD due to victimization by others or by natural or accidental traumas. This book is an attempt to begin to lay the foundation for future research. Enough information has accumulated to justify further investigation. That information from the literature has been consolidated, along with various possible explanations and confounding variables that have been compiled from several years of conversations and presentations with other scholars on this subject.

REFERENCES

American Psychiatric Association. (1994). *Diagnostic and statistical manual of mental disorders* (4th ed.). Washington, DC: Author.

Gaudium et Spes [Constitution of the Church in the Modern World]. (1965). Rome: Second Vatican Council.

Green, B.L. (1990). Defining trauma: Terminology and generic stressor dimensions. *Journal of Applied Social Psychology, 20,* 1632–1642.

Grossman, D. (1995). *On killing: The psychological cost of learning to kill in war and society.* Boston: Little, Brown and Company.

Hall, H.V., & Hall, F.L. (1987). Post-traumatic Stress Disorder as a legal defense in criminal trials. *American Journal of Forensic Psychology, 5,* 45–53.

Janoff-Bulman, R. (1985). The aftermath of victimization: Rebuilding shattered assumptions. In C. Figley (Ed.), *Trauma and its wake: The study and treatment of Posttraumatic Stress Disorder* (pp. 14–35). New York: Brunner/Mazel.

Johnson, E.C. (1960). *Jane Addams: A centennial reader* (pp. 272–273). New York: Macmillan.

Kulka, R.A., Schlenger, W.E., Fairbank, J.A., Hough, R.L., Jordan, B.K., Marmar, C.R., & Weiss, D.S. (1990). *Trauma and the Vietnam war generation: Report on the findings from the National Vietnam Veterans Readjustment Study.* New York: Brunner/Mazel.

Marmar, C.R., Weiss, D.S., Metzler, T.J., & Delucchi, K. (1996). Characteristics of emergency services personnel related to peritraumatic dissociation during critical incident exposure. *American Journal of Psychiatry, 153,* 94–102.

Marmar, C.R., Weiss, D.S., Schlenger, W.E., Fairbank, J.A., Jordan, B.K., Kulka, R.A., & Hough, R.L. (1994). Peritraumatic dissociation and posttraumatic stress in male Vietnam theater veterans. *American Journal of Psychiatry, 151,* 902–907.

Marshall, R.D., Olfson, M., Hellman, F., Blanco, C., Guardino, M., & Struening, E. (2001). Comorbidity, impairment, and suicidality in subthreshold PTSD. *American Journal of Psychiatry, 158,* 1467–1473.

Nader, K.O., Pynoos, R.S., Fairbanks, L.A., Al-Ajeel, M., & Al-Asfour, A. (1993). A preliminary study of PTSD and grief among the children of Kuwait following the Gulf crisis. *British Journal of Clinical Psychology, 32,* 407–416.

Varela, R.E., & Matchinsky D.J. (1995). Posttraumatic Stress Disorder: Physiological vulnerability and temperament. Unpublished manuscript, Emporia State University, Kansas.

World Health Organization. (1992). *International statistical classification of diseases and related health problems* (10th revision). Geneva, Switzerland.

Young, A. (1995). *The harmony of illusions: Inventing Posttraumatic Stress Disorder.* New Jersey: Princeton University Press.

Chapter 2

Combat Veterans

KILLING AS STRESSOR

Peace activist Jane Addams (Johnson, 1960) described symptoms of PTSD during World War I and ascribed the symptoms to the act of killing. In addition, there were a few early scholarly articles noting the distinction between passive victimization and active causing of the trauma before the American Psychiatric Association published the term and diagnostic criteria for PTSD in *DSM-III* in 1980.

Haley (1974) and Shatan (1978) separately pointed out that when the patient reports atrocities, therapists have more trouble listening. This could, of course, make patients less likely to report such events. If so, gaining knowledge of the psychological aftereffects of participating could be impaired.

Strayer and Ellenhorn (1975) found that participation in atrocities brought more symptoms in terms of withdrawal, hostility, and life-outcome maladjustment. Introversion accentuated the problems, but those with the authoritarian personality had the opposite reaction and had good life-outcome adjustment. Whether the latter finding has any validity in other samples has not been pursued.

Breslau and Davis (1987) commented that participation in atrocities and the cumulative exposure to combat stressors, each independently of the other, conferred a significant risk for PTSD. Hendin and Haas (1984) make a similar case, but from the opposite direction. They say, "we will discuss our study of combat veterans who have not developed posttraumatic stress. It is significant that none of the veterans in that group was involved in non-military violence" (p. 28).

Several studies have also noted the correlation of "atrocities exposure" to PTSD even when battle intensity is controlled, but the measure of exposure combines witnessing with actual participation (e.g., Beckham, Feldman, & Kirby, 1998; King et al., 1995).

A book on assessing adult posttraumatic conditions published by the American Psychological Association (Briere, 1997) discusses "specific stressors known to produce posttraumatic states." In a subsection on war, it says, "War involves a very wide range of violent and traumatic experiences, including . . . involvement in injuring or killing others (both combatants and civilians), witnessing or participating in atrocities, acts of rape" (p. 4). Thus, perpetration-induced trauma is covered for war situations, though nonwar perpetration situations are still not considered. Earlier, Lund et al. (1984) constructed a Combat Exposure Scale in which the factor of participation in abusive violence was included, with the idea that it would be a stressor that could lead to later psychological problems.

As discussed in the first chapter and further below, Lt. Col. Grossman (1995) wrote an entire book on PTSD as a result of committing violence, entitled *On Killing: The Psychological Cost of Learning to Kill in War and Society*. This book is the only major source to detail at length the subject of killing as ordinarily required in combat, not just atrocity, as a source of PTSD.

SUGGESTED CHARACTERISTICS ASSOCIATED WITH AFTERMATH OF COMBAT KILLING

Yager, Laufer, and Gallops (1984) found greater marijuana and heroin use, but not greater drinking, among participants in abusive violence. Compared to those who had only been exposed to combat, they found a higher arrest record, much higher distrust, and higher stress symptoms. Blacks had worse symptoms than Whites, which the authors accounted for from their interviews by saying that Blacks had more trouble with violence and dehumanization, and more regard for the Vietnamese.

Hendin and Haas (1984, p. 31) note that aggression—often explosive—is a common feature with combat veterans. Unlike concentration camp survivors, for example, for whom such outbursts would be maladaptive, those who used aggression in combat continue to use it in peacetime. The authors observed that "comparably, veterans who had traumatic combat experiences but never fired a weapon are a minority whose posttraumatic stress disorders do not include explosive expressions of anger" (pp. 27–28).

Glover (1985) did a qualitative study of Vietnam veterans, in which there is some material on dreams and intrusive thoughts of killers. He does not mention PTSD, but finds guilt more related to depression and lack of guilt more related to paranoia.

Hendin and Haas (1984), with their psychiatric qualitative study of just over a hundred combat veterans, also found a distinction between paranoia and depression, and devoted a chapter to each. They are tellingly entitled, "Combat Never Ends: The Paranoid Adaptation," and "Mourning Never Ends: The Depressive Adaptation." The difference is defined this way: "The paranoid response involves a perception of combat as never ending, a perception that requires vigilance and counterattack to survive; the depressive response reflects a perception of irretrievable loss, a triumph of death over life" (p. 129).

A personality characteristic that has been considered is introversion. Studies have varied in their findings of the relationship of this factor to the development of PTSD. Some (Dalton et al., 1993; Breslau et al., 1991; Orr et al., 1990) find introversion higher for those with PTSD, but not all do (Schnurr, Friedman, & Rosenberg, 1993). The findings are not consistent; greater depth is required to make distinctions. Some of the variances come from the different samples, and some from the different tests. The distinction between perpetration-induced and passive-victim forms of PTSD might be a prime place where the influence of introversion might differ.

STRUCTURAL EQUATION MODELS

Using government data on veterans of the American war in Vietnam, as detailed in the next section, two structural equation models have been done which do include killing as one of the variables that can lead to PTSD. Both such models have shown a significant and strong path (King et al., 1995; Fontana & Rosenheck, 1999), treating killing as one variable among many that lead to PTSD. They were not attending to the differences that killing as a causal mechanism might have in comparison with other mechanisms.

These two studies dealt quite differently with the variable of "atrocities." For King et al. (1995), the "atrocities" variable covered killing, primarily in its more extreme and militarily unjustified forms, with the killing of traditional combat not distinguished. They did not differentiate between exposure to atrocities and actual participation, but used the scores as an ordinal scale. Higher scores indicated more participation.

For Fontana & Rosenheck (1999), killing/injuring was one variable and "atrocities" was designed to be an orthogonal different variable. It therefore excluded killing and measured instead the items of harassment of civilians, destruction of property, and the mutilation of corpses. Measured this way, the variable turned out to be an insignificant path to PTSD and was therefore dropped from the structural equation model. The bivariate correlation was lower than most of the other variables, while that for killing/injuring was among the highest.

This leads to the suggestion that forms of perpetration that are not connected to violence against living persons may have a much lesser effect as a form of trauma. Of course, there can be a tremendous psychological difference between the property destruction of blowing up a pile of enemy weapons as opposed to setting fire to a family's house while they watch. These kinds of distinctions were not made in the data.

THE NVVRS AND TESTING HYPOTHESES FROM THE LITERATURE

Unlike the groups discussed in the following chapters, veterans are the one group on which sufficient quantitative data is available to allow for some generalizations, at least to similar veterans. The largest study of any at-risk population for PITS was a United States government-commissioned survey of veterans of the American war in Vietnam, done in the 1980s (Kulka et al., 1990). The National Vietnam Veterans Readjustment Study (NVVRS) used a stratified random sample of Vietnam-era veterans and a comparison group of veterans. I have performed a large secondary analysis of this data, using the 1,638 theater veterans (MacNair, 1999). There were some simple tests of severity and of previous hypotheses from the above literature. There was also exploratory discriminant function analysis and factor analysis to establish findings upon which to base further research, covered in the next section. Below is a summary; for further details on the statistics, see the Appendix.

PTSD scores, as measured with a modified Mississippi Scale for combat-related PTSD, were indeed more severe among the perpetration groups compared to the control groups; see Table A.1 in the Appendix. This is consistent with the consensus of previous literature (Strayer & Ellenhorn, 1975; Yager, Laufer, & Gallops, 1984; Hendin & Haas, 1984; Laufer, Gallops, & Frey-Wouters, 1984; Green, 1990; Grossman, 1995). In a subset given psychiatric interviews, PTSD diagnostic scores were also higher for those who said they had killed. In a different subset given the widely used scale called the Minnesota Multiphasic Personality Inventory (MMPI), scores on the MMPI's PTSD subscale were also higher. Effect sizes were very high in the main group, being close to an entire standard deviation of difference (Cohen's d = .97). The effect sizes were moderate in the subsets, which were selected for including people more likely to have PTSD. The finding of greater severity is robust in the NVVRS sample, cross-validated in various ways.

The greater severity was not merely due to the level of battle intensity, as remembered and rated by the veterans. Killing could simply be a marker for having been in heavier combat, and the intensity of the combat has always been associated with more severe PTSD. This would be expected, if PTSD were in fact a response to trauma; the heavier the trauma, the heavier the response. However, those who had killed in light combat had a higher mean score than those who had not killed in heavy combat. As seen in Table A.2 in the Appendix, scores for PTSD rise as expected from light combat to heavy combat for those who say they did not kill, then start at a higher level and rise for those who said they did. Those who did not kill in light combat had a mean score of 70.6, and this rose with the intensity of combat, so that in heavy combat the mean average was 80.3. Those who said they killed, and rated battle intensity as light, had an average PTSD score of 85.5. Scores then rise with battle intensity, as would be expected, but this rise started with a higher mean score than was the highest mean score for those who did not kill. Multiple regression with self-assessed memory of battle intensity also showed that the variable of killing still added explanation once battle intensity was controlled, as shown in Table A.3 in the Appendix. The same was true not just for overall PTSD scores, but also for factors within PTSD, as shown in Table A.4.

In both univariate analysis and the discriminant function analyses, the hypothesis of greater explosive outbursts as compared with other symptoms was confirmed. As measured by individual items and a factor for rage or temper, this was much higher than other symptoms. This point has important therapy implications and also relates to the question of prevention; violent outbursts can lead to violent activity.

One group of researchers found in their patients that those who engaged in violence have greater marijuana and heroin use, but not greater alcohol use (Yager, Laufer, & Gallops, 1984). However, in a subset of the NVVRS veterans given psychiatric interviews, the difference in the alcohol score between the killing and non-killing group was actually greater than in either cannabis or opioid. It was a moderate effect size for alcohol (Cohen's d = .5) and a small effect size for the other drugs (Cohen's d = .2). These scores are in Table A.6 of the Appendix. This was based on a distinction of killing and not killing, whereas the other researchers were looking at commission or noncommission of atrocities (a related distinction, but not the same). Additionally, scores were based on psychiatric assessments for addiction and dependency, rather than on level of usage.

Another suggestion from the previous researchers was that there are racial differences in severity. They reported that Black perpetrators suffered more, had stronger guilt feelings and more intrusive imagery than Whites (Yager, Laufer, & Gallops, 1984; Laufer, Gallops, & Frey-Wouters, 1984; Laufer, Brett, & Gallops, 1985). In the NVVRS, the mean scores for PTSD and for the one item on guilt were higher for Blacks who said yes on killing than for Whites who did so, but the effect size was small (Cohen's d = .2). In the case of the intrusive imagery items, there was no significance between the yes-on-killing and no-on-killing groups. For those who answered "directly involved" on killing civilians, prisoners, or women, children, or elderly people, the difference in mean scores between Blacks and Whites on all these scores was insignificant (see Table A.7 in the Appendix). Inasmuch as there are racial differences, they are small in this stratified random sample. The sample in which such differences were initially suggested was one of treatment-seeking veterans. The level of distress a veteran may have before seeking help may be a confounding variable on racial differences.

A subset of the veterans were given the MMPI, and the same division of the group based on the question of whether or not they had killed was done. On the two constructs of paranoia and depression, the MMPI subscales are positive but fairly small, r = .25.

On the matter of social introversion, in which previous literature had given inconsistent views as outlined above, the scores on the MMPI subscales actually showed no significant difference between the killing and nonkilling groups. This is particularly noteworthy in contrast to the higher scores on other subscales.

Those who said yes on killing are higher on most subscales of the MMPI. The exceptions are the L (lie) scale and the social introversion scale, in which there are no differences, and the K scale for defensiveness, in which those who said no on killing actually score higher. See Table A.5 in the Appendix for the figures on MMPI scores.

An alternative explanation of higher PTSD scores is that, rather than those who killed actually having more symptoms, they simply report more symptoms. That is, there may be an association with negative affectivity, or perhaps a negative response bias. The L-scale in the MMPI subset is designed to measure this. However, the difference between those who said yes on killing and those who said no was not significant. The other test of this explanation is in three items included in an extensive list of symptoms. While most of the list dealt with PTSD, these three items have nothing to do with PTSD and were therefore not expected to differ between those who answered yes on the killing item and those who answered no. These are: retarded pace of actions, tremors or tics, and clumsiness or carelessness. Tests on these three items did, in fact, show no statistically significant differences. The lack of difference in these three items and in the L-scale is not consistent with an explanation of over-reporting, negative affectivity, or a negative response bias.

THE NVVRS AND EXPLORATORY ANALYSES

In this same U.S. government database of 1,638 Vietnam combat veterans, the factor structure of PTSD for those who said they killed was not meaningfully different from those who said they did not. Though there are differences in patterns such that an analysis can use factors to distinguish the two groups, the symptom items do not coalesce differently (MacNair, 1999).

In the discriminant function analysis, both individual items and factors of various scales were carried out in the main set of veterans and in two subsets (see Tables A.8 through A.12 in the Appendix). The item of never telling anyone about something that was done in the military always loaded on the side of the perpetration group in whatever way that was measured. Intrusive imagery also always loaded high as a discriminator. Violent outbursts always loaded on the perpetration groups, either as an individual item or as a factor of temper.

Also commonly loading on the perpetration groups, but not as strongly, were hypervigilance, alienation, and survivor guilt. The issue of justified guilt was not covered in the database; only a reverse-scored item on not feeling guilt was included, and it never entered in the analysis.

Avoidance items were less consistent, sometimes appearing for perpetration, sometimes nonperpetration, and often not entering at all. In this study, the same veterans were asked about how they coped in Vietnam, and an analysis of their answers showed that avoidance was a coping mechanism more for those who did not kill than for those who did. There is some intuitive sense to this, that avoidance behavior would be more characteristic of those who avoided killing. Therefore, those who kill may already be at a lower threshold of avoidant behavior as a personality disposition, and this helps account for the inconsistency on these items. Perhaps they require a greater level of avoidant symptomatology to surpass a group that started off with more than they had.

A surprising finding was that concentration and memory problems, both as items and as a factor, consistently loaded on the side of the nonperpetration groups. This was a strong finding that was not predicted. It could have implications for determining the physical and psychological causality of individual symptoms. If the more active are less inclined toward concentration or memory problems, and those who tend to be passive are more so inclined, then the search for the underlying causal mechanisms can be directed along more fruitful avenues. Of course, the causality could be in the opposite direction, that preceding concentration and memory problems interfere with getting into situations in which one kills. This finding is based on self-report, but one advantage of concentration or memory problems is that they are much easier to measure objectively or in the laboratory.

Suicidal thoughts, or to feel like killing one's self, tended to load on the side of those who said they did not kill. This loaded weakly, with the size of the effect being so small, and the number who reported the problem being such a tiny portion, that from a purely statistical point of view it would not receive much attention. However, suicide among veterans is a major problem, the nature of which is quite peculiar compared with other symptoms, because its more severe forms could be absent from the data set. This is on the simple grounds that those who have suffered from the more severe forms of this problem have, in fact, successfully committed suicide and consequently cannot be part of the sample.

It could therefore be the weaker form of suicidal thought, the form that does not lead to actual suicide, which does get represented in the database. In this way, even though the items load weakly on the side of those who say they did not kill, the symptom may follow the pattern of other symptoms and be more severe in those who killed. There has been a finding that when PTSD is at subthreshold levels, there is a linear increase of suicidal thoughts, along with impairment and comorbidity, as the number of symptoms increases (Marshall et al., 2001). This means that suicidality is present though lower with a smaller number of symptoms, and increases as the symptoms multiply. Unlike all the other symptoms, the manifestation of greatest severity—actual suicide—can take people entirely out of the sample being studied.

One study did do a structural equation model with suicide attempts as the dependent variable (Fontana & Rosenheck, 1995). It found that participation in atrocities (defined as terrorizing, wounding, or killing civilians or prisoners and mutilating bodies) contributed to PTSD and other psychiatric disorders, but only contributed to suicide attempts through the psychiatric disorders, not through the PTSD. The inclusion of mutilation of bodies may dilute the variable of participation in atrocities, as shown by the authors' later work (1999) in which atrocities were defined to be orthogonal with killing and thereby resulted in lower scores. In any event, this was done with the same NVVRS database, so the same problem applies. The dependent variable was suicide attempts, not actual suicides, which are not represented in the database at all. Research on suicide directly would be necessary before any conclusions could be drawn on this point.

Finally, only one scale used in a subset had the component labeled disintegration. The factor included the items of a sense of unreality, experience of depersonalization, unrealistic distortion of meanings, restlessness or agitation, self-hatred, hostility toward a part of the body, perception of high pressure, panic, and disintegration. This set of symptoms is not normally included in PTSD scales and is not in the official definition. However, when included in a discriminant function analysis, this factor was second only to the intrusion factor. This suggests that this construct may be very important in the population of those who killed. If so, it deserves much more research attention.

INTRUSIVE IMAGERY

Laufer, Brett, and Gallops (1985) proposed that the intrusive imagery degraded over time for those engaged in "abusive violence." The researchers thought those veterans had more reason to suppress such imagery and accordingly were more successful in doing so. In this NVVRS data set, the best way to look at this question was to compare the "lifetime" and "current" set of symptoms (MacNair, 1999). The comparison of the discriminant function analyses shows that there were two items which were present in lifetime symptoms but dropped out as discriminators for the current symptoms: "avoidance" dropped as an indicator for the no-on-killing group, and "watchful when no reason to be" dropped as an indicator of the yes-on-killing group. The intrusion items did not drop; see Table A.12 in the Appendix. Furthermore, the factors including intrusion did remain in both the lifetime and the current lists as discriminators between yes-on-killing and no-on-killing.

This way of looking at the data does not offer support for the deteriorating imagery thesis that Laufer, Brett, and Gallops (1985) proposed. However, it was not designed to answer this question and is weak for the purpose; amount or quality of intrusive imagery is not addressed. A set of other studies designed for the purpose can give a stronger conclusion. The best that can be said here is that the phenomenon is not clear enough to come through when looking at the NVVRS data in this manner.

Another point to mention is the recent conceptual model in which veterans are seen as going through cycling stages of PTSD, a process of worsening and improving and worsening and improving again (Wang, Wilson, & Mason, 1996). If this is the case, then the list of "current" symptoms could depend heavily on what stage the veteran is in at the time. The lifetime symptoms could include those that happen during the worst stage, which has happened several times before and will happen several times again. This is entirely different from having more severe symptoms that degrade over time. In fact, if this model were to be determined sound and the cycling found to be more severe for those who killed, this could be the explanation for the findings of Laufer, Brett, and Gallops (1985). Perhaps they were talking to the veterans when they were in the less severe part of the cycle. The fact that they were talking to them at all indicates this is a possibility, since the worst part of the cycle for this disorder could make veterans more uncommunicative.

Another complication is that it is not uncommon to have delayed reactions. It has been reported that veterans who have shown little sign of PTSD symptomatology over their working lives have started showing signs of it at retirement (e.g., Sleek, 1998). Delayed reactions are part of the definition of PTSD in both the *DSM-IV* and *ICD-10*.

DIFFERENCE OF "ATROCITIES" AND TRADITIONAL COMBAT

Since much of the literature looks at what is normally called "atrocities," defined as the killing of innocent civilians or of prisoners, the distinction between this and other killing must be considered. In the NVVRS Secondary Analysis, the PTSD scores were clearly higher for those directly involved than for those who killed in other contexts (MacNair, 1999). There was no way to ascertain if the higher PTSD scores are due to the greater likelihood of seeing the results, the cognitive component, the difference in social support or disapproval, or simply that this is a measure of greater frequency in killing.

Three discriminant function analyses were conducted of the NVVRS that addressed this question. In the primary analysis, those who answered "directly involved" to any of the atrocity items were removed. Thus, this was a straight comparison to those who killed (presumably in traditional combat situations) as opposed to those who did not kill. The possible confounding of the atrocity group was handled by simply removing the group. The results of the discriminant analysis on individual items of the scale were practically the same, as shown in Table A.9 in the appendix. The presence of the atrocity group did not skew the results.

On the other hand, another analysis did show that the atrocity group differed from the one that only saw (as opposed to being directly involved) and answered yes on whether they had killed. They differed on the variables of being unable to tell about what they had done and on nightmares of things that had happened. As shown in Table A.11 in the Appendix, the classification results and variance accounted for were poorer than in other analyses, and both of these items were among those that differentiated the yes-on-killing group with "directly involved" removed from the no-on-killing group. These two items were even more extreme for the directly involved group.

The two items that distinguished the perpetration groups might be related. It is not puzzling that those who were involved in atrocities might feel more strongly that they can never tell anyone what they did. The very use of the word "atrocity" for this behavior in the scholarly literature, in which nomenclature is usually more subdued, indicates the greater likelihood that participants would feel this way. The higher score for nightmares is less clear. Perhaps there is a cognitive component—they were more likely to see what they did, or the sights were more graphic, and this led to the nightmares.

These are both quite plausible, but another possibility is that the two items are connected. Perhaps the lack of expression contributes to the presence of the nightmares. Quite a bit of work on stress suggests that expression is therapeutic and lack of it makes the situation worse. A psychiatrist working with Vietnam veterans also suggests that "narrative can transform involuntary reexperiencing of traumatic events into memory of the events, thereby reestablishing authority over memory" (Shay, 1994, p. 192).

Since the item about never telling what one saw in the military is not directly a PTSD symptom, and it had a tendency to overpower, it was removed and another discriminant analysis was run without it in the same groups. This time, three items entered, all as characteristic of the pattern of those who were directly involved. As worded in the code book, these are: "dreams so real waken in sweat & stay awake," "certain situations make me feel back in military," and "unexpected noises make me jump." The first two are intrusion symptoms, in *DSM-IV* cluster B, and the third is symptom D(5) of an exaggerated startle response, a matter of increased arousal.

The connections of these to the presumably more extreme form of perpetration, and the question of whether less ability to express the memories exacerbates the intrusive imagery or not, await further research. At this point, only the questions can be raised. Data sets different from this one will be required to answer them, because the NVVRS data was not designed to answer questions involving PITS. The analysis was done only to establish what could be known from already existing data in order to establish a foundation for future research.

BOMBING

Another obvious question lies at the other end of the spectrum: what about killing in a context where the results are never seen? Bombing from an airplane, for example, might have different psychological consequences than killing on the ground. There are many anecdotes from Vietnam of airplane bombers who were comfortable with their work until they were shot down and faced on the ground with the actual results. The visual stimulus of bombing usually does not comport with killing in contexts in which the results are immediately seen. In fact, viewed from the other direction, being bombed has not led to as many psychiatric casualties as face-to-face killers have (Grossman, 1995).

It was difficult to study the psychological consequences of bombing in the NVVRS. There was no variable for bombing from an airplane, only the item on whether or not a fixed-wing airplane was flown. There was no designation as to whether this was for bombing, carrying supplies or personnel, reconnaissance, or medical missions. The group who answered yes was therefore cross-tabulated with the item of whether or not they had killed or thought they killed anyone in Vietnam. This brought the sample size down to 144, about evenly split (73 said no, 71 said yes). The mean scores on the PTSD measure were practically indistinguishable from those of the overall group. The group that said no on killing had a mean of 72.4 when the overall mean was 71.9, and the group that said yes on killing had a mean of 92.0 compared with the overall mean of 93.4. The effect size for the difference between those who said they killed and those who said they did not was the same.

In other words, when taking out this subsample of the larger group, the results were the same as those for the group as a whole. There is no information on whether those who answered yes to killing had done so in the context of bombing, or whether they are referring to incidents that have nothing to do with their flying airplanes. Nor do we know how well those who bombed actually understood themselves as engaged in killing, as the surprised shot-down pilots can attest.

The psychology literature makes little mention of impacts of bombing on the bombers. There is a short mention of fighter pilots having a reaction to killing in terms of downed aircraft (Grossman, 1995). More distinctly, a history professor noted from her interviews that:

technology still failed to render the dead completely faceless. Combatants used their imagination to "see" the impact of their weapons on other men, to construct elaborate, precise, and self-conscious fantasies about the effects of their destructive weapons, especially when the impact of their actions was beyond their immediate vision. . . . So while technology was used to facilitate mass human destruction, it did very little to reduce the awareness that dead human beings were the end product. (Bourke, 1999, pp. xviii–xix)

She cites a poem written by William J. Simon in which an airplane pilot named "Chopper Jockey" says that in the jungle below, "with blood of men I have killed, I see the faces of men I have never seen" (Simon, 1972, p. 42).

A small amount of qualitative data suggests the possibility that those who do not see the results nevertheless suffer PITS symptoms, at least in intrusive imagery. A small amount of quantitative data is at least consistent with this possibility. This point requires much more exploration.

RAGE

Symptom D(2) of the official definition of *DSM-IV* (1994) is "irritability or outbursts of anger." Hendin and Haas (1984) suggested on the basis of their observations that those who had killed were especially characterized by violent outbursts. Univariate and multivariate analyses of the National Vietnam Veterans Readjustment Study have in various ways confirmed this as a major difference. Both individual items and a factor labeled temper were consistently high in discriminant function analyses. In the multiple regression using factors, the variable of self-rated battle intensity did not enter as a predictor for the factor of temper. However, the variable of killing did, as shown in Table A.4 of the Appendix. This further suggests that the phenomenon is strongly attached to having killed.

When the temper factor was forced to join others by limiting to two or four factors, the items in it did not enter with the intrusion/avoidance/hypervigilance factor. This is where "reenactment" symptoms would be found. Instead, the items entered the deadened or nonsocial feelings factor, where numbing symptoms are found.

This finding is consistent with factor analyses in other populations, in which the role of hyperarousal varies but irritability always loads with numbing symptoms. Taylor et al. (1998) divided PTSD symptoms into the two factors of intrusion/avoidance and hypervigilance/numbing, and reported that in two sets of motor vehicle accident victims the increased irritability symptom loaded on the numbing factor. They reported this true with even a stronger loading among a sample of 419 peacekeepers in Bosnia. In a sample of 405 American veterans from Vietnam, Silva, and Iacono (1994) also found that "Reexperiencing the Trauma" was one factor and "Detachment and Anger" went together as another; this included both numbing and hyperarousal items. In a different study of female victims of rape and nonsexual assault (Foa, Riggs, & Gershuny, 1995), authors were somewhat surprised to find that the increased irritability/anger loaded with numbing, separate from an arousal factor. They suggest that there is a difference between angry arousal and anxious arousal, and that both numbing and anger may serve to ameliorate anxious arousal when effortful avoidance fails.

There are several other possible explanations for the violent outbursts. Hendin and Haas (1984), when observing that this behavior seemed more common among those who had killed, pointed out that such outbursts would have been maladaptive for concentration camp inhabitants, but perhaps more adaptive for those in combat situations. Alternatively, these angry flare-ups could indicate a latent personality disposition that made it more likely for soldiers to get themselves into situations in which they killed.

The outbursts could also be something that was not present before the event and resulted from it. Shay (1994) suggests this in his book about Vietnam veterans that compared their expression of feelings with passages from the *Iliad*.

He did not deal with a perpetrator/non-perpetrator distinction explicitly. How-ever, based on his psychiatric experience, he said:

Some survivors, having learned the untrustworthiness of words, conclude that the only way to be heard is through action—guerrilla theater. Intimidation, "acting out," and creating impossible situations sometimes aim at coercing the therapist to feel the fear and helplessness that the survivor felt. This is coercive communalization. It recreates terror and helplessness at work, in the family, on the street or in the clinic. Like Achilles (1:292f), these survivors have flung the heralds' staff to the ground. Words mean nothing; only actions count. In this coercive communalization the audience is no longer made up of listeners; the survivor has made them victims. They most assuredly feel the emotions. Aloneness is broken here, too, but the inner presence of the perpetrator has taken over. Healing does not occur. (Shay, 1994, p. 191)

In one way, this interpretation seems to suggest that the violent outbursts or temper factor could be part of the intrusive imagery/reenactment cluster, and are independent of whether one was a perpetrator or a passive victim in the battle situation. The last two sentences, however, indicate why this may be more as-sociated with the sense of alienation, rather than with intrusive imagery and other kinds of reenactment (nightmares and flashbacks).

A different approach is suggested by William Chamberlin, a staff psychologist at the PTSD unit at the Veteran's Administration Hospital in Montrose, New York. In discussing the symptom of constricted affect (blocking of emotions), he says:

My experience with PITS veterans indicates that they are very in touch with their anger. By being in touch with their anger, the temptation is to think they would have little difficulty controlling or regulating their anger. But this is not the case. They are made anxious by getting in touch with their anger because they are afraid for themselves! They have little confidence they can manage intense angry states because they are uncertain of the consequences of their behavior. Their conclusion is that if their anger/rage becomes intense, they will kill someone. If you look a little deeper, they are terrified their rage will separate them from the rest of humanity. . . . Anger serves as a cover for their guilt. As a result, their anger is projected guilt. Their harsh judgmental view of others is only a mirror of how judgmental they are towards themselves but unable to acknowledge. The guilt is pervasive, inescapable. Heroic efforts to constrict their guilt are only partially successful. They live with it. They suffer . . . Being out of touch with your feelings can be very adaptive at times. (W. Chamberlin, personal communication, March 25, 2001)

Glover (1985) makes a similar point about rage's connection to guilt in what he calls the category of "violence-prone veterans":

Aggression serves a number of functions for them, including a defense against the feeling of guilt for having murdered civilians or having been involved in other war related atrocities. Aggression directed towards others represents their projected feelings of self-hatred. These same acts are oftentimes provocative, and are carried out with the intentions of eliciting retaliatory responses. Acting in a threatening and violent manner also dramatizes their negative identities as murderers. A frequent form this takes is for the veterans to express wishes or intentions to become mercenaries. (Glover, 1985, p. 16)

Another possibility is simply that during an intense and memorable part of their lives, those with explosive outbursts learned that aggressiveness works well and they continue behaving in accordance with what they have learned. As Glover (1985) put it:

other veterans are more likely to expect that problems with the environment can be resolved as quickly as they were in Vietnam, where the law of the land was settled without question and where there was instant gratification. The experience of having wielded considerable fire power in the Vietnam War has had a major impact on the lives of these men. The exhilaration and sense of power which attended this experience seems to have reinforced any previous predilection they may have had toward acting aggressively. They are more inclined to explode in frustration and rage when events in their lives do not turn out as they wish. (Glover, 1985, p. 17)

Whether in war or other contexts, violence is very often done for the purpose of more quickly achieving a certain goal, and inasmuch as it is successful in doing so, learning to use violence can also be associated with impatience.

The point about rage also relates to the question of prevention. Violent outbursts can underlie domestic abuse and other forms of violent criminal activity. In addition to the importance of avoiding violence itself, such activities can also be traumas that cause others to get PTSD, thus widening the circle. Effective therapeutic intervention and understanding of the origin and dynamics helps not only the veteran, but also potentially helps prevent further victimization of others.

This finding on temper so far applies only to veterans. Its possible application or lack of application to other groups of perpetrators awaits further study. The extent to which it does or does not apply in differing groups can provide further insight as to its cause and treatment.

QUALITATIVE WORK DESCRIBING THE EXPERIENCE

The best sources for qualitative data and case studies of the psychological consequences of killing for American war veterans are three books in which PTSD as a result of killing is attended to: *On Killing: The Psychological Cost of Learning to Kill in War and Society* (Grossman, 1995); *Wounds of War: The Psychological Aftermath of Combat in Vietnam* (Hendin & Haas, 1984); and *Hell, Healing, and Resistance* (Hallock, 1998). The first two are written by psychological professionals who are drawing from their long therapeutic experience. The third comes from interviews that were done for the purpose of writing a book.

Grossman's book is the best for focusing on killing as a stressor capable of causing PTSD. Hendin and Haas go from the opposite direction: they are interested in what it is that causes veterans *not* to get PTSD, and one of their criteria was to not have "committed non-military violence." At one point, Hallock says: "Without a doubt, PTSD is most acute in veterans who have seen or participated in the killing of defenseless people, especially women and children. . . . In the final analysis, lives were ruined on all sides" (Hallock, 1998, p. 103). He does not back this statement up with any documentation, but does illustrate it with a case of someone who had killed many civilians at the massacre at My Lai.

Additionally, a historian has done in-depth interviews with veterans of the two world wars as well as the war in Vietnam, which she organizes in a book called *An Intimate History of Killing: Face-to-Face Killing in Twentieth-Century Warfare* (Bourke, 1999). Her interest in PTSD, or "war neurosis," is in how the historical interplay of the concept impacts attitudes of all involved.

The qualitative data is unencumbered by quantitative needs for standardized categorization or comparisons, and so can go into greater depth. It catches more nuances and individual differences. Qualitative data also allows for more exploration of the veterans' own understanding of the causes of their distress, while results of quantitative checklists can find only correlations. The expression by the veterans of the details of their problems provides a different kind of insight than asking them to check off items on paper. We are studying real people who have real pain.

REFERENCES

American Psychiatric Association. (1994). *Diagnostic and statistical manual of mental disorders* (4th ed.). Washington, DC: Author.

Beckham, J.C., Feldman, M.E., & Kirby, A.C. (1998). Atrocities exposure in Vietnam combat veterans with chronic Posttraumatic Stress Disorder: Relationship to combat exposure, symptom severity, guilt, and interpersonal violence. *Journal of Traumatic Stress, 11*, 777–784.

Bourke, J. (1999). *An intimate history of killing: Face-to-face killing in twentieth-century warfare*. Great Britain: Granta Books.

Breslau, N., & Davis, G.C. (1987). Posttraumatic Stress Disorder: The etiologic specificity of wartime stressors. *American Journal of Psychiatry, 144*, 578–583.

Breslau, N., Davis, G.C., Andreski, P., & Peterson, E. (1991). Traumatic events and Posttraumatic Stress Disorder in an urban population of young adults. *Archives of General Psychiatry, 48*, 216–222.

Briere, J. (1997). *Psychological assessment of adult posttraumatic states*. Washington, DC: American Psychological Association.

Dalton, J.E., Aubuchon, I., Agnes, T., & Pederson, S.L. (1993). MBTI profiles of Vietnam veterans with Post-traumatic Stress Disorder. *Journal of Psychological Type, 26*, 3–8.

Foa, E.B., Riggs, D.S., & Gershuny, B.S. (1995). Arousal, numbing, and intrusion: Symptom structure of PTSD following assault. *American Journal of Psychiatry, 152*, 116–120.

Fontana, A., & Rosenheck, R. (1995). Attempted suicide among Vietnam veterans: A model of etiology in a community sample. *American Journal of Psychiatry, 152,* 102–109.

―――. (1999). A model of war zone stressors and Posttraumatic Stress Disorder. *Journal of Traumatic Stress, 12,* 111–126.

Glover, H. (1985). Guilt and aggression in Vietnam veterans. *American Journal of Social Psychiatry, 1,* 15–18.

Green, B.L. (1990). Defining trauma: Terminology and generic stressor dimensions. *Journal of Applied Social Psychology, 20,* 1632–1642.

Grossman, D. (1995). *On killing: The psychological cost of learning to kill in war and society.* Boston: Little, Brown and Company.

Haley, S.A. (1974). When the patient reports atrocities. *Archives of General Psychiatry, 30,* 191–196.

Hallock, D. (1998). *Hell, healing, and resistance.* Farmington, PA: The Plough Publishing House.

Hendin. H., & Haas, A.P. (1984). *Wounds of war: The psychological aftermath of combat in Vietnam.* New York: Basic Books.

Johnson, E.C. (1960). *Jane Addams: A centennial reader* (pp. 272–273). New York: Macmillan.

Keane, T.M., Caddell, J.M., & Taylor, K.L. (1988). Mississippi scale for combat-related Posttraumatic Stress Disorder: Three studies in reliability and validity. *Journal of Consulting and Clinical Psychology, 56,* 85–90.

King, D.W., King, L.A., Gudanowski, D.M., & Vreven, D.L. (1995). Alternative representations of war zone stressors: Relationships to Posttraumatic Stress Disorder in male and female Vietnam veterans. *Journal of Abnormal Psychology, 104,* 184–196.

Kulka, R.A., Schlenger, W.E., Fairbank, J.A., Hough, R.L., Jordan, B.K., Marmar, C.R., & Weiss, D.S. (1990). *Trauma and the Vietnam War generation: Report on the findings from the National Vietnam Veterans Readjustment Study.* New York: Brunner/Mazel.

Laufer, R.S., Brett, E., & Gallops, M.S. (1985). Dimensions of Posttraumatic Stress Disorder among Vietnam veterans. *Journal of Nervous and Mental Disease, 173,* 538–545.

Laufer, R.S., Gallops, M.S., & Frey-Wouters, E. (1984). War stress and trauma: The Vietnam veteran experience. *Journal of Health and Social Behavior, 25,* 65–85.

Lund, M., Foy, D., Sipprelle, C., & Strachan, A. (1984). The combat exposure scale: A systematic assessment of trauma in the Vietnam War. *Journal of Clinical Psychology, 40,* 1323–1328.

MacNair, R.M. (1999). *Symptom pattern differences for Perpetration-Induced Traumatic Stress in veterans: Probing the National Vietnam Veterans Readjustment Study.* Doctoral dissertation, University of Kansas City, Missouri.

Marshall, R.D., Olfson, M., Hellman, F., Blanco, C., Guardino, M., & Struening, E. (2001). Comorbidity, impairment, and suicidality in subthreshold PTSD. *American Journal of Psychiatry, 158,* 1467–1473.

Orr, S.P., Claiborn, J.M., Altman, B., Forgue, D.F., de Jong, J.B., & Pitman, R.K. (1990). Psychometric profile of Posttraumatic Stress Disorder, anxious and healthy Vietnam veterans: Correlations with psychophysiologic responses. *Journal of Consulting and Clinical Psychology, 3,* 329–335.

Schnurr, P.P., Friedman, M.J., & Rosenberg, S.D. (1993). Preliminary MMPI scores as predictors of combat-related PTSD symptoms. *American Journal of Psychiatry, 150*, 479–483.

Shatan, C. (1978). Stress disorders among Vietnam veterans: The emotional context of combat continues. In C.R. Figley (Ed.), *Stress disorders among Vietnam veterans: Theory, research, and treatment.* New York: Brunner/Mazel.

Shay, J. (1994). *Achilles in Vietnam: Combat trauma and the undoing of character.* Toronto: Maxwell MacMillan.

Silva, S.M., & Iacono, C.U. (1994). Factor-analytic support for DSM-III's Posttraumatic Stress Disorder for Vietnam veterans. *Journal of Clinical Psychology, 40*, 5–14.

Simon, W.J. (1972). My country. In L. Rottman, J. Barry, & B.T. Paquet (Eds.), *Winning hearts and minds: War poems by Vietnam veterans* (p. 42). New York: McGraw-Hill.

Sleek, S. (1998). Older vets just now feeling pain of war. *APA Monitor, 29*, 1, 28.

Strayer, R., & Ellenhorn, L. (1975). Vietnam veterans: A study exploring adjustment patterns and attitudes. *Journal of Social Issues, 31*, 81–93.

Taylor, S., Koch, W.J., Kuch, K., Crockett, D.J., & Passey, G. (1998). The structure of posttraumatic stress symptoms. *Journal of Abnormal Psychology, 107*, 154–160.

Wang, S., Wilson, J.P., & Mason, J.W. (1996). Stages of decompensation in combat-related Posttraumatic Stress Disorder: A new conceptual model. *Integrative Physiological and Behavioral Science, 31*, 237–253.

Yager, T., Laufer, R., & Gallops, M. (1984). Some problems associated with war experience in men of the Vietnam generation. *Archives of General Psychiatry, 41*, 327–333.

Chapter 3

Executioners

THE NATURE OF THE EVIDENCE

Is there evidence that carrying out executions constitutes a traumatic event to those who participate? The symptoms of PTSD are used here as a theme. Descriptions of symptoms are sought, but full diagnoses are neither possible nor desirable. The clinical dichotomy is not relevant, inasmuch as symptoms that a psychiatrist would regard as being at a subclinical level are also of interest on a continuum of psychological reactions. Furthermore, none of the people are being subjected to the kind of interview or psychometric scale that would be necessary to ascertain what level of symptomatology they have. The idea is that if the symptoms are in fact strong and widespread, then documentary evidence should occasionally surface.

This evidence will be in a different vocabulary from that which psychiatrists use. Individuals express their own experience in their own words, and with few exceptions no professional is intervening to ascertain the extent to which the lay terms fit the professional nomenclature for the experience.

Prevalence rates for those with PTSD symptoms are always only a portion of those who have been subjected to similar traumas, so there can be no expectations that such symptoms must necessarily always be present. Additionally, while some signs of trauma can manifest themselves immediately, it is quite common to have a delayed reaction in which symptoms do not appear until well after a traumatic event. Furthermore, many of those who undergo the experience may have an interest in believing that it does not affect them, and that makes it all the harder to get information. This is already difficult in that very few researchers have looked at the matter.

IMMEDIATE TRAUMATIC REACTIONS TO EXECUTIONS

The first thing that must be established is whether or not the event which causes later symptoms is traumatic and would ordinarily be seen as such. If the event is either not traumatic or imaginary, then the symptoms must be interpreted in some manner other than PTSD. In the current definition of *DSM-IV*, there are two requirements to determine a traumatic event. The first one—an event involving the death of another—is clearly met in the case of executions. The second requirement—a response of fear, helplessness, or horror—replaces the standards of an earlier version, which said only that the trauma had to be "outside the realm of ordinary experience" (American Psychiatric Association, 1987). They realized that, unfortunately, too many traumas cannot fit that criterion. Furthermore, different people have different ideas of what is traumatic, and the requirement of the most recent version was intended to add that subjective component.

Is there evidence of such reactions at the time of executions? Do some of the symptoms associated with traumatic events occur at the time of executions among those witnessing and participating in them? After all, there are many people who have continued conducting many executions over the course of years, so "helplessness" is not an expected component. Expected components would be sense of anxiety, dissociation, numbing, and physiological reactivity.

There are many sources that suggest a sense of anxiety or horror accompanying executions. When *Corrections Today*, a popular style magazine for prison professionals, ran a series of articles on "Managing Death Row" in 1993, the view that executions are much more anxiety provoking than other prison work was presented without opposition. In a highlighted quotation, one warden said, "For most of the members of the execution team, the procedure is a gut-wrenching, highly emotional experience" (Thigpen, 1993, p. 56). Another warden put it this way: "The next four weeks were among the most difficult of my life. Like many of you, I have seen riots, grisly murder scenes and other prison crises. Yet the impending execution weighed on my mind constantly . . . [it would] nearly consume me with personal anxiety and concern for our people" (Martin, 1993, pp. 62, 64). In his own book, another warden said simply, "Try as I might, I could not separate myself from the horribleness of it all" (Cabana, 1996, p. 17).

Sleep problems related to anxiety would be expected, and wardens have also reported this in connection to executions: "In the weeks since the most recent execution, I had slept with troubled dreams, fitfully trying to make sense of the whole thing. Looking at the man in front of me, I wondered if I would ever sleep peacefully again" (Cabana, 1996, p. 16). Another warden said: "I didn't sleep well that night. I didn't sleep well the night before either. I'd sleep a bit, then wake up. When I think about this, it washes over you, it comes in a jumbled up mess of things" (Johnson, 1998, p. 179).

Peritraumatic dissociation (dissociation at the time of the event) is a major predictor for PTSD. Dissociative symptoms include time distortion, a sense of unreality, and detachment from the event and from other people. In a study of retrospective reports of such dissociation among Vietnam veterans, researchers concluded that "the tendency to dissociate during a traumatic event, although affording the victim some degree of detachment, distancing, and unreality, does not confer long-term protection against, but rather constitutes a risk factor for, subsequent PTSD" (Marmar et al., 1994, p. 906).

Warden Cabana (1996) especially has several illustrative passages noting the time distortion and unreality: "How long the final minutes would be for both of us! . . . The telephone was still ringing, but somehow it sounded far away" (pp. 12–13). "In a quivering, staccato voice, I read for what seemed an eternity" (p. 14). "The 'last mile' seemed an eternity, every step a painful reminder of what waited at the end of the walk" (p. 187). "Although the struggle seemed to go on forever, it was, in reality, over quickly. . . . It had taken barely a minute for Connie Ray Evans to lapse into unconsciousness" (p. 189).

A reporter talking with officers also noted that when conducting an execution, "a minute is a lifetime" (Trombley, 1992, p. 212). In a composite portrait of three witnessed executions, a researcher notes: "Jones sat perfectly still for what seemed an eternity but was in fact no more than thirty seconds" (Johnson, 1998, p. 177).

A study was done on media witnesses to an execution (Freinkel, Koopman, & Spiegel, 1994). Though these people were not active participants in causing the death of the condemned, their reactions are instructive. The study was done to see the psychological consequences of witnessing violence under circumstances in which one is not threatened personally, and in which psychological preparation is possible since the fact and timing of the event is known in advance. Fifteen journalists filled out questionnaires ten weeks after the event, and twelve of those also responded to semi-structured interviews. The interviews showed that the dissociative symptoms might be greater than the questionnaires would reveal, and more than half of the journalists did report these symptoms. Long-term follow-up has not been reported.

Physiological reactivity to the event would primarily be manifested in increased heart rate. There are other kinds of reactivity (skin conductance, blood pressure, even brain wave patterns), but measuring them requires equipment and this is normally done for PTSD diagnostic purposes long after the event. Only one case of measuring equipment was found in the execution literature, and this was for a staff member who had volunteered to play the role of the condemned during a practice of the procedure; he showed wildly erratic electrocardiogram [EKG] results (Cabana, 1996, p. 161).

However, when people can hear their hearts pounding, this can be a sign of psychophysiological reactivity. Trombley (1992), for example, reports one officer as saying: "I could hear my own heart beating more than anything else that I'm conscious of in that last three, four, five minutes after the execution warrant has been read" (p. 213). Warden Cabana gives a more detailed illustration of physiological reactivity at the time of the event, right before the execution as he approaches the cell of the condemned:

The officers on the block were closing the windows along the top of the tier. The heavy old steel-framed windows made a loud noise as they were slammed shut one by one. Each time I heard the noise echo up and down the tier, my skin crawled and I jumped just a little. The electric lock released the door at the end of the tier with a crack. Everything seemed magnified—every sound, every whisper. Though it was only a few feet to the cell where Connie had spent the last seventy-two hours, I moved more slowly than usual. My feet were heavy, I felt as though I had to force my legs to move, and I could feel my heart pounding in my chest. (Cabana, 1996, p. 185)

The jumpiness at loud noises is especially noteworthy, and common in reactions to trauma.

Numbing is another expected reaction. In lay terms, this can be expressed as being "blank," as the chaplain of Potosi Prison explains how he finds executions:

Exhausting. You're running on adrenaline. You're stressed out. And when it's all said and done, because you're running on the adrenaline of stress, it's anticlimactic. . . . I've talked to Mr. Roper . . . I said, "How do you feel?" And he said, "Blank." I said, "Blank? That's it?" And he said, *"That's all I'm feeling. Blank."* There's nothing there. You keep thinking there's going to be some emotion. You're searching for something. . . . It's just a blank. (Trombley, 1992, pp. 274–275; emphasis in original)

Johnson (1998) found a similar reaction, quoting an officer: "I just cannot feel anything. And that was what bothered me. I thought I would feel something, but I didn't feel anything" (p. 181).

Thus, the acute reactions to executions do exist. Prevalence and severity have not been studied, but the prerequisite for regarding subsequent chronic symptoms as being due to an etiological traumatic event seems to be present. The long-term effects are not due to unusual reactions to that which would not ordinarily be deemed traumatic.

CHRONIC SYMPTOMS

Throughout history, it has been common for executioners to be illiterate men of low socioeconomic class, who were given to substance abuse. In some cases, men have received reprieves from their own executions by serving as executioners themselves. Accordingly, the historical evidence looking for a clear articulation of psychological reaction is likely to be more recent, when executions became more bureaucratized and professionalized.

One of the most comprehensive historical sources is derived from the extensive diary kept by James Berry, who served as primary hangman in Great Britain from 1884 to 1892. A book based on these diaries, called *The Reluctant Hangman* (Atholl, 1956), gives a wealth of information. The author says: "The conversations and thoughts I attribute to Berry are based on his own words as recorded, reported and remembered. He discussed his work and his feelings without inhibition and it has not been necessary to invent" (p. 10). Berry's thoughts ran the gamut of posttrauma reactions, and so his thoughts can be used extensively. Additionally, current publications of execution officers speaking in their own words will be used to illustrate symptoms.

The aversion of James Berry to his work was mentioned throughout his diaries. In keeping with the language of the time, it was frequently referred to as a case of nerves:

Berry . . . never lost an opportunity of praising his wife for . . . the way she sustained him, especially at times when he was deeply depressed and near a nervous breakdown as a result of some experience at a hanging. Indeed, he recorded that on occasions when he should be setting out for an execution and the whole idea nauseated him, it was only his wife's reminder of his duty that enabled him to go through with it. (Atholl, 1956, p. 60)

According to the *DSM-IV* psychiatric definition, the first symptom in persistently reexperiencing the event is "recurrent and intrusive distressing recollections of the event, including images, thoughts, or perceptions." The intrusiveness of these thoughts tends to be recordings of emotional states, and wordless because words were not used in processing the experience; they are unmodified by the passage of time (van der Kolk & Fisler, 1995, p. 520).

James Berry noted the experience with one of his hanging victims: "For the rest of his life, Berry was haunted by Lee. Haunted not merely by that terrible half hour in Exeter Prison which he re-lived a hundred times" (Atholl, 1956, p. 131). Warden Thigpen put it this way: "I witnessed eight human beings move from life to death. . . . Those experiences remain indelibly imprinted in my mind" (Thigpen, 1993, p. 58).

The following testimony comes from Larry Myers on June 28, 1991, before the State of Nebraska Pardons Board. He reports that in 1959, John Greenholtz was the assistant warden at the Nebraska Penal Complex, the official in charge of an execution in Nebraska.

[In 1971,] John and I were chatting about various subjects when "out of the blue" he asked me if I had ever witnessed an execution. . . . John continued on to describe the gruesome details of the execution. . . . I want to emphasize that John's words flowed out like a "stream of consciousness," as if he wanted to tell me some things in order to "get it off his chest." . . . He said that he was physically sick for two days afterwards, he was vomiting and had fits of depression. He said he had nightmares for years after, and that the gruesome images still haunted him, even 12 years later! And then he cried. . . . John Greenholtz was a good man, but he had psychological and emotional scars for the rest of his life. (pp. 35–37)

National Public Radio broadcast an interview with Fred Allen on its program called *All Things Considered* on October 12, 2000. Allen was part of the tie-down team in about 120 executions, but had stopped three years earlier. His description of why he stopped follows:

I was just working in the shop, then all of a sudden something just triggered in me and I started shaking and I walked back into the house, and my wife asked, "What's the matter?" and I said, "I don't feel good," and tears, uncontrollable tears, was coming out of my eyes. And she said, "What's the matter?" and I said, "I just thought about that execution that I did two days ago, and everybody else's that I was involved with." And what it was, was something triggered within and it just—everybody, all of these executions, all of a sudden all sprung forward.

In his first willingness to talk about the aftermath in public, he explained his current state that shows expressions of intrusive imagery, the kind of memories that are copies of the experience:

Just like taking slides in a film projector and having a button and just pushing a button and just watching over and over, him, him, him. I don't know if it's a mental breakdown, I don't know if—it will probably be classified more as a traumatic stress, similar to what the individuals in war had, you know, and they'd come back from the war and it might be three months, it might be two years, it might be five years, all of a sudden they relive it again, and all that has to come out. You see, I can barely even talk because I'm thinking more and more of it, you know. There was just so many of them.

As a similar intrusion, the next symptom listed in the psychiatric manual is recurrent distressing dreams of the event (American Psychiatric Association, 1994, p. 427). An anti-death penalty newsletter published this from former Canadian executioner John Robert Radclive: "I used to say to condemned persons as I beckoned with my hand, 'Come with me.' Now at night when I lie down, I start up with a roar as victim after victim comes up before me. I can see them on the trap, waiting a second before they face their Maker. They haunt me and taunt me until I am nearly crazy with an unearthly fear. I am two hundred times a murderer, but I won't kill another man" (Johnson, 1998, p. 190).

Another symptom, acting or feeling as if the traumatic event were recurring, can involve hallucinations or flashbacks. People who have these are disinclined to mention them, but James Berry did refer to the "victims I sometimes see in my waking dreams" (Atholl, 1956, p. 140). The term "waking dreams" may indicate this kind of experience. There is even suggestion in the literature on PTSD that flashbacks may be the emergence into wakefulness of a form of mentation otherwise associated with REM sleep, that is, with dreams (Ross et al., 1989).

Symptom B(4) is "intense psychological distress at exposure to internal or external cues that symbolize or resemble an aspect of the traumatic event." This is best illustrated in the case of James Berry:

It is worth noting that when, eventually, revulsion set in, one of his first actions was to sweep from the house everything that reminded him of his hangings. His explanation was an almost superstitious one, that these things had brought him "bad luck." What had been souvenirs of duty competently done became reminders of a past which weighed heavily on him. The result of getting rid of the relics and momentos was like laying a ghost. He never forgot his victims or any details of their end, but he was no longer proud of them. "It was a different house when they were gone," he wrote. "I found I could sleep and no longer had an uncanny feeling when I entered a room where they were kept," and he talked of "the evil influence of my victims clinging to these relics." (Atholl, 1956, p. 53)

This passage illustrates several of the symptoms in this intrusion cluster of symptoms: the sleep problems, the uncanny feeling, the evil influence; these also suggest a high probability of the fifth symptom in the cluster, B(5): "physiological reactivity on exposure to internal or external cues that symbolize or resemble an aspect of the traumatic event."

A journalist reporting on a Missouri prison gives a couple of examples of avoidance strategies. One officer said, "When I went to Vietnam . . . I knew that people were going to be killed. . . . So I think the preparedness that I go through might be something similar. I don't consciously think about Vietnam because I pretty well put up a mental block and let that be past history, and to forget about it" (Trombley, 1992, p. 215). The relationship of being an executioner to having been a combat veteran is of particular interest, and has not been adequately studied. In the other example, a homicide investigator is speaking: "Things affect me. And that's why I can't watch those police drama type of movies. It's not that you don't like your profession. But you have to have that certain curtain that you put down, and that's your psychological self protecting itself" (Trombley, 1992, p. 118).

However, intrusion and avoidance are not mutually exclusive. They can go together, because avoidance can be strongest when intrusion is strongest. Warden Cabana shows how this works:

Although it seems like yesterday, eight years have passed since the execution of Edward Earl Johnson and Connie Ray Evans. Following Connie's execution, I plunged back into my work with a sense of urgency. For a time, it must have seemed that I was pursuing my duties with a vitality and determination not seen before. In a very real sense, I was. Each new day's crises kept me from having to think or remember. But nothing could dispel the feelings I harbored inside. Try as I did, I could not remove the lingering doubt or bewilderment. (Cabana, 1996, p. 191)

This also shows that posttrauma symptoms, contrary to the psychiatric definition that requires "clinically significant distress or impairment," can manifest without actually being a disorder that interferes with functioning. In fact, one study of men at Harvard who had fought in World War II showed that those with more PTSD symptoms were actually more likely to be listed in *Who's Who of America* (Lee et al., 1995). They had worked hard at their jobs because it was a good avoidance strategy, as the previous quotation from Warden Cabana illustrates.

The idea that the job of executioner might lead to PTSD is not a claim peculiar to opponents of the death penalty by any means. Just as with the police officers who have shot someone in the line of duty, there are those who sympathize and work with the execution staff, and believe these reactions to be an occupational hazard of men who are doing their job. At California State Prison in San Quentin, for example, Staff Psychologist Maurice Lyons conducts regular training on handling traumatic events such as executions. The "sessions are intended to help staff understand post-trauma syndrome and its normal course of development" (Vasquez, 1993, p. 70).

THE HANGMAN'S ACCOUNT

As mentioned above, James Berry was a hangman in Great Britain from 1884 to 1892. He was unusual among executioners in keeping an extensive diary that included his feelings. Justin Atholl wrote a book based on this diary, published in 1956.

There was, of course, no concept of PTSD in the nineteenth century when Berry was doing his work. There was barely such a concept when the book was written in the 1950s. Atholl makes no reference to any similarities to feelings of combat veterans. He states an interest in why someone who had spent so much time in this occupation would later campaign against it.

The fact that Atholl was not looking at the diaries with the symptom definitions in mind was both a disadvantage and an advantage. He could have missed important points that would back up or refute the thesis, but also he was not biasing his report in favor of showing the presence or absence of the symptom definitions.

Erving Goffman, a prominent sociological thinker, cited Atholl's book as a case of how people manage a stigma. There is quite a bit of information on how Berry handled the disdain against the executioner even in a society that demanded that kind of work be done (Goffman, 1963). This shows that scholars can look at the same material and identify different aspects of the social and psychological dynamics in Berry's experience.

Signs of substance abuse and irritability surfaced over the course of time:

After a hundred hangings, signs began to appear that Berry's nerves were being affected. He had been a teetotaler when he started. Now he was drinking a good deal. Where formerly he had always been genial he was inclined to become snappy with reporters. His nights were sometimes sleepless and when he slept he was agitated by dreams. When he started as an executioner his nightmares had been the products of his secret fears that things would go wrong, "of things that never happened and never could happen," as he put it. Now they were not products of imagination, but the re-playing by shadowy figures of real scenes which needed no embellishment from a troubled mind to make them nightmares. (Atholl, 1956, p. 158)

The form of eidetic dreams, the playing of a videotape in the head during sleep, is here expressed and connected to other symptoms.

In one case, Joseph Lowson had at first treated his own imminent hanging as a joke, but then let loose of a string of "foul and blasphemous" language coming through the cloth covering his head. What happened next was a case of time distortion during the event:

The moment which turned Berry's dream into a nightmare was that when he was pulling the lever and it would not move while the man on the trap continued to talk. It was probably only seconds before signs from a warder reminded Berry that in his nervousness he was trying to move the lever the wrong way, but it seemed like an eternity, and when the man fell Berry had to prop himself against the wall to avoid fainting. In his sleep the sweat would break out on him again as it had done that morning in Durham. (Atholl, 1956, p. 160)

Berry interpreted and dealt with the intrusive imagery differently over the course of time:

A curious point was that while at the beginning of his career he had proclaimed he was completely without superstitions and thought dreams and omens all nonsense, he had come to be haunted not merely by memories, but by relics. I have mentioned that he had many "souvenirs" of the men and women he had hanged. He came to have the idea that these were responsible for the nightmares that disturbed his nights and in 1880 he sold them all to Madame Tussaud's. He said the effect was immediate and beneficial, that his depression lifted and a curse seemed to have gone from the house. (Atholl, 1956, p. 167)

Outwardly, however, there were few signs for outsiders to know what Berry was writing in his diary about his feelings. For years, he had times when he thought he would quit, but he had nevertheless continued. He never missed an execution on grounds of health, even though there were some that involved a "nervous breakdown" from which he took two or three weeks to recover. He was successful in hiding this from the public and officials. H. Snowden Ward worked with him on a book and found him genial and humorous. If we now know from his diary what it was that was being concealed, this does suggest that the mere outward appearance of a lack of problems in an individual is insufficient to establish an actual lack of such symptoms. It may require either

deeper discussion with the individual, or the individual's own retrospective reflections at a later time, to uncover the presence of symptoms.

EXCEPTIONS

Some of the writings on staff reactions insist that there are none. Even if it
were the case that posttrauma reactions are common, this would be expected,
for four major reasons: (1) people who expect stress but instead get a blank
feeling, the feeling of numbness as discussed above, may interpret that as not
having any problem; (2) the delayed reaction that is common, a feature to be
specified as present or absent in diagnosis; (3) with any trauma, a portion of the
people gets symptoms, but not all do; and (4) there is the basic social psychology
of cognitive dissonance: people who are engaged in an activity have an interest
in asserting that the activity is justified, and if they see the presence of symptoms
as a threat, they have a strong interest in denying it.

Justin Atholl, the same man who wrote the biography of reluctant hangman
James Berry, wrote an earlier book in 1954, when hangings were still being
practiced in Great Britain. He interviewed people involved and reported that
execution "has been so effectively humanized that it does not even appear to
place any particular strain on those who have to be present at it" (Atholl, 1954,
p. 132). He further elucidates: "Mr. Pierrepointe was asked whether he found
his duties very trying . . . and replied, 'I am accustomed to it now,' and to the
further question, 'You do not turn a hair?' answered with a simple 'No'" (p.
132). Three other statements from prison officers also indicated a lack of being
affected.

Atholl's book two years later, which indicates that hangman Berry did have
some problems, is not actually in contradiction to this, in that Berry had worked
in the previous century and Atholl was only claiming the lack of problems for
the contemporary situation. However, Atholl's interviewee, Albert Pierrepointe,
like James Berry, did later come out as a strong advocate against the death
penalty, and that may serve to temper Pierrepointe's previous statement somewhat.

The other counterarguments to posttrauma reactions came from the journalist
reporting on Potosi Prison in Missouri. As can be seen from previous quotes in
this chapter, he also documented that there were many such problems. However,
since he was particularly interested in the subject of staff reactions and reporting
all he was told, he naturally came across resistance to the idea that there should
be any aftereffects.

One particularly telling case was that of Don:

He told me about a Department of Corrections stress seminar he attended with the prison
psychologist, Betty Weber. . . . There were six groups in all, from prisons around the
state . . . he said, "So at this seminar, each of the groups had to list, in order of priority,
the six most stressful work situations. . . . [W]e couldn't figure out number six, so we

put down, going through an execution. Out of the six groups the other five felt that going through an execution was number one. But none of them were from Potosi, and none had any experience. When it's done as professionally as we do it here at Potosi, there's very little stress . . . it doesn't bother me . . . I know my duty. These people killed somebody. I didn't. All I'm doing is a job that the state says I should do." (Trombley, 1992, pp. 204–205)

The wording at the end indicates why there is a need to deny being bothered, but the rest of the interview is even more telling about what this man is going through. After a discussion of constant fear, attributed to danger of inmates, which could be due to such fear but could also be attributed to symptom D(4), hypervigilance: "There is no doubt in my mind that if someone spits on me, my anger is going to flare, because I'm a human being. And I'm afraid somebody is going to get the crap knocked out of them . . . there's times when possibly there is an excessive use of force because of an incident where an inmate spits on someone" (Trombley, 1992, p. 206). This statement no longer portrays professionalism. It looks more like the explosive outbursts of symptom D(2) in the *DSM-IV*, a symptom that was found in veterans to be especially applicable to those who have killed (see Chapter 2).

The journalist goes on to discuss matters with the prison psychologist, Betty Weber. When executions started, Weber did a survey in June 1990, to measure psychological effects on staff. It had thirty-four responses on fourteen yes/no questions. Seven of those questions were given: second thoughts about accepting execution assignment, family problems, whether they would volunteer for the assignment, understanding the appeals process, wanting training on the appeals process, reservations about the guilt of some inmates, and the need to talk to someone afterward (Trombley, 1992, pp. 217–218). This leaves only seven unspecified questions for posttrauma reactions, with no wording given to see how well they covered that. The result was: "Betty Weber reported that the overall consensus of opinion was that the problems expected, i.e. stress, guilt, depression, etc. did not occur following the executions" (Trombley, 1992, p. 218).

This is not a survey that would be taken seriously in the PTSD literature because of its yes/no format, small sample size, one-time administration with no consideration of delayed or long-term effects, no psychometric validation, and probably no consideration of emotional numbing. Still, it is the only mention of quantitative data on actual executioners that was found.

In addition to these problems, a further difficulty with the data comes later when the journalist, while talking with Weber, returns to the survey and wonders if there were staff concerns for which a brief questionnaire would be insufficient. Her response was "Everybody says we ought to have all these problems. I've always said no, I don't think so. Because we can opt out at any time and not participate" (Trombley, 1992, p. 223). A bias on the part of the researcher toward what the results ought to be could mean the results are methodologically flawed.

In his research among execution staff, Johnson also reports that the view that there would be no scars left was prevalent, but "problems would surface for some of the officers, I learned from my research, with the passage of time" (Johnson, 1998, p. 181). He went on to detail several such problems, from recurring fear to a fear of a delayed reaction of guilt.

In summary, while it is always harder to establish an absence of symptoms than to establish a presence, the evidence for an absence is actually very meager. The very fact that the question comes up, and is answered with such vehemence, shows that the presence of some kind of psychological scars is an idea that has occurred to participants. Its actual prevalence and depth await further study, in research designs that are more rigorously done.

REFERENCES

American Psychiatric Association. (1987). *Diagnostic and statistical manual of mental disorders* (3rd ed., revised). Washington, DC: Author.

————. (1994). *Diagnostic and statistical manual of mental disorders* (4th ed.). Washington, DC: Author.

Atholl, J. (1954). *Shadow of the gallows*. London: John Long Limited.

————. (1956). *The reluctant hangman: The story of James Berry, executioner 1884–1892*. London: John Long Limited.

Cabana, D.A. (1996). *Death at midnight: The confession of an executioner*. Boston: Northeastern University Press.

Freinkel, A., Koopman, C., & Spiegel, D. (1994). Dissociative symptoms in media eye-witnesses of an execution. *American Journal of Psychiatry, 151*, 1335–1339.

Goffman, E. (1963). *Stigma: Notes on the management of spoiled identity*. Englewood Cliffs, NJ: Prentice-Hall.

Johnson, E.C. (1960). *Jane Addams: A centennial reader*. New York: Macmillan.

Johnson, R. (1998). *Death work: A study of the modern execution process*. Belmont, CA: Wadsworth.

Lee, K.A., Vaillant, G.E., Torrey, W.C., & Elder, G.H. (1995). A 50-year prospective study of the psychological sequelae of World War II combat. *American Journal of Psychiatry, 152*, 516–522.

Marmar, C.R., Weiss, D.S., Schlenger, W.E., Fairbank, J.A., Jordan, B.K., Kulka, R.A., & Hough, R.L. (1994). Peritraumatic dissociation and posttraumatic stress in male Vietnam theater veterans. *American Journal of Psychiatry, 151*, 902–907.

Martin, G.N. (1993). A warden's reflections: Enforcing the death penalty with competence, compassion. *Corrections Today*, July, 60, 62, 64.

Ross, R.J., Ball, W.A., Sullivan, K.A., & Caroff, S.N. (1989). Sleep disturbance as a hallmark of Posttraumatic Stress Disorder. *American Journal of Psychiatry, 146*, 697–707.

Thigpen, M.L. (1993). A tough assignment. *Corrections Today*, July, 56, 58.

Trombley, S. (1992). *The execution protocol: Inside America's capital punishment industry*. New York: Crown.

van der Kolk, B.A., & Fisler, R. (1995). Dissociation and the fragmentary nature of traumatic memories: Overview and exploratory study. *Journal of Traumatic Stress, 8*, 505–525.

Vasquez, D.B. (1993). Helping prison staff handle the stress of an execution. *Corrections Today,* July, 70, 72.

Chapter 4

A Historical Case: The Nazis

USING HISTORICAL DOCUMENTS

The Nazis are a group well known for containing large numbers of perpetrators of a genocidal level of violence. Unlike most veterans, the Nazis did this usually with minimal danger to themselves. The graphic scenes they witnessed were ones they caused, with the confounding variable of concurrent dangers as possible etiological traumas being much less in this than in other groups. However, the confounding variable of previous traumatization remains, which was amply provided by World War I. Additionally, German interwar psychiatrists treated PTSD harshly, believing its root cause was a desire for compensation or coddling.

Unlike most historical instances of genocide, the Nazis left a large number of documents behind which can be utilized in the search. The information on psychological consequences of mass murder to those who carried it out is available through diaries, court transcripts, memoranda, and interviews, which have been well researched, analyzed, and consolidated in numerous secondary sources. Were posttrauma symptoms among Nazi perpetrators sufficiently intense or widespread enough to allow us to find evidence of them?

As with the historical executioners, a diagnosis cannot be given to historical figures because no interaction is possible; they cannot respond to clarifying questions. We must be satisfied to glean whatever information is suggested from what they did choose to leave behind. Additionally, many of the secondary sources that discuss the historical documents were done by authors with varying perspectives; none of them has had the documentation of PITS as an interest.

The symptoms can be treated as an interpretive theme. Posttrauma symptoms can be inferred from historical documents, both from writings by those who may have suffered from it, and from other people's descriptions of their behavior. The distinction between full-blown PTSD and subclinical levels of the disorder, after all, is of more interest to professionals treating individuals in the present. From the point of view of helping to explain historical circumstances, the distinction is not relevant.

There are many obstacles in the way of finding what actually happened. The Nazis destroyed a large number of documents to avoid having the documents used against them in court. Other documents never came into existence. This was either for the same reason or because the defeat of the Nazis removed motivation for the writing of documents that would otherwise have occurred. Some documents, such as the reminisces of Pery Broad, a participant at Auschwitz, use postwar interpretation of the activities as criminal and the perpetrators as villainous—and therefore too callous to have psychological consequences (Bezwinska & Czech, 1972). In any event, the subject of descriptions of individuals' reactions to events and emotional responses naturally make up only a very small portion of historical material.

Furthermore, as would be the case in all searches for posttrauma symptoms in history, the symptoms themselves include a desire to avoid reminders of the trauma and dissociation. Along with the natural human predilection for denial of responsibility, the denial of memory that goes with trauma adds a substantial barrier to the existence of appropriate historical materials.

Finally, the vocabulary must be inferred. The modern terms of PTSD—"dissociation," "psychic numbing," "intrusive thoughts," "reexperiencing of events," and "flashbacks"—are not used in historical documents. Terms like "shell shock," "soldier's heart," and "battle fatigue" can be expected to be primitive, imprecise translations of the modern terms. However, even those terms imply more of an understanding of a clear phenomenon than can be expected in most historical eras.

Among the most likely candidates for concepts that may lead to passages thematically related to posttrauma symptoms are hallucinations, dreams and nightmares, nervous breakdowns, bad nerves, and anything indicating a sense of unreality about situations that onlookers would reasonably describe as traumatic. Substance abuse is also strongly correlated with PTSD, and comments on excessive use of alcohol and drugs can be found.

THE EINSATZGRUPPEN

The Einsatzgruppen were groups of soldiers or police charged with the assignment of directly shooting and killing Jews who had been rounded up for the purpose. Victims were immediately buried in mass graves. Commonly mentioned in histories of the Holocaust, many secondary sources document that these murder squads had major psychological difficulties. This was the reason that the more costly move to gas chambers had to be utilized, allowing for distance between executioner and victim. While commonly put in terms of breakdown or revulsion, these psychological reactions are what one would expect when looking for posttrauma symptoms.

Browning documents extensively how much a certain police battalion hated the duty and resented its captain for being absent (Browning, 1992, pp. 55–70). On one occasion, Jews who had been rounded up were let go, apparently because other shooters didn't show up and that captain was not going to put his men through this again (p. 77). Citing Nazi documents, Hilberg (1961) reports, "every once in a while a man did have a nervous breakdown," and "in several units the use of alcohol became routine" (p. 218).

In his autobiography, Rudolf Hoess (1959) reported what he had heard from Gestapo officer and "Jewish specialist" Adolf Eichmann's descriptions: "Many members of the Einsatzkommandos, unable to endure wading through blood any longer, had committed suicide. Some had even gone mad. Most of the members of these Kommandos had to rely on alcohol when carrying out their horrible work" (p. 163).

An oft-repeated quotation comes from one of the officers in charge of the Eisentzgruppen, von dem Bach-Zelewski. When Heinrich Himmler, Leader of the SS (SchutzStaffel, the organization responsible for all police activity of the Third Reich) visited, Bach-Zelewski said to him: "Look at the eyes of the men in this Kommando, how deeply shaken they are! These men are finished for the rest of their lives. What kind of followers are we training here? Either neurotics or savages!" (Hilberg, 1961, p. 218).

The same report expressed that Himmler was badly shaken up from watching the work of the shooting squads on this visit. Himmler indicated in his subsequent pep talk to the troops that he knew this was a repulsive duty, that he hated this bloody business, and that he had been aroused in the depths of his soul. The conclusion was that this sacrifice made it all the more noble an endeavor. It was because of how ill he felt on this visit that he ordered a "more humane" way of doing the killings, which led to using gas chambers that allowed for greater distances between killer and victim.

The head SS doctor, Dr. Grawitz, later reported to Himmler that von dem Bach-Zelewski "is suffering particularly from hallucinations connected with the shootings of Jews which he himself carried out" (Hohne, 1969, p. 363). Hallucinations are included in PTSD symptom B(3) in the *Diagnostic and Statistical Manual of Mental Disorders* (*DSM-IV*) (American Psychiatric Association, 1994).

Symptom B(2), recurrent distressing dreams of the event, is mentioned here in several instances. Hilberg (1961) notes that "One of the officers who one day had been commanded to watch the shootings suffered the most horrible dreams during the following night" (p. 215). On the same subject of those executing at point-blank range, Steiner (1967) remarks: "This personalization of the act was accompanied by a physical proximity, since the executioner stood less than a yard away from his victim. Of course, he did not see him from the front, but it was discovered that necks, like faces, also individualize people . . . these necks came to haunt their dreams" (p. 73).

Browning (1992), while mentioning how much participants avoided talking about the subject, related that after a graphic incident: "The massacre was simply not discussed. . . . But repression during waking hours could not stop the nightmares. During the first night back from Jozefow, one policeman awoke firing his gun into the ceiling of the barracks" (p. 69). This form of acting out from the dreams is also common for those suffering posttrauma reactions.

Robert Jay Lifton, a psychiatrist who formally interviewed large numbers of Nazi doctors, reports more evidence of such reactions. Lifton (1986) says that an unnamed Nazi neuropsychiatrist who had treated many of the Einsatzgruppen members told him "that these disorders resembled combat reactions of ordinary troops: severe anxiety, nightmares, tremors, and numerous bodily complaints" (p. 15). For what the Nazi psychiatrist called the "killer troops," the "symptoms tended to last longer and to be more severe." Relating this in detached clinical tones, the Nazi also indicated that they did what they could to relieve symptoms and return men to duty, in line with German psychiatric practice since the First World War (p. 454).

The Nazi psychiatrist estimated prevalence of the disorder at 20% of the troops, with half attributing it to unpleasantness and half to guilt. The normal estimate of prevalence of PTSD for those who have been exposed to traumas is in the range of 25%. Given that these are both imprecise estimates, they would be roughly equivalent. This is interesting, since soldiers in combat have the additional factor of danger to themselves, whereas the shooting squads had a remarkable lack of casualties. If the symptoms were more severe, it would be due to action rather than danger. The revulsion resulted not from the passive sight of friends dying but from active killing of strangers.

THE NAZI DOCTORS

Lifton has done the most thorough work on the psychology of the doctors who did killing-related work at death camps such as Auschwitz. He did extensive interviews with such doctors, in the interest of finding out how they were able to do what they did. He documented a great deal of "psychic numbing" and sense of unreality, which are PTSD symptoms (Lifton, 1986, pp. 442–447). He also suggested "doubling" (pp. 422–429), which is a special form of dissociation, also a common posttrauma reaction.

Ironically, Lifton never mentions the possibility of PTSD. He did not solicit information from the doctors that would have given more information about it, such as presence of flashbacks or trauma-related dreams. Only in the one case of a doctor who was more humanitarian and did what he could within his authority to help the prisoners at Auschwitz did Lifton deal with high-anxiety dreams. He did relate PTSD to killing activities in the case of Vietnam veterans, and has contributed quite a bit of the scholarly literature on PTSD; he simply does not utilize this work in his book on Nazi doctors.

THE RORSCHACH

One of the few quantitative methods for assessing psychological consequences, in something resembling a standard manner that can be compared with others, is the Rorschach inkblot test. A psychometric test utilizing projection to ascertain personality traits and disorders, the Rorschach was, of course, unavailable before the twentieth century, but the Nazis are one of the few historical cases in which there are a few such tests available. One set was done for a group of sixteen men about to face trial after the war in Nuremburg, and another of about 200 Danish collaborators for lower-ranking Nazis. This allows a small expansion beyond the narrative wording of documents into a possibility of a more standardized kind of documentation.

In 1945, after they were captured but well before the actual trials began, sixteen Nazi war criminals were administered the Rorschach. These men were primarily administrators, and with the exceptions discussed below, they did not see as much graphic violence as those they were administering to carry out the violence. If the men did see any killing, it was someone else doing the violence under their orders. If they did not see the events they caused, they may be psychologically more similar to those airplane pilots who bomb targets without the visual feedback that makes the results of their actions unambiguous; some preliminary evidence suggests that there may still be posttrauma symptom consequences to this, as covered in Chapter 2. In any event, the tests of these men can serve as a beginning in trying to understand the role of PITS among Nazis in a way that goes beyond the narrative reports. The Nazis making those reports, after all, had no concept of PITS and an ideological commitment that would not have been philosophically compatible with the existence of such a phenomenon.

The entire transcripts of the responses of the sixteen men tried at Nuremburg can be found in the appendix of *The Quest for the Nazi Personality* (Zillmer et al., 1995). Very little was done to analyze these for several years; experts declined the opportunity. Miale and Selzer finally put out a book in 1975 on how the responses showed these men to be psychopaths. However, they have been roundly criticized for drawing conclusions because certain answers were not given, and for doing an analysis in full knowledge of who the respondents were.

The next year, Harrower (1976) selected eight of the Nazi records and eight Rorschach responses of other people from the normal population to serve as controls. She then sent these to be analyzed by ten experts who had no knowledge that any of the respondents were Nazis. She concluded that this was not a homogeneous group and that with few exceptions these were not psychopaths. In other words, it took the passage of almost thirty years before the climate of opinion was such that viewing the Nazis as something other than unambiguous subhuman monsters could be contemplated in the study of the Rorschachs.

Soon thereafter, Ritzler (1978) revisited the question by having the control group matched for age and for known pathology. He compared the sixteen Nazi records to a control group of sixteen on quantitative scores, and concluded that the Nazis did deviate from normal, but not as much as suggested by Miale and Selzer.

In the meantime, a more comprehensive method of scoring was devised by Exner, which has pretty much universally replaced the several scoring systems that preceded it to become the standard. Therefore, the standard scores are published and can be analyzed. Zillmer, Archer, and Castino (1989) published individual scores of the eight Nazis who received death sentences, leaving out those who were either acquitted or received a few years in prison. Resnick and Nunno (1991) published mean scores for the group as a whole. Ritzler, Zillmer, and Belevich (1993) published comparisons of different ways of scoring, so that scholars by discussion could come to agreement.

This is of interest to this study because there has been some preliminary work by Levin (1993) on which Exner scores would be related to Posttraumatic Stress Disorder. Therefore, comparisons can be made. One of Levin's hypotheses, confirmed in her sample, is that CF+C should be greater than FC for those with PTSD. To explain simply, color is used more than form, a lack of structuring that is accounted as "failure to use available resources in a manner which can invoke emotional modulation"—that is, restricted range of affect. This turned out to be true for five of the Nazis: Hoess, Kaltenbrunner, Keitel, Rosenburg, and Saukel.

Another of Levin's hypotheses was that the Afr, which stands for Affective Ratio, would be lower in those with PTSD. This was quite clear in six of the eight Nazis (Frank, Hoess, Kaltenbrunner, Rosenberg, Seyss-Inquart, and Saukel). Normal Afr is .66, and theirs ranged from .38 to .46. Only one, Keitel, had a normal level at .63. Goering's was actually quite elevated, at .89.

Being at the opposite extreme from normal does not mean being all the more opposite of PTSD, however. Several symptoms are bimodal at the extremes. The overall average of the full sixteen respondents was not different from normal, but this includes the eight who were not executed and whose crimes were therefore not as serious. It also includes Goering's score, serving as an outlier that brings up the average for those who were low.

Those with PTSD would be expected to be more "ambitent" rather than introtensive or extratensive in their approach to problem solving. That is to say, they have a thinking style that would take more time to achieve solutions or integrate traumatic experiences, as opposed to using their inner lives or interactions with their environments to do so more efficiently. This is shown on the Rorschach by the EB (Experience Balance) score, and it did show the group to be unusually ambitent compared to groups from the general population.

Another confirmed hypothesis is a significant elevation in inanimate movement, seen by some as related to dissociation. The average score did not differ from the norm of 1.3, but Keitel was a little higher at 3, Hoess was higher yet at 5, and Frank was remarkably high at 13.

Indeed, Frank is the most interesting case as an exception, since this group is not composed of those who committed the direct violence. The rest of the men never administered the gas pellets directly. They were the people who decided the pellets would be used and made arrangements. Frank was the exception; in his diary, he mentioned committing several ruthless, brutal acts. His scores are the most in line with the PTSD Rorschach profile: an inordinately high score of 13 on inanimate movement when 1.3 is the norm; a remarkably low Afr of .40 when .66 is the norm, and the highest score with four mentions of morbid content. The prison psychiatrist concluded from many conversations with him that he was a tortured soul (Zillmer, Archer, & Castino, 1989).

For more rank-and-file Nazis, about 200 Rorschachs done on Danish collaborators have recently been analyzed (Zillmer et al., 1995). Some of these respondents committed murders and torture, while others merely did sabotage or provided otherwise mundane services. Scores are reported only as averages for the entire group, without those committing violence differentiated from those who did not. The one exception is that the content scores for aggression and morbid content were higher in the violent group, which is not surprising. Overall, however, the CF+C scores were in fact higher than the FC (p. 113). Additionally, the percentage of the group with EB scores for an ambient problem-solving style was also much greater than the general population. These findings suggest that a further probing of this heterogeneous group for differences on PTSD-related scores, especially with a division of the violent from those not violent, would be fruitful.

Of course, alternative explanations are readily available for the above findings, offered by the researchers that presented the figures. They all related the characteristics found to permanent personality traits that antedated the Nazi activities of the individuals and helped to account for those activities.

Either a diagnosis or a scientific finding would require further probing of living individuals to preclude alternative explanations. While this may be a limitation of historical research, such research nevertheless overcomes the limiting of study to the living. This is a restriction far too binding for this particular subject.

PRE-NAZI PTSD

Erich Maria Remarque wrote the novel *All Quiet on the Western Front* from the point of view of a German soldier in World War I. Since the protagonist died at the end, this included nothing about long-term consequences like PTSD. Some of symptoms could be seen in acute form, such as the sense of foreshortened future. The Nazis banned the novel as being a negative view of the soldiers' experience, and the author had to flee. The very admission of PTSD symptoms would not be tolerated as the Nazis rose to power.

As mentioned above, after World War I, the psychiatrists of Germany who treated soldiers with PTSD believed it was caused by a desire for compensation or for coddling. Their primary method of treatment was to send them back into battle at the time of the war, and when there was no battle to send them back into, they otherwise tried to stiffen their resolves. The militaristic culture fosters a belief that war is a manly endeavor, and those who react negatively need to be helped to be combat-ready again. This means that the German veterans of World War I received what by today's standards would be regarded as counterproductive treatment.

In the case of the Nazi troops who were shooting Jews into pits, Robert Jay Lifton gives an illustration from his interviews as to how this counterproductive treatment was done:

The *Wehrmacht* neuropsychiatrist who had treated these psychological difficulties in *Einsatzgruppen* troops described them to me—the general manifestations of anxiety, including anxiety dreams—in the most detached clinical tones. When I asked him whether he had ever experienced anxiety dreams in response to all this killing or to his treating the killers, he answered that he had not: "I never killed anybody"; and, "As doctors . . . we were outsiders." It also became clear that he and his colleagues did not alter their medical approach in any significant way when treating these "killer troops" (as he called them during our interviews) but simply did what they could to relieve symptoms and help the men to return to duty. He would even sometimes gently warn them, "Be careful now, you're complaining but you're well." He was trying to suggest to me that, in doing so, he was considering the interests of the individual killer soldier. But there was no doubt that he was playing the role of the physician suspicious of malingering, who insisted upon holding to strictly medical criteria in decisions concerning sending these men back to duty where they could continue their killing. (Lifton, 1986, p. 454)

This is a clear continuation of the attitude among German psychiatrists that had been prevalent during the youth of the Nazi leaders.

What kind of effect did this form of treatment have in forming the attitudes of these leaders? It clearly bolstered beliefs and attitudes that favor the kind of views they held about war. It was both a result of and a continuing source of such attitudes, as would be expected under normal rules of socialization. Could counterproductive treatment also have been one of the many problems in the environment explaining why they engaged in such widespread killing?

Symptoms of PTSD can underlie future violent activity. Constricted affect (the blocking of emotions) and numbing are common predecessors to committing violence. Outbursts of irritability and rage are also possibilities for this. There is markedly diminished interest in significant activities and a sense of foreshortened future. Especially important is the sense of being detached or estranged from others. Even a sense of hypervigilance, which would involve constant fear, can contribute to the sense that a violent response is justified, as well as giving the emotional undercurrent necessary to carry it out. Much more would be necessary to move people to performing violent acts, but posttrauma symptoms could be one contributor.

The possible role of PTSD is not limited to combat veterans from World War I. In 1924, one of the Nazi war criminals, Hoess, received a ten-year sentence for a savage murder. The following passage is a memory that comes from that time of imprisonment. After his early release by amnesty, he rose in the Nazi hierarchy. He later assumed command of Auschwitz and oversaw the gassing of approximately two million people from July 1941 to the end of 1943. He wrote his autobiography while in prison awaiting trial for war crimes in 1947, and was executed by hanging soon thereafter. The extent to which his autobiography reflects his true feelings and the extent to which he is conscious of how he looks to others is of course a caveat to be aware of when reading his story:

Toward the end of the first two years, which had passed monotonously and without any special incident, I was overcome by a most peculiar state of mind. I became very irritable, nervous, and excited. I felt a disinclination to work, although I was in the tailoring shop at the time and had hitherto thoroughly enjoyed this work. I could no longer eat and I brought up every mouthful that I forced myself to swallow. I could not read any more and became completely unable to concentrate. I paced up and down my cell like a wild animal. I lay awake all night, although I had up to then always fallen at once into a deep and almost dreamless sleep. I had to get out of bed and walk round my cell, and was unable to lie still. Then I would sink exhausted on to the bed and fall asleep, only to wake again after a short time bathed in sweat from my nightmares. In those confused dreams I was always being pursued and killed, or falling over a precipice. The hours of darkness became a torment. Night after night I heard the clocks strike the hour. As morning approached, my dread increased. I feared the light of day and the people I should have to see once more. I felt incapable of seeing them again. I tried with all my strength to pull myself together, but without success. I wanted to pray, but my prayers dissolved into a distressed stammering. I had forgotten how to pray, and had lost the way to God. In my misery I believed that God had no wish to help me, since I had forsaken Him. I was tormented by the memory of my definite secession from the Church in 1922. Yet this had been the ratification of a state of affairs that had existed since the end of the war. In my heart I was already leaving the Church during the last years of the war. I reproached myself bitterly for not having followed the wishes of my parents, for my lack of piety. It was strange how all this worried me while I was in this plight.

My nervous agitation increased day to day, even from hour to hour. I nearly went raving mad. My health gave way. My foreman noticed my unaccustomed absent-mindedness and the mess I made of even the simplest tasks, and although I worked furiously I could not finish my daily task.

For several days I had fasted, thinking that after this I would be able to eat once more. The guard in charge of my section caught me in the act of throwing my dinner into the garbage pail. Although he usually did his job in a weary and indifferent manner, and hardly bothered about the prisoners, yet even he had noticed my behavior and appearance, and on this account had been keeping a sharp watch over me, as he later told me. I was taken immediately to the doctor. He was an elderly man who had been attached to the prison staff for a great many years. He listened patiently to my story, thumbed through the pages of my file and then said with the greatest nonchalance, "Prison psychosis. You'll get over it. It's not serious!" (Hoess, 1959)

The psychiatrist's response indicates this is not all that uncommon a condition in what he sees. He attributes it to prison, which may indeed be the case. PITS is another possible interpretation.

As stated above, Hoess was one of the Nuremberg war criminals who was given a Rorschach test, and his responses were consistent with someone who suffers from PTSD. He used color more than form, suggesting constricted affect, and he had a low Afr score indicating something similar. He had elevation in inanimate movement, with a score of 5 when 1.3 is normal. This indicates a possibility of dissociation.

Hoess is no longer available for a proper interview and diagnosis. There is at least some evidence of PTSD symptoms before he rose in Nazi ranks, and there is at least some evidence of it afterwards. In both cases, perpetration as the etiological trauma is plausible—a criminal homicide before his rise, and administration of a mass killing center after his rise. What caused what and when has been lost in the mists of time, but Hoess's case illustrates the possibility that knowledge of PITS serves not only as a way of dealing with those who suffer from it, but perhaps also as an important tool in prevention efforts.

REFERENCES

American Psychiatric Association. (1994). *Diagnostic and statistical manual of mental disorders* (4th ed.). Washington, DC: Author.

Bezwinska, J., & Czech, D. (Eds.). (1972). *KL Auschwitz seen by SS: Hoess, Broad, Kremer*. Panstwowe Muzeum w Osweicimiu, Poland.

Browning, C.R. (1992). *Ordinary men: Reserve Police Battalion 101 and the Final Solution in Poland*. New York: HarperCollins.

Harrower, M. (1976). Rorschach records of the Nazi war criminals: An experimental study after thirty years. *Journal of Personality Assessment, 40*, 341–351.

Hilberg, R. (1961). *The destruction of European Jews*. Chicago: Quadrangle Books.

Hoess, R. (1959). *Commandant of Auschwitz: The autobiography of Rudolf Hoess*, C. FitzGibbon (Trans.). London: Weidenfeld and Nicolson.

Hohne, H. (1969). *The order of death's hand: The story of Hitler's SS*, R. Barry (Trans.). Mcann, NY: Coward.

Levin, P. (1993). Assessing Posttraumatic Stress Disorder with the Rorschach projective technique. In J.P. Wilson & B. Raphael (Eds.), *International handbook of traumatic stress syndromes* (pp. 189–200). New York: Plenum.

Lifton, R.J. (1986). *The Nazi doctors: Medical killing and the psychology of genocide*. New York: Basic Books.

Miale, F.R., & Selzer, M. (1975). *The Nuremberg mind*. New York: Quadrangle.

Resnick, M.N., & Nunno, V.J. (1991). The Nuremberg mind redeemed: A comprehensive analysis of the Rorschachs of Nazi war criminals. *Journal of Personality Assessment, 57*, 19–29.

Ritzler, B.A. (1978). The Nuremberg mind revisited: A quantitative approach to Nazi Rorschachs. *Journal of Personality Assessment, 42,* 344–353.

Ritzler, B.A., Zillmer, E., & Belevich, A. (1993). Comprehensive system scoring discrepancies on Nazi Rorschachs: A comment. *Journal of Personality Assessment, 61,* 576–583.

Steiner, J. (1967). *Treblinka.* New York: Simon & Schuster.

Zillmer, E.A., Archer, R.P., & Castino, R. (1989). Rorschach records of Nazi war criminals: A reanalysis using current scoring and interpretation practices. *Journal of Personality Assessment, 53,* 85–99.

Zillmer, E.A., Harrower, M., Ritzler, B.A., & Archer, R.P. (1995). *The quest for the Nazi personality: A psychological investigation of Nazi war criminals.* Hillsdale, NJ: Lawrence Erlbaum Associates.

Chapter 5

Both Sides of Law Enforcement

POLICE

While it is common that active participation in the trauma is not attended to as a possible etiological stressor for PTSD, the case of police who shoot in the line of duty is the exception that proves the rule. It is readily admitted that police get PTSD from such incidents, and it is a particular kind of PTSD that is worse than what comes from being shot at. This has been clearly asserted in several studies (Carson, 1982; Loo, 1986; Mann & Neece, 1990; Manolias & Hyatt-Williams, 1993; Martin, McKean, & Vetkamp, 1986; Neilson, 1981; Stratton, Parker, & Snibbe, 1984).

In this case, the blame for the officer having to shoot is placed with the criminal(s) who created the traumatic situation. The officer's traumatic symptoms are viewed as a sign of virtue and sacrifice for being a good officer. In contrast to the soldier, the police officer is treated as someone who naturally would find shooting someone to be repulsive. Unlike military action, there is no social interference in admitting to it and sympathizing with the officer accordingly. The attitude is one of sympathy toward the officer who was put in a situation in which it was necessary to shoot.

The officer is seen as already being a victim because the trauma was bad enough to make shooting necessary. Shooting is to be avoided if at all possible; therefore, if it happens to a good officer doing his or her duty, acknowledging psychological difficulties is no insult. Unlike the soldier, who is expected to be fierce in battle, the idea of psychological difficulties for the police officer is a mark of virtue. It is, after all, the criminal who is blamed for causing the shooting. The officer has been victimized by being put in the situation where shooting could not be avoided. It is perceived as one of the reasons to be sympathetic to police officers.

There are some differences between police officers and others. Because the incident occurs in a context of an occupation that they continue to pursue, there is a constant reminder of possible trauma. Police have a self-image of being in control that is important to them, and an incident or incidents may cause additional stress if it counters that self-image. There are commonly legal repercussions in the form of hearings following the incident, which exacerbate the stress. In addition to the stress of the hearing itself, the determination of whether the shooting was justified by necessity or unjustified is likely to make a major difference in the psychological aftermath to the officer. Whether the officer agrees or disagrees with the assessment will also make a difference.

As with all cases of Perpetration-Induced Traumatic Stress (PITS), there are confounding possibilities on having PTSD before the incident. Police officers are disproportionately likely to be combat veterans. Like anyone else, they may have suffered child abuse, accidents, natural disasters, or been victims of crime. They are frequently targets of criminals simply by virtue of being police officers. They also can be exposed to more traumas by virtue of being emergency personnel—rescuers deliberately called in to handle already existing traumatizing situations. They have to deal at length with the aftermath of traumatization to others (e.g., Follette, Polusny, & Milbeck, 1994; Hallet, 1996). The extent to which PTSD symptomatology already exists before a shooting incident complicates the study of the etiological nature of the shooting incident itself.

PTSD is an important area of study not only in understanding the therapeutic needs of such officers, but in understanding how it can cause violence by police. Some studies on veterans have suggested a possibility that the presence of PTSD can contribute to the commission of violent crimes (e.g., Davis & Breslau, 1994; Hall & Hall, 1987; Hiley-Young et al., 1995; Lasko et al., 1994; Wilson & Zigelbam, 1983). An analogous process could happen with police officers. There can be a psychological need to master the trauma, or a related sensation-seeking syndrome. Arousal and lack of self-control, a survivor mode, hypervigilance, and readily available trauma reminders can lead to overreaction in situations. Constricted affect or depression can negatively impact appropriate judgments. The possibility of outbursts of rage is clearly counterproductive for avoiding unnecessary incidents.

Therefore, the study of PTSD is necessary both for the benefit of the officers and for the purpose of having their jobs done well and appropriately. Fortunately, this is one area where this is understood. There is no blind spot, and while there certainly needs to be more research than there is, it is not an area that is being ignored.

CASE STUDY: A TELEVISED REPORT

The NBC news program *Dateline* (2000) presented a case of a New York City police officer, Sal Glibbery, with a clear case of PTSD resulting from an incident in which he had shot a man. Kotbe is the reporter on this story:

Sal said he was OK, but his wife, Nancy, began to notice subtle changes. He seemed a little edgy and was slightly more irritable with the kids. And then there was this: Sal had begun a folder documenting the shooting, which he showed to Nancy and even their friends. In it, to Nancy's horror, was this: a close-up photograph of the man he'd shot just moments after he died. And there was something else Sal saved a copy of: the police dispatch tape, which he listened to over and over again. . . . Sal wasn't telling anyone, even his wife, what he was really going through: flashbacks, horrifying nightmares of the shooting, panic attacks triggered by sirens or cop shows on TV. These he kept secret from everyone. . . . Nancy was prepared for many things in her marriage, but not for this. Gradually, over the next few years, she watched as Sal became jumpy and developed insomnia, symptoms of a mental disorder they wouldn't learn about for several years. But even now, Sal still wasn't going for help, and when he finally did tell Nancy about his haunting symptoms, she didn't push him to go get help, either. (*Dateline* NBC, 2000)

Sal did finally go to the department's psychological services, and they diagnosed him as having PTSD. They also explicitly said that the shooting caused his disorder. One of his doctors, Dr. William Kaplan, said that the terror of looking down at the face of the man he had just shot and having the face looking up at him was the kind of image that is indelibly impressed upon those with PTSD.

He had several diagnoses of PTSD from different people, and was originally approved for a pension based on his line-of-duty injury. The doctors on the pension board, however, were charged with cutting costs for the department and declared that he did not have PTSD, despite the many diagnoses. They even indicated at one point that an ex-Marine who had been trained to kill would not be bothered that much by just one death. The additional stress and lack of recognition led to the officer's suicide.

Clearly, a greater understanding of PTSD as the result of killing is crucial, not just for treatment considerations but for public policy as well. It is not only the scholarly literature that clearly states an active shooting can cause PTSD. There is also no controversy on this point in the popular literature, which is aimed at police and, like this television program, at the general public. However, there are bureaucratic decision makers for whom this point is not yet established.

Note also that the officer suffered symptoms for years without telling anyone, not even his wife. This reticence is common and helps account for why the problem is not better known. It also suggests that the officer would have benefited from having information about PTSD as part of his training, so he would have been more aware of what was happening and sought therapeutic help sooner.

CONVICTS

It would seem logical, if one wishes to do a thorough study of the idea that that involvement in perpetration itself can be traumatic, to look at that group which is most commonly given the name of perpetrators: criminals who go through the court system and spend terms in prison.

In this case, the element of socially sanctioned behavior is generally absent. There could be a sense of social approval in some cases, such as those who have a relationship with a gang or a politically motivated militant group, or those who have the assumptions of one's family associations. However, such approval is clearly lacking from the society as a whole. This is one of the variables that might make a difference in symptomatology. Whether social approval of killing, as with executions, lessens the symptoms or not, or whether social disapproval exacerbates the symptoms, is not yet known. The studies have not yet been done. Comparisons of this group with others may help to establish this point.

Another major element of difference is the familiarity with the victim. Soldiers and police officers who kill are usually killing someone who they do not know well. Those who carry out executions may or may not be familiar with those to be executed, but if they are, they generally meet them in the knowledge that there is an execution expected. While many criminal homicides are of strangers, a larger portion of this form of killing involves people the perpetrator knows and has known in social, non-threatening settings. Offenders are also much less likely under current conditions to have had prior training or knowledge about PTSD symptom aftereffects.

Hall and Hall (1987) recognized the possibility of PTSD being a result rather than a precursor. They said that in court cases it had to be established that "the PTSD existed at the time of the violent crime and did not stem from it" (p. 49). Kruppa (1991) published a case study of a sexual homicide perpetrator with intrusive images and flashbacks to the actual killing. In a later sample of hospital patients, seven out of forty-four (16%) had a lifetime diagnosis of PTSD with the trauma being the offense itself. However, Kruppa pointed out that offenders are motivated to report their offense as being "traumatic" to indicate progress toward rehabilitation. This gives various advantages outside of an ability to get treatment (Kruppa, Hickey, & Hubbard, 1995). Steiner, Garcia, and Matthews (1997) in a sample of juvenile delinquents found that 5% were "traumatized by their own violent committing offense" (p. 361). This was noting the primary form of traumatization, so that if previous abuse was reported, traumatization due to the offense itself would not be included. It also included lesser violence than killing. Hambridge (1994), in discussing treatment of this population, suggested that those patients who get PTSD as a result of the killing may benefit from reassurance that this is a normal response to their experience.

Collins and Bailey (1990) did a large study of 1,140 felons. They analyzed separately those who used violence to achieve goals, called "instrumental violence," from those for whom the violence was the goal, called "expressive violence." They found 15% of those who had trauma symptoms and had been arrested for expressive (not instrumental) violence had the symptoms *after* the arrest. The remaining 85% had symptoms preceding the crime. However, the authors did not look at whether the act may have added severity or additional symptoms. Since PTSD symptomatology can be cumulative, becoming more severe with additional traumas, this is important. They did find only 2.3% of their sample having a full diagnosis of PTSD, but 70% having some symptoms. This bolsters the case for the importance of looking for a continuum of symptomatology rather than an extreme of strictly defined disorder in order to understand this phenomenon.

Pollock (1999) is much more direct and is specifically interested in the committing of homicide as a traumatic event. He especially looks at the issue of whether the violence was instrumental or reactive. Instrumental violence is planned with a specific goal in mind, whereas "reactive violence" is unplanned and done in a state of anger (the same as "expressive" violence as distinguished by Collins and Bailey). He studied eighty convicts, all of whom admitted to the crime, and hypothesized that those with reactive violence would be much more likely to have higher scores on PTSD scales. Results confirmed this consistently, on the entire scale and on subscales, with the difference on intrusive imagery being especially high.

He also looked at a four-part typology of perpetrators and found that those who were more psychotic were more likely to have been traumatized previous to the crime, to not be traumatized by the crime itself, and to have engaged in instrumental violence. The more "over-controlled" were more likely to report no pre-offense traumatization, to have used reactive violence, and to have suffered trauma symptoms from the incident itself. Thus, both the kind of violence and personality variables related to it made a large and significant difference in posttrauma stress symptoms This is one of the few studies that clearly looks at the confounding variable of previous traumatization, a point that has important applicability across all the perpetration groups, such as veterans and executioners.

Instrumental violence that is socially obligatory may bring different results than that which is planned contrary to social expectation. While there are psychotic people who join the military, for example, their proportion in the armed forces is not the same as their proportion in the prison population—and does not have the same meaning. The distinction between instrumental and reactive or expressive violence may have different results across groups, but in the criminal homicide group it is clearly a major factor. Similarities in other groups need to be explored.

There is another aspect to the question of posttrauma stress symptoms from the crime itself that can have applicability in law enforcement. Schacter (1986) discusses the phenomenon of limited amnesia for a specific episode of committing murder. He never mentions the possibility of a connection to PTSD.

Such a connection is suggested by the fact that this reference is found in a later list of various populations that suffer amnesia for their differing traumatic events (van der Kolk, McFarlane, & Weisaeth, 1996, p. 285). Schacter (1986) reports that the few studies which have been done show some consistency: samples range from 23% to 65% of individuals claiming amnesia of some form, usually "patchy" or "hazy," regarding the crime. One of the major points in the article is to try to ascertain how to tell if the murderers are lying, since they certainly have ample motivation to do so. Therefore, adding a possible connection to PTSD might be very fruitful. Since PTSD has various objective physiological and hormonal markers that can be revealed by tests, a rich store of information could be found by utilizing those tests in that situation.

Lisak (2000) has counseled murderers on death row. In this case, of course, the danger of being put to death at a certain time serves as a trauma in and of itself. He discusses the additional complication that many murderers have spent their lives steeped in violence, as *both* victims and perpetrators:

[I]t is fair to ask how one could ever separate the psychological legacy of victimization from that of perpetration. Since most murderers have experienced both, how can we ever know whether the act of murder can traumatize the perpetrator? This is a profound confound. Both clinical findings and our rapidly evolving understanding of neurobiology tell us that victimization and violence often inhabit and spring from the same areas of the brain. Victimization evokes overwhelming states of terror and rage, states which are very often the wellspring of terrible acts of violence. (Lisak, 2000)

To untangle this confound will require future studies, but Lisak offers case studies from his own experience: "In these examples, I think you will see how clinical evidence—post-traumatic symptoms themselves—can offer strong evidence as to their source; evidence that the act of murder can indeed traumatize the murderer." He concludes, "They were the creators of these scenes of horror, but they were by definition also witnesses to them. The images seared them no less than those images would sear any witness."

Studies on this point will be complicated by the task of ascertaining the true population. It is common for criminals to deny that they actually committed the crime or crimes. The courts, in theory, are supposed to convict and imprison only those that are guilty beyond a reasonable doubt, but they are not entirely reliable in this regard. Innocent people convicted of crimes will obviously have high levels of stress that can be accounted for in ways other than PITS. Those actual criminals that the court does convict may be a skewed sample, not best representative of those who commit violent crimes as a whole. Imprisonment itself provides another stressor, and additional traumatic events may be more common there than elsewhere. Furthermore, ethical considerations in the research, always present in a study of PITS, are especially important if participants are current prisoners, and ensuring informed consent is therefore problematic.

Lisak (2000) also addresses another crucial point: beyond theoretical considerations, why should we care?

I will begin by stating the obvious: Most of us do not lie awake at night worrying about whether murderers suffer from post-traumatic symptoms as a result of the murders they have committed. Some of you may be wondering why such a question should even be addressed. . . . I think such a question belies a common belief about murder and murderers . . . that murderers, by virtue of their deeds, have crossed over some threshold dividing us from 'them.' . . . It is so much harder to acknowledge, to truly understand, that murderers are humans, just like us. But once you truly accept this, the question posed by this talk becomes a simple one to answer. Can murderers be traumatized by the murder they commit? Of course . . . the killer is human, subject to the same psychological and neurobiological consequences as the rest of us when confronted by violence and death. Our assumption that only the victim of such violence would be traumatized is fundamentally based on our exclusion of the murderer from us—our category. An understandable reaction, but not one that is scientifically valid. (Lisak, 2000)

HISTORICAL FICTIONAL DESCRIPTIONS OF MURDERERS

It is difficult to find direct writings from those who have committed criminal homicide about the emotional aftereffect the act had on them. This is not difficult to account for. Those who have never been caught have a strong interest in not giving any evidence that they were connected to the crime. Those who have been caught, and not quickly executed, generally have the confounding variable of being punished, which is often an additional traumatization itself. They are not especially encouraged to write about their feelings, and if they do, it can be seen as a self-serving play for sympathy. Because there is a lack of public interest, for reasons discussed above, these writings are infrequently published.

Historically, the best material on the possibility of PITS resulting from criminal homicide comes from fiction writers. As far as establishing evidence for the condition, of course, fiction is useless. However, if the condition does exist and is sufficiently widespread, then it would be expected to be portrayed occasionally in those keen observers of life whose insight into the human condition has earned their writings the status of classics. Its absence would weaken the theory.

Fyodor Dostoevsky spent a few years in prison in Siberia on a sentence of engaging in subversive activity against the czar of Russia in the nineteenth century. He accordingly had the opportunity to observe a large number of men convicted of murder in the years following their crimes. His famous novel, *Crime and Punishment*, shows some sense of perpetration-induced PTSD symptoms, though not clearly in distinct, quotable passages. More to the point, his fictionalized autobiography, *Notes from the House of the Dead*, is closer to his real-life observations. The introduction to that novel would be an excellent case study of PTSD symptoms, especially detachment and estrangement from others, if it were reporting actual observations rather than being a fictionalized account.

One passage in that book has the following incident occur in the Siberian prison: "The convicts heard him cry out one night in his sleep: 'Hold him, hold him! Chop off his head, his head, his head!' Almost all the convicts raved and talked in their sleep. Oaths, thieves' slang, knives, axes were what come most frequently to their tongues in their sleep. 'We are a beaten lot,' they used to say; 'our guts have been knocked out, that's why we shout at night.'" (Dostoevsky, n.d., p. 15). This not only indicates the symptoms of intrusive imagery, especially active during sleep, but it also shows that explanations are found for the behavior under circumstances in which the concept of PTSD does not yet exist.

Also from the nineteenth century, Freidrich Nietzsche had served as a medic during the Franco-Prussian War, but otherwise his biography gives no indication of experience with others having PTSD. This is a passage from his work, *Thus Spoke Zarathustra*, in the chapter "On the Pale Criminal": "But thought is one thing, the deed is another: and the image of the deed still another . . . An image made this pale man pale. He was equal to his deed when he did it; but he could not bear its image after it was done. Now he always saw himself as the doer of one deed. Madness I call this . . . madness *after* the deed I call this" (Nietzsche, 1967). The intrusive imagery may be a fictionalized report of something Nietzsche had observed, but of course it could also be nothing more than a form of moralizing. There is no claim made of direct observation of reality.

Edgar Allan Poe is known for a fictionalized form of dwelling on the aftermath of violence for those who commit it. His short story, "The Tell-Tale Heart," seems to indicate definite intrusive imagery after a criminal homicide. However, the motivation for the homicide in that case gave an indication that the narrator of the story had additional mental problems. The intrusive imagery is also on display in "The Imp of the Perverse," in which a man who committed a sophisticated murder to get an inheritance has for several years gone entirely undetected:

At first, I made an effort to shake off this nightmare of the soul. I walked vigorously—faster—still faster—at length I ran. I felt a maddening desire to shriek aloud. Every succeeding wave of thought overwhelmed me with new terror, for, alas! I well, too well understood that to *think*, in my situations, was to be lost. I still quickened my pace. I bounded like a madman through the crowded thoroughfares. At length, the populace took the alarm, and pursued me. I felt *then* the consummation of my fate. Could I have torn out my tongue, I would have done it, but a rough voice resounded in my ears—a rougher grasp seized me by the shoulder. I turned—I gasped for breath. For a moment I experienced all the pangs of suffocation; I became blind, and deaf, and giddy; and then some invisible fiend, I thought, struck me with his broad palm upon the back. The long imprisoned secret burst forth from my soul. (Poe, 1845/1978, p. 1226)

The first half of the entire story is taken up with a philosophical discourse on why this confession that was so contrary to his self-interest would have been so compelling—hence the title of the story. Poe's biography also gives no clear-cut cases of direct observation, but his location in the nineteenth-century South of the United States would have been likely to give him opportunity to know relevant people firsthand.

Finally, one of the most famous cases of negative psychological aftermath for criminal homicide in the history of fiction is William Shakespeare's *Macbeth*. In this play, we find examples of sleep problems, intrusive imagery, outbursts of anger, numbness, and a sense of foreshortened future. This will be covered in more detail in the section on PITS in artistic literature in Chapter 9.

As evidence, fiction is not as good as first-person accounts or observations of others, which are intended to be accurate and not converted to fictionalized form. Psychologists would be more inclined to consult fictional accounts in order to understand people's ideas about criminals, rather than to understand the actual psychology of the criminals themselves. Fiction writers are more likely to be interested in philosophical points, and the point that people should not commit criminal homicides is a widely accepted one. To warn of negative aftereffects could be a form of preaching.

Still, the theory that a good portion of those who commit such crimes will find posttrauma symptoms as an aftermath to those acts would be weakened if the keen observers of human foibles who have written the world's extensive artistic literature had never noticed or in any way expressed the phenomenon. Scientific and artistic ways of considering the same state can be expected to differ.

CASE STUDIES OF TREATMENT

Two case studies of treatment in offenders who were diagnosed as having PTSD resulting from their offense have been published, and they offer quite different circumstances and methods of treatment. One involves a British woman who had been suffering from depression and stabbed her employer in an unplanned fit of rage (Rogers et al., 2000). The other involves an American man who was a member of an organized criminal group and engaged in many violent acts, including the premeditated shooting of a man (Pollock, 2000). One case is expressive violence done by someone who was filled with remorse, and the other was instrumental violence done by someone who claimed to normally not be bothered by reflecting on his violent actions.

The first patient, CH, was convicted of manslaughter on grounds of reduced mental capacity. Her treatment was intended to lead to discharge from the mental hospital. She had an extreme fear and avoidance of knives, which of course reminded her of the event. She had similar fears of other reminders of the event, such as the smell of the victim's perfume or movies in which stabbing occurred. She also reported intrusive thoughts, weekly nightmares of the event, and flashbacks such that when holding a knife she saw herself stabbing the victim. Because she needed to use knives in her cooking work, her inability to deal with them was a significant impairment. No traumas previous to the incident were identified.

Therapists used a procedure of systematic desensitization in this case. There has been some question as to whether methods involving exposure to reminders of the trauma are a good idea when the trauma involved perpetration, but it was tried in this case. Over the course of many sessions, CH was gradually exposed to minor reminders, such as the smell of the perfume, and then to more major reminders. Measurements of PTSD and depression over the course of the treatment showed improvement. Of course, in a single case, naturally occurring changes over time cannot be precluded as an explanation. Expanding beyond single-case studies for treatment in this population has not been published as of this writing.

The other case involved a man, R, who had planned and carried out the shooting of a specified individual:

Following the murder, R reported experiencing a vivid, intrusive image of the victim's face, re-experiencing the crime scene in repetitive flashbacks and nightmares. He would become physically agitated and anxious, commonly drinking alcohol "to the point where I was oblivious." . . . Prior to treatment, R maintained a diary of symptoms over a 6-week period and this assessment showed that R experienced a recurrent flashback of a single image of the offense and a repetitive nightmare that included an image of the victim's face before the murder. He reported that the vividness of the images was the most distressing aspect. (Pollock, 2000, p. 179)

R was diagnosed with PTSD, with no other forms of mental disorder observed. He had tried to commit suicide, not out of a sense of guilt or self-punishment, but because it was the only way he could see out of his predicament.

In this case, therapists used a different form of desensitization technique: Eye Movement Desensitization and Reprocessing (EMDR). EMDR is a procedure used when the PTSD is caused by a specific, known incident (Shapiro, 1995). This means of treatment for PTSD has been used on various populations and has been widely studied, with mixed results. The theory uses an information-processing model of trauma, whereby traumatic memories involve neurophysiological imbalances. Patients think of the trauma while doing an eye movement, typically following the back-and-forth slow movement of the therapist's finger with their eyes. Discussion during the procedure deals with re-processing the information, so that much of what occurs is similar to ordinary therapy. The addition of the eye movement in theory provides a biological way of resolving the biological part of the problem.

The results of the procedure in this case were that:

the composite image reported by R at the beginning of the procedure changed dramatically in terms of its form and vividness. The image initially became "hazy," the victim's face blurred and became unrecognizable. He then reported that the image had become distant, in "silhouette" and "as if it was a picture of two people in the distance, I don't know what exactly is going on, it's not me involved in it, it's like glancing at a horror film on the TV but not knowing what the story is really about." At the end of the desensitization procedure, R claimed that all details were diluted, difficult to focus on and not distressing. In fact, R expressed himself as feeling "troubled" that he could not produce the original intrusive image. (Pollock, 2000, p. 181)

This form of decrease in intensity is typical of the procedure.

This leads to the question about whether or not treatment of homicide offenders is a good idea, given an ethical consideration to prevent further violence. Kruppa, Hickey, and Hubbard (1995) address this point directly: Do untreated PTSD symptoms provide a constant reminder of the offense, and thereby inhibit further offending because of this repeated unpleasant reminder? Would they instead increase the chance of offending again? There are many arguments in favor of the proposition that PTSD symptoms can contribute to further acts of violence, but that may apply to social conditions overall. In individual cases, there may be differing effects. A person like CH, who strongly does not want such an incident to happen again, may be made less likely to do so with treatment. This may not be true for someone like R, who has already claimed to be emotionally unaffected in several previous instances and might be delighted to place this incident in the same category. Much more research needs to be done to ascertain the relationship of treating PTSD symptoms and avoiding further violence in the differing circumstances under which criminal homicides occur.

In the case of R, the treatment focused on his intrusive imagery, and not on his apparent sense of detachment and estrangement from others. This numbing symptom may be much more of a problem in terms of committing more violence, especially in instrumental instances approved in his subculture, including the subculture of prison. The symptoms that the patient reports as most distressful may not be the ones most urgently in need of treatment from a violence-prevention point of view.

The form of treatment is also of crucial importance here. If someone has developed a fear of knives because of having used one in a stabbing, it may be more ethical in some cases to leave her with a strong desire to avoid them. This is especially true if she has no remorse and may be inclined to use the knife in the same way again. Is it helpful to acclimate her to movies in which stabbing occurs rather than having her continue to avoid such movies? An exposure to the stimulus for purposes of desensitizing could amount to something similar to the form of operant conditioning that trains soldiers to kill more effectively.

Most of the cases in which the eye-movement technique is used involve victims of trauma, for whom it can be quite beneficial when it works as intended. The case of R is unusual in the use of EMDR on a perpetrator of violence. EMDR does not necessarily have a connection to conditioning for action the way systematic desensitization by exposure to the stimuli does. On the other hand, we do not have enough experience to know if this is entirely true.

Could this be the treatment that those who would like to continue in violent activity without posttrauma symptom problems are looking for? Would the ability to decrease the vividness of the imagery and nightmares through a neurophysiological technique help to put soldiers back into combat, or put those who are expected to torture prisoners or to carry out executions back to work?

It may be that the opposite is the case. Perhaps the technique erases the habituation to the stressor that has built up. It may put people back at the beginning, so that they experience the committing of violence the way they did the first time they did it, before they got accustomed to it. The repulsion that has been overcome throughout the course of continued practice may be reestablished.

Alternatively, of course, it may be that neither of these possibilities is correct, and the sessions merely have the effect of suppressing symptoms the same way alcohol does, more permanently and without the side effect of intoxication. It may have no significant effect on further acts of violence.

It could also be that it varies with the kind of violence; EMDR may lead to lowering acts of unplanned violence by alleviating PTSD symptoms that contribute to them, but have no effect on planned acts of violence such as premeditated murder, execution, or battle. In those cases, the very planned nature of the action brings in other variables for causation besides PTSD symptoms.

Unlike the research on treatment of combat veterans, which is at a rather advanced stage, the research is very preliminary on treatment of those who commit criminal homicide. Veterans who are treated successfully may have lower risk of committing further acts of violence by virtue of removing PTSD symptoms that could contribute to such acts. Whether treatment of those who have committed criminal homicide would have the same effect is simply not known. Would it be effective to treat the numbing, detachment, and anger but not the avoidance strategies, or would treatment of all symptoms help? Which methods of treatment have the best preventative effects? Does it depend on the planned or unplanned nature of the crime, whether it was instrumental or expressive, whether guilt is felt, or whether the crime involved someone familiar or a stranger? The connection of PTSD to other mental illnesses as a comorbid condition also needs to be taken into account, along with the effect of the prison conditions under which a majority of those convicted of homicide will be expected to live. All these questions are added to the simple question of which treatments are in fact most effective for this population.

REFERENCES

Carson, S. (1982). Post-shooting stress reaction. *The Police Chief,* October, 66–68.

Collins, J.J., & Bailey, S.L. (1990). Traumatic stress disorder and violent behavior. *Journal of Traumatic Stress, 3*, 203–220.

Dateline NBC. (2000). *NYPD Blues* (transcript). December 26. Livingston, NJ: Burrelle's Information Services.

Davis, G.C., & Breslau, N. (1994). Post-traumatic Stress Disorder in victims of civilian trauma and criminal violence. *Psychiatric Clinics of North America, 17*, 289–299.

Dostoevsky, F. (n.d.). *Notes from the house of the dead*, C. Garnett (Trans.). New York: Grove Press.

Follette, V.M., Polusny, M.M., & Milbeck, K. (1994). Mental health and law enforcement professionals: Trauma history, psychological symptoms, and impact of providing services to child sexual abuse survivors. *Professional Psychology: Research and Practice, 3*, 275–282.

Hall, H.V., & Hall, F.L. (1987). Posttraumatic Stress Disorder as a legal defense in criminal trials. *American Journal of Forensic Psychology, 5*, 45–53.

Hallet, S.J. (1996). Trauma and coping in homicide and sexual abuse detectives. Dissertation, California School of Professional Psychology.

Hambridge, J.A. (1994). Treating mentally abnormal killers in a regional secure unit: Some suggested guidelines. *Medicine, Science and the Law, 34*, 237–241.

Hiley-Young, B., Blake, D.D., Abueg, F.R., Rozynko, V., & Dusman, F.D. (1995). War zone violence in Vietnam: An examination of premilitary, military, and postmilitary factors of PTSD in-patients. *Journal of Traumatic Stress, 8*, 125–140.

Kruppa, I. (1991). The perpetrator suffers too. *The Psychologist, 4*, 401–403.

Kruppa, I., Hickey, N., & Hubbard, C. (1995). The prevalence of Post Traumatic Stress Disorder in a special hospital population of legal psychopaths. *Psychology, Crime & Law, 2*, 131–141.

Lasko, N.B., Gurvits, T.V., Kuhne, A.A., Orr, S.P., & Pitman, R.K. (1994). Aggression and its correlates in Vietnam veterans with and without chronic Posttraumatic Stress Disorder. *Comprehensive Psychiatry, 35*, 373–381.

Lisak, D. (2000). Can murder traumatize the murderer? Answers from death row. Paper presented at the 108th Annual Convention of the American Psychological Association, Washington, DC.

Loo, R. (1986). Post-shooting stress reactions among police officers. *Journal of Human Stress, 12*, 27–31.

Mann, J.P., & Neece, J. (1990). Workers' compensation for law enforcement related Posttraumatic Stress Disorder. *Behavioral Sciences and the Law, 8*, 447–456.

Manolias, M.B., & Hyatt-Williams, A. (1993). Effects of postshooting experiences on police-authorized firearms officers in the United Kingdom. In J.P. Wilson & B. Raphael (Eds.), *International handbook of traumatic stress syndromes* (pp. 386–394). New York: Plenum Press.

Martin, C.A., McKean, H.E., & Vetkamp, L.J. (1986). Posttraumatic Stress Disorder in police and working with victims: A pilot study. *Journal of Police Science and Administration, 14*, 98–101.

Neilson, E. (1981). The law enforcement officer's use of deadly force and post-shooting trauma. Dissertation, University of Utah.

Nietzsche, F. (1967). *Thus Spake Zarathustra*. New York: Heritage Press.

Poe, E.A. (1845/1978). The Imp of the Perverse. In T.O. Mabbot (Ed.), *Collected works of Edgar Allen Poe and sketches 1843–1849, vol. 3* (pp. 1224–1226). Cambridge, MA: Belknap Press of Harvard University Press.

Pollock, P.H. (1999). When the killer suffers: Post-traumatic stress reactions following homicide. *Legal and Criminological Psychology, 4*, 185–202.

———. (2000). Eye movement desensitization and reprocessing (EMDR) for Posttraumatic Stress Disorder (PTSD) following homicide. *Journal of Forensic Psychiatry, 11*, 176–184.

Rogers, P., Gray, N.S., Williams, T., & Kitchiner, N. (2000). Behavioral treatment of

PTSD in a perpetrator of manslaughter: A single case study. *Journal of Traumatic Stress, 13*, 511–519.

Schacter, D.L. (1986). Amnesia and crime: How much do we really know? *American Psychologist, 41*, 286–295.

Shapiro, F. (1995). *Eye movement desensitization and reprocessing: Basic principles, protocols, and procedures*. London: Guilford Press.

Steiner, H., Garcia, I.G., & Matthews, Z. (1997). Post-traumatic Stress Disorder in incarcerated juvenile delinquents. *Journal of the American Academy of Child and Adolescent Psychiatry, 36*, 357–365.

Stratton, J.G., Parker, D.A., & Snibbe, J.R. (1984). Post-traumatic stress: Study of police officers involved in shootings. *Psychological Reports, 55*, 127–131.

van der Kolk, B.A., McFarlane, A.C., & Weisaeth, L. (Eds.). (1996). *Traumatic stress: The effects of overwhelming experience on mind, body, and society*. New York: Guilford Press.

Wilson, J.P., & Zigelbam, S.D. (1983). The Vietnam veteran on trial: The relation of Post-traumatic Stress Disorder to criminal behavior. *Behavioral Sciences and the Law, 1*, 69–82.

Chapter 6

Is It Violence?: Abortion
Practitioners

SCHOLARLY STUDIES

Defenders of abortion believe that it is a form of medicine. Opponents believe
it to be killing. If abortion is the taking of a human life, then the psychological
consequences of PITS could be expected among those who perform abortions.
If we find no such aftermath, the case is strengthened that abortion is not violence at all. In this way, psychological research can add insight to the debate.

Such research is yet to be done in a way that could be considered conclusive
to policymakers and citizenry. Nevertheless, a review of what is known so far
is worthwhile.

Some scholars have proposed that women who undergo abortion have a var-
iant of PTSD, which they call Post Abortion Syndrome. Controversy rages over
whether this exists or not. Some studies show that it does, others show that it
appears not to, and there seems to be a high correlation between the bias of the
researcher and the results. Opponents of the concept of postabortion problems
believe that proponents are trying to undermine the actual benefits of abortion.
Proponents, on the other hand, believe that people who are making a profit or
have an ideological commitment are trying to ignore the negative. Over 300
studies with varying outcomes have been done on this matter, and it is subject
to intense debate.

However, remarkably little study has been done of the doctors, nurses, counselors, and other staff in abortion clinics and hospitals. Such studies exist, but
they are very few and hard to find. In fact, if it is narrowed down to scientific
studies done by researchers who do not work in the abortion field and which

look at a large number of people, there are really only two (Such-Baer, 1974; Roe, 1989).

One feature of those two studies is that they were conducted by people with an explicitly stated bias in favor of abortion availability. Yet, in contrast to the studies of postaborted women, they both note the high prevalence of symptoms that fit under Posttraumatic Stress Disorder. The one published in 1974, before the term PTSD was adopted, noted that "obsessional thinking about abortion, depression, fatigue, anger, lowered self-esteem, and identity conflicts were prominent. The symptom complex was considered a 'transient reactive disorder,' similar to 'combat fatigue'" (Such-Baer, 1974).

The other study did not mention the old term for PTSD, but did list symptoms:

Ambivalent periods were characterized by a variety of otherwise uncharacteristic feelings and behavior including withdrawal from colleagues, resistance to going to work, lack of energy, impatience with clients and an overall sense of uneasiness. Nightmares, images that could not be shaken and preoccupation were commonly reported. Also common was the deep and lonely privacy within which practitioners had grappled with their ambivalence. (Roe, 1989)

IS ABORTION PRACTICE A STRESSOR?

It is necessary first to establish that the stressor is sufficiently traumatic to be etiological for the symptoms. Events that are merely unpleasant, or mildly traumatic but not extraordinary, are insufficient. Everyone has arguments and bruises. Many have divorces and broken legs. Does performing abortions lead to more than these normal stresses? Do abortion staffs ever express it that way?

The reaction to the work itself is examined in an article written in the *American Medical News*, published by the American Medical Association, which reports on a meeting of the National Abortion Federation. It says that the discussions "illuminate a rarely heard side of the abortion debate: the conflicting feelings that plague many providers . . . The notion that the nurses, doctors, counselors and others who work in the abortion field have qualms about the work they do is a well-kept secret" (Gianelli, 1993).

In a paper given by Dr. Warren Hern to the Association of Planned Parenthood Physicians, he says of his staff, "Attitudes toward the doctor were those of sympathy, wonder at how he could perform the procedure at all, and a desire to protect him from the trauma. Two felt that it must eventually damage him psychologically" (Hern and Corrigan, 1978). In this case, he was referring to late-term abortions. However, it is not ordinary for medical staff to regard surgery as a trauma. Dr. Hern is still an abortion specialist at this writing, and he gave this paper in front of other abortion specialists.

Another example from the article in the *American Medical News* states: "A New Mexico physician said he was sometimes surprised by the anger a late-term abortion can arouse in him. On the one hand, the physician said, he is angry at the woman. 'But paradoxically,' he added, 'I have angry feelings at myself for feeling good about grasping the calvaria, for feeling good about doing a technically good procedure which destroys a fetus, kills a baby" (Gianelli, 1993). This doctor is angry at his own patients, and also with himself. Doctors are not ordinarily angry with themselves for doing their work well. The way he worded the problem gives an unmistakable clue as to why this would be, but only hints at the complexity. There seem to be some negative emotions that have not been explored.

Sallie Tisdale was a nurse in an abortion clinic for a time. After she left, she wrote about her experience in *Harper's* magazine:

There are weary, grim moments when I think I cannot bear another basin of bloody remains, utter another kind phrase of reassurance. . . . I prepare myself for another basin, another brief and chafing loss. "How can you stand it?" Even the clients ask . . . I watch a woman's swollen abdomen sink to softness in a few stuttering moments and my own belly flip-flops with sorrow. . . . It is a sweet brutality we practice here, a stark and loving dispassion. (Tisdale, 1987)

This woman is a nurse, so she is accustomed to ordinary medicine and all its normal squeamish details. These words suggest more stress than would be common in practicing ordinary medicine.

When the *American Medical News* looked at a workshop at the National Abortion Federation, it entitled the report "Abortion Providers Share Inner Conflicts." It says: "A nurse who had worked in an abortion clinic for less than a year said her most troubling moments came not in the procedure room but afterwards. Many times, she said, women who had just had abortions would lie in the recovery room and cry, 'I've just killed my baby. I've just killed my baby.' 'I don't know what to say to these women,' the nurse told the group. 'Part of me thinks, Maybe they're right'" (Gianelli, 1993). Again, this is an atypical remark for a nurse.

Warren Hern, an abortion specialist, gave a paper to the Association of Planned Parenthood Physicians in which he had studied his own staff:

We have produced an unusual dilemma. A procedure is rapidly becoming recognized as the procedure of choice in late abortion, but those capable of performing or assisting with the procedure are having strong personal reservations about participating in an operation which they view as destructive and violent. . . . Some part of our cultural and perhaps even biological heritage recoils at a destructive operation on a form that is similar to our own, even while we may know that the act has a positive effect for a living person. No one who has not performed this procedure can know what it is like or what it means; but having performed it, we are bewildered by the possibilities of interpretation. We have reached a point in this particular technology where there is no possibility of denial of an act of destruction by the operator. It is before one's eyes. The sensations of dismemberment flow through the forceps like an electric current . . . The more we seem to solve the problem, the more intractable it becomes. (Hern and Corrigan, 1978)

Hern is a doctor who is saying outright that this is unusual and stressful.

Don Sloan, another abortion doctor, in a book that vigorously asserts the need for abortion to be available, also indicates its stressful nature in contrast to ordinary medical practice: "As the pregnancy advances, the idea of abortion becomes more and more repugnant to a lot of people, medical personnel included. Clinicians try to divorce themselves from the method." He goes into graphic detail and describes the need to check the body parts to make sure everything is out. "Want to do abortion? Pay the price. There is an old saying in medicine: If you want to work in the kitchen, you may have to break an egg. The stove gets hot. Prepare to get burned" (Sloan and Hartz, 1992, pp. 239–240).

These doctors and nurses were still quite firm in their belief in the need for abortion at the time they made these statements. Their idea that dealing with abortion constantly was an unusual and significant stressor, more so than ordinary medicine, did not by any means come from opposition to abortion.

On the other hand, there is a book entitled *Abortion, A Positive Decision* (Lunnenborg, 1992), which includes qualitative data in the form of interviews from a specific abortion clinic. The author concludes that the consequences of abortions are positive for both patients and the staff who provide them. The absence of negative sequelae is, of course, much more difficult to document and less likely to be of interest to researchers because of the nature of research. A lower amount of anecdotal material on how something is not a stressor than how something is a stressor is not surprising and means little. More vigorous study with appropriate quantitative research design is necessary to truly address the question.

REEXPERIENCING AND DREAMS

Having recurrent, intrusive recollections of the trauma is one of the PTSD symptoms. Hern's paper said: "Six respondents denied any preoccupation . . . outside the clinic. Several others felt that the emotional strain affected interpersonal relationships significantly or resulted in other behavior such as an obsessive need to talk about the experience" (Hern and Corrigan, 1978).

Those symptoms may not seem to show much, since many people will have those kinds of problems with more minor events throughout their lives. However, one symptom is unmistakable and remarkably widespread: dreams. Dreams are so common that a mention of them, even a slight one, can be expected in almost all presentations on the subject of abortion staff's emotional reactions.

From academic literature, for example, comes this case from an editorial discussing sessions in which abortion staff members are talking about their feelings. The author supports these sessions as a way to keep abortion staff doing the work:

Their distress was typified by one nurse's dream. This involved an antique vase she had recently wished to purchase. In the dream she was stuffing a baby into the mouth of the vase. The baby was looking at her with a pleading expression. Around the vase was a white ring. She interpreted this as representing the other nurses looking upon her act with condemnation. One can clearly see the feelings of shame and guilt reflected in this dream. But more importantly, the dream shows that unconsciously the act of abortion was experienced as an act of murder. It should be noted that this nurse was strongly committed intellectually to the new abortion law. Her reaction was typical. Regardless of one's religious or philosophic orientation, the unconscious view of abortion remains the same. This was the most significant thing that was learned as a result of these sessions. (Kibel, 1972)

In another case, several doctors looked at the emotional impact on staff of late-term abortions with the D and E (dilation and extraction) procedure. They published this in the *American Journal of Obstetrics and Gynecology*: "The two physicians who have done all the D and E procedures in our study support each other and rely on a strong sense of social conscience focused on the health and desires of the women. They feel technically competent but note strong emotional reactions during or following the procedures and occasional disquieting dreams" (Kaltreider, Goldsmith, & Margolis, 1979, p. 237). The same authors discussed dreams in a 1977 paper presented to the annual meeting of Planned Parenthood physicians: "As the doctor tends to take responsibility and assume guilt for the procedure, she or he may have disturbing and recurrent ruminations or dreams" (Goldsmith, Kaltreider, & Margolis, 1977, p. 6).

The *American Medical News* reported this from the National Abortion Federation workshop: "They wonder if the fetus feels pain. They talk about the soul and where it goes. And about their dreams, in which aborted fetuses stare at them with ancient eyes and perfectly shaped hands and feet asking, 'Why? Why did you do this to me?'" (Gianelli, 1993). A news item in the *ObGyn News* on emotional reactions to the late-term D and E procedures reports that one-fourth of the staff members reported an increase in abortion-related dreams and/or nightmares (Jancin, 1981).

Hern's paper recounts more dreams:

Two respondents described dreams which they had related to the procedure. Both described dreams of vomiting fetuses along with a sense of horror. Other dreams revolved around a need to protect others from viewing fetal parts, dreaming that she herself was pregnant and needed an abortion or was having a baby. . . . In general, it appears that the more direct the physical and visual involvement (i.e., nurses, doctor), the more stress experienced. This is evident both in conscious stress and in unconscious manifestations such as dreams. At least, both individuals who reported several significant dreams were in these roles. (Hern & Corrigan, 1978)

Former abortion doctor McArthur Hill gave his story at an anti-abortion conference:

We used medications to try to stop the labor of women in premature labor so that the pregnancy could progress to term. Sometimes, the aborted babies were bigger than the premature ones which we took to the nursery. It was at this point that I began to have nightmares . . . In my nightmares, I would deliver a healthy newborn baby. And I would take that healthy newborn baby, and I would hold it up. And I would face a jury of faceless people and ask them to tell me what to do with this baby. They were to go thumbs up or thumbs down, and if they made a thumbs down indication, then I was to drop the baby into a bucket of water which was present. I never did reach the point of dropping the baby into the bucket, because I'd always wake up at that point. (Pro-Life Action League, 1989)

Bernard Nathanson, speaking of the time when he was a pioneer in setting up abortion clinics, spoke of nightmares of a clinic doctor:

I also recall well being cornered by the wife of one doctor at the cocktail party we gave when the Sixty-second Street clinic opened. She drew me aside and talked in a decidedly agitated manner of the increasingly frequent nightmares her husband had been having. He had confessed to her that the dreams were filled with blood and children, and that he had latterly become obsessed with the notion that some terrible justice would soon be inflicted upon his own children in payment for what he was doing. (Nathanson, 1979, p. 141)

The fate of the fetus is the most common theme, but Sallie Tisdale reports another effect:

I have fetus dreams, we all do here: dreams of abortions one after the other; of buckets of blood splashed on the walls; trees full of crawling fetuses. I dreamed that two men grabbed me and began to drag me away. "Let's do an abortion," they said with a sickening leer, and I began to scream, plunged into a vision of sucking, scraping pain, of being spread and torn by impartial instruments that do only what they are bidden. I woke from this dream barely able to breathe and thought of kitchen tables and coat hangers, knitting needles striped with blood, and women all alone clutching a pillow in their teeth to keep the screams from piercing the apartment-house walls. Abortion is the narrowest edge between kindness and cruelty. Done as well as it can be, it is still violence— merciful violence, like putting a suffering animal to death. (Tisdale, 1987)

The image of the men grabbing her and forcing her through pain in private parts of her body suggests that in this dream, abortion is associated with rape.

Only two of these cases, Nathanson and Hill, are given by people who now oppose abortion. The remaining ones are from people who still advocated for it at the time the dreams were reported.

NUMBING

Markedly diminished interest in significant activities is a symptom of numbing, as is a more constricted expression on the face. Both of those symptoms can easily be due to other things, and can be a matter of interpretation. Feeling detached or estranged from other people may also be due to different causes, but there is also quite a bit of evidence for it coming from abortion work. In fact, the method of doing abortions in an assembly-line fashion could well be a manifestation of this. When this is done, most commonly the doctor has no contact with the patient until her legs are up in the stirrups. Unlike most of medicine, being detached from the patient is built into the system.

Nurse Sallie Tisdale talks of numbness: "There is a numbing sameness lurking in this job; the same questions, the same answers, even the same trembling tone in the voices." The numbness is not merely in the sameness, though. "Still, I've cultivated a certain disregard. It isn't negligence, but I don't always pay attention" (Tisdale, 1987).

This kind of symptom naturally will be reported more by the people who have left the field than by the people who are still in it. After all, it is part of the symptom to avoid noticing what is happening. Talking with those who have left does lead to a rich set of illustrations of the point, as the following shows:

"We don't have conversations," said Joy Davis, a former employee of Dr. Tucker. "Sometimes, the employees faint. Sometimes they throw up. Sometimes, they have to leave the room. It's just problems that we deal with, but it's not talked about." She goes on:

[I]f you really dwell on it, and talk about it all the time, then it gets more personal. It gets more real to you. You just don't talk about it, try not to think about it. . . . If Dr. Tucker ever caught you discussing something like that—is this right what we're doing?— he'd fire you. When I was active in the abortion clinics, I don't know that any of us had any feelings about anything. We didn't really have a lot of feelings about the women, about the moral issues.

Judith Fetrow worked at a clinic in San Francisco. Later, at a pro-life conference, she offered an analysis: "When I started at Planned Parenthood, I saw two types of women working at the clinic. One group were women who had found some way to deal with the emotional and spiritual toll of working abortion. The second group were women who had closed themselves off emotionally. They were the walking wounded. You could look in their eyes, and see that they were emotionally dead" (Pro-Life Action League, 1993).

In a telephone conversation, a woman who worked for a doctor in Louisiana for a few months recounted an incident:

The one thing that sticks out in my mind the most, that really upset me the most, was that he had done an abortion, he had a fetus wrapped inside of a blue paper. He stuck it inside of a surgical glove and put another glove over it. He was standing in the hall, speaking with myself and two of his assistants. He was tossing the fetus up in the air, and catching it. Like it was a rubber ball. I just looked at him, and it's like, doctor, please. And he laughed. He says, "Nobody knows what this is."

Doctors who are accustomed to surgically removing body parts do not generally toss those body parts around like a toy. This doctor seems to have a numbed attitude toward the fetus, an attitude of emotional anesthesia.

Luhra Tivis worked for George Tiller of Kansas, and was asked in a taped interview about whether she saw any sign of him being detached from others:

He had this weird thing. It was a small office, there weren't that many people there. I did all of his correspondence and everything, but if I had a certain kind of a question or procedural change, I was supposed to go through my supervisor, and she would go to him. I mean, it's ridiculous, because it was a small office. And then sometimes he would circumvent that himself, and then I'd get in trouble. So it was like he was trying to hold people off, and not have to deal with any more of the staff than he absolutely had to.

This estrangement from others can be expected to have a negative impact on the quality of the medical care. As one example, Judith Fetrow reported from her former work at a San Francisco Planned Parenthood clinic: "The most horrifying complication that I witnessed was a woman who stopped breathing during the abortion. [The doctor] just walked out of the room when he was finished. Despite my telling him that the client was not breathing, he left me alone with her. When [the doctor] was forced to return, we didn't even follow emergency protocol for that situation. It was a miracle that this woman didn't die" (Pro-Life Action League, 1993).

In her book, Carol Everett tells how she administered several abortion clinics in Dallas, and eventually came to oppose abortion. She describes a case in which the doctor telephoned and said:

"The coroner called with the results of the autopsy. The cause of death was hemorrhaging from a cervical tear." I went numb. "We could have saved [her] life!" my mind screamed. We only needed to have sutured her cervix. We had everything we needed in the clinic to save [her] life, with one exception—a doctor willing to take the time to re-examine his patient to determine the cause of the bleeding. . . . Even a first-year intern would have checked for the source of such profuse bleeding. (Everett & Shaw, 1992, p. 21)

It is common, when telling these stories, to interpret this kind of callous disregard as just being sloppy, or as incompetence. That judgment may be truer in some cases and less true in others. However, this does fit into the pattern of being a symptom of Posttraumatic Stress Disorder.

PREVALENCE

On the question of troubling dreams, Dr. Hern said that two out of twenty-three workers reported them (Hern & Corrigan, 1978). An item in the *ObGyn News* that focused on late-term abortions said one-fourth of the workers had them (Jancin, 1981). Nurse Sallie Tisdale's remark that they all had them at her clinic was probably poetic license. That symptom is clearly common enough that it should be expected to arise among a good-sized group, but not among all individuals.

There is much less data for other symptoms, many of which are fairly subjective, and any one of them can be caused by a lot of different things. Having a professional psychologist or psychiatrist look over individual cases with these symptoms in mind has not been done for abortion staff. The studies have noted the symptoms without saying how common they are.

However, looking at "negative emotions" as a whole provides some information from the academic studies. The study done in 1974, which was very soon after the countrywide legalization, reported: "A total number of sixty-six questionnaires were distributed, and forty-two were returned . . . In this particular sample, almost all professionals involved in abortion work reacted with more or less negative feelings" (Such-Baer, 1974, p. 438). The article also reports that those who have contact with the fetal remains have more negative feelings than those who do not, as would be expected if abortion practice leads to PTSD symptomatology: "Whether the professional had contact with the fetus significantly affected emotional reaction. Those staff members who had contact with the fetus reacted with much more discomfort to abortion work. Additionally, among the group of professionals who had fetus contact, there was very little variability in emotional response: All emotional reactions were unanimously extremely negative" (Such-Baer, 1974, p. 439). This figure comes from an article whose concern is to ease the problem in order to make abortion workers more available. This one sample, with a two-thirds response rate, and taken by people whose sympathies were with abortion work, found negative emotions among all workers with fetal contact.

The largest published study involved interviews with 130 abortion workers in San Francisco between January 1984 and March 1985 (Roe, 1989). Unfortunately, the study did not report on the prevalence of the symptoms, but only noted that they were widespread. Authors did ascertain differing definitions of what was going on in abortion work, and they were not expecting to find what they found:

Particularly striking was the fact that discomfort with abortion clients or procedures was reported by practitioners who strongly supported abortion rights and expressed strong commitment to their work. This preliminary finding suggested that even those who support a woman's right to terminate a pregnancy may be struggling with an important tension between their formal beliefs and the situated experience of their abortion work. . . . At this point in the research, the methodological decision was made to interview only practitioners who identified themselves as pro-choice and were committed to continuing their abortion work for at least six months . . . It was felt that these practitioners, most free of pre-existing anti-choice sentiments and most resistant to their potential influence, would provide rich insight into the current dilemmas and dynamics of legal abortion work. (Roe, 1989)

This lowered the sample to 105 workers. Results showed that 77% bring up the theme of abortion as a destructive act, as destroying a living thing. As for murder: "This theme was unexpected among pro-choice practitioners, yet 18% of the respondents talked about involvement with abortion this way at some point in the interview. This theme tended to emerge slowly in the interviews and was always presented with obvious discomfort." If this were the case, one would expect it to arise much less frequently on written surveys and question-naires.

In talking about how abortion providers share inner conflicts, the *American Medical News* referred to abortion clinics as "America's most controversial bat-tlegrounds" in a "political war." If Posttraumatic Stress Disorder is prevalent, then the term "battleground" may be more real, less of a metaphor, than is commonly thought.

ALTERNATIVE EXPLANATIONS

Two alternative explanations have been offered in the literature. One is simply that the phenomenon is actually burnout, as is frequently found in the helping professions. For those who believe abortion provision is a helping profession, this explanation has obvious appeal. It is also a more easily solvable problem. It only requires vacation breaks and rotation of duties. Burnout can be an ex-planation for numbing and for irritable outbursts. Considering the high-volume, high-speed nature of most abortion practice, there is no reason to discount the phenomenon of burnout as a possibility, especially among counselors. However, its presence does not preclude the possibility of PTSD. It may only provide a confounding variable to consider in analysis. More importantly, burnout does not explain dreams or other forms of intrusive imagery.

The other alternative explanation has been suggested in the scholarly literature to account for the prevalence of the dreams. In one editorial: "Whether it is properly explained by parents or haphazardly accumulated in a piece-meal fash-ion, the child inevitably mixes fact with fantasy. Unable to conceptualize the whole process in sophisticated terms, the child thinks in concrete terms. He visualized an 'egg' in 'the stomach' and believes that a formed baby develops at the outset, growing for nine months into a full size infant." The author be-lieves this is the way to account for the dreams:

As one grows one's intellectual concept of reproduction matures. But the primitive fan-tasies remain in the unconscious. . . . Therefore, even those who become intellectually committed to abortion have to contend with their own unconscious view of a fetus as a real baby. The emotional trauma observed in these nurses was a result of the psychic conflict between their intellectual commitment, on the one hand, and their unconscious views, on the other. Inwardly, they experience themselves as participating in an act of murder. (Kibel, 1972)

If seeing the fetus as a baby is merely a figment of the imagination, a symbol, an oversimplification, then the solution is simple. The best way to counter a fantasy is to show the reality. Modern technology shows photographs of embryos and fetuses, and sonograms show their movements in real time. A strong dose of reality should put a fantasy to rest. However, this technique seems to be counterproductive (e.g., see the editorial "Warns of Negative Psychological Impact of Sonography in Abortion," *ObGyn News*, 1986).

The case for widespread PTSD among abortion practitioners, including both clinical and subclinical levels, cannot yet be strongly made. However, the evidence so far accumulated shows that the effort required for further research is certainly warranted.

There are some major confounding variables in any study. One is the fact that it may be difficult to ascertain who is and who is not doing abortions. Not all those participating are willing to say so; some do not care to admit it, and some are suspicious about revealing it to others. Since it stands to reason that a greater amount of practice may lead to greater severity of symptoms, it would be necessary in a study to ascertain how frequently respondents perform abortions, and simply asking them may not provide strictly accurate answers. This has long been a problem in studying the emotional aftereffects of women who have had abortions, so the possibility that it would be problematic in this case also should be considered.

Another variable is the direction of causation. Might those people who have been through traumatic events already be more inclined to participate in abortions? If numbing is a response to trauma, then those who were abused as a child or who might have been a combat veteran could be overrepresented among those who do abortions. Even if it were established that PTSD symptoms are higher among such doctors and nurses than among others in the field, this is a variable that would need to be statistically controlled and otherwise taken into account.

Finally, the very nature of the current political debate can impact the study. Abortion providers are likely to be suspicious of the motives of researchers who are clearly abortion opponents, and scholars are likely to be suspicious of results if there is a clear bias. Those who are advocates of abortion legalization, however, will also have a bias that can influence interpretation of results. The ideal situation would involve a research team which includes people of both positions, who can serve as checks and balances on each other. Failing that, at least increasing accumulation of evidence over time may lead to greater interest among different perspectives, which can then offer different and innovative strategies for study.

REFERENCES

American Psychiatric Association. (1994). *Diagnostic and statistical manual of mental disorders* (4th ed.). Washington, DC: Author.

Everett, C., & Shaw, J. (1992). *Blood money*. Oregon: Multnomah Press Books.

Gianelli, D.M. (1993). Abortion providers share inner conflicts. *American Medical News*, July 12.

Goldsmith, S., Kaltreider, N.B., & Margolis, A.J. (1977). Second trimester abortion by dilation and extraction (D and E) surgical techniques and psychological reactions. Unpublished paper.

Hern, W.M., & Corrigan, B. (1978). What about us? Staff reactions to the D and E procedure. Presented at the 1978 meeting of the Association of Planned Parenthood Physicians, San Diego, October 26.

Jancin, B. (1981). Emotional turmoil of physicians, staff held biggest D and E problem. *ObGyn News, 16*, 15–31.

Kaltreider, N.B., Goldsmith, S., & Margolis, A.J. (1979). The impact of midtrimester abortion techniques on patients and staff. *American Journal of Obstetrics and Gynecology, 135*, 235–238.

Kibel, H.D. (1972). Editorial: Staff reactions to abortion. *Obstetrics and Gynecology, 39*, 1.

Lunnenborg, P. (1992). *Abortion, a positive decision*. New York: Bergin & Garvey.

Nathanson, B.N. (1979). *Aborting America*. Toronto: Life Cycle Books.

ObGyn News. (1986). Warns of negative psychological impact of sonography in abortion. February, 15–28.

Pro-Life Action League. (1989). [Videotape]. *Meet the abortion providers*. Chicago: Author.

————. (1993). [Audiotape]. *Meet the abortion providers III: The promoters*. Chicago: Author.

Roe, K.M. (1989). Private troubles and public issues: Providing abortion amid competing definitions. *Social Science and Medicine, 29*, 1191–1198.

Sloan, D., & Hartz, P. (1992). *Abortion: A doctor's perspective, a woman's dilemma*. New York: Donald I. Fine.

Such-Baer, M. (1974). Professional staff reaction to abortion work. *Social Casework*, July, 435–441.

Tisdale, S. (1987). We do abortions here. *Harper's*, October, 66–70.

Chapter 7

Other Groups to Study

NONKILLING VIOLENCE: TORTURE AND ABUSE

People who commit deliberate torture on prisoners at the behest of their governments are an obvious example of those who commit extreme violence without necessarily killing. The very training of such people can involve deliberate traumatization.

When studying this, a precautionary note is in order: Care must be taken with the sensibilities of those who advocate on behalf of torture victims. Many have expressed resentment at the idea that the perpetrators are traumatized, and perceive the very idea as a suggestion of sympathy for them. Yet the ability to understand and treat torture perpetrators has promise as one of many methods to stop the practice of torture, since it can be exacerbated by the presence of PTSD symptoms of numbing, rage, and reenactment of the trauma. Understanding this is also necessary to society-wide reconciliation efforts. With a clearer understanding, the knowledge may also have a preventative aspect, in that those who practice or order the practice of torture currently are thinking in terms of an ability to do it with impunity. An understanding that natural psychological consequences accrue, even without legal repercussions, can serve as a contribution to prevention efforts. The same reasoning applies to clandestine operatives who engage in violent activities.

A case study of a man involved in torture activities was reported from a psychiatrist practicing during revolutionary activity against the French in Algeria (Fanon, 1968). By the time the book was written in French in 1963, the author's sympathies were with the rebels. The case report gives a short mention of sleep troubles and nightmares, but the symptom of explosive outbursts in inappropriate situations is especially prominent here. The connection of the symptom to the perpetration of domestic abuse is also explicit.

The thirty-year-old man was a European police inspector who was dealing with getting information out of Algerian rebels through the use of torture. He came of his own accord to get psychiatric services. He had lost his appetite, and his sleep was frequently disturbed by nightmares with no special distinguishing features. The reason he had come was what he called "fits of madness," which seem to fit the category of explosive outbursts:

Can you give me an explanation for this, doctor: as soon as someone goes against me I want to hit him. Even outside my job. I feel I want to settle the fellows who get in my way, even for nothing at all. Look here, for example, suppose I go to the kiosk to buy the papers. There's a lot of people. Of course you have to wait. I hold out my hand (the chap who keeps the kiosk is a pal of mine) to take my papers. Someone in the line gives me a challenging look and says "Wait your turn." Well, I feel I want to beat him up and I say to myself, "If I had you for a few hours my fine fellow you wouldn't look so clever afterwards." (Fanon, 1968, p. 267)

The case report indicates that these outbursts were not limited to thoughts, but led to domestic abuse:

The patient dislikes noise. At home he wants to hit everybody all the time. In fact, he does hit his children, even the baby of twenty months, with unaccustomed savagery. But what really frightened him was one evening when his wife had criticized him particularly for hitting his children too much. (She had even said to him, "My word, anyone'd think you were going mad.") He threw himself upon her, beat her, and tied her to a chair, saying to himself "I'll teach her once and for all that I'm master in this house." Fortunately his children began roaring and crying. He then realized the full gravity of his behavior, untied his wife and the next day decided to consult a doctor, "a nerve specialist." (Fanon, 1968, pp. 267–268)

He told the doctors that he had not been like this before, rarely punishing his children or fighting with his wife. This had only started "since the troubles."

The man could not get sick leave, and he did not want to be declared as having psychological problems, so he requested treatment while he continued to work. The psychiatrist comments on this:

The weaknesses of such a procedure may easily be imagined. This man knew perfectly well that his disorders were directly caused by the kind of activity that went on inside the rooms where interrogations were carried out, even though he tried to throw the responsibility totally upon "present troubles." As he could not see his way to stopping torturing people (that made no sense to him for in that case he would have to resign) he asked me without beating about the bush to help him to go on torturing Algerian patriots without any prickings of conscience, without any behavior problems, and with complete equanimity. (Fanon, 1968, p. 269)

Whether or not the treatment was successful is not reported, but certain ethical problems are indicated here. This is more thoroughly discussed with regard to criminal offenders in Chapter 5.

Beyond the question of deliberate torture, the atmosphere in prison often can be abusive. A study of guards at such institutions with reputations for harshness may offer useful information, compared to those with more lenient policies.

In the experimental literature, there is one case of a simulated prison in which conditions became crueler than experimenters had anticipated, called the Stanford Prison Experiment (a full explanation of the experiment, complete with narrated slide show, can be found on its official website, www.prisonexp.org). The simulation was supposed to last for two weeks, but it was shut down after six days. The experimenters concluded that the dehumanization had gotten out of hand. One of the experimenters, Craig Haney, wrote several years later about a symptom of trauma that occurred as an acute response at the time:

As the prison atmosphere evolved and became thick and real, I sensed the growing hostility and distrust on all sides. On one of the nights that it was my turn to sleep overnight at the prison, I had a terribly realistic dream in which I was suddenly imprisoned by guards in an actual prison that Zimbardo, Banks, and I supposedly had created. Some of the prisoners in our study, the ones who in retrospect had impressed me as most in distress, were now decked out in elaborately militaristic guard uniforms. They were my most angry and abusive captors, and I had the unmistakable sense that there was to be no escape or release from this awful place. I awoke drenched in sweat and shaken from the experience. The dream required no psychoanalytic acumen to interpret and should have given me some pause about what we were doing. But it didn't. I pressed on without reflection. After all, we had a prison to run and too many day-to-day crises and decisions to allow myself the luxury of pondering the ultimate wisdom of this noble endeavor that had already started to go wrong. (Haney, 2000, pp. 226–227)

Since this was a simulation, there are problems with drawing too many conclusions about real-life situations. Haney does not report long-term chronic consequences, but this was only a short simulation and there was a debriefing afterward in which everyone calmed down. This is not an ordinary procedure for harsh prisons. Haney does at least offer some insight into why people continue to engage in violent behavior even if they do suffer acute symptoms at the time. This also suggests that the absence of such symptoms cannot be assumed merely because a person does continue in the activity.

There are many other categories in which the violence is less than killing, but may be sufficient to cause some PTSD symptomatology. There are those who commit abuses in institutions in which clientele are relatively helpless— mental facilities, nursing homes, as well as prisons. Those who engage in domestic abuse of partners or children in the home would also fit into this category. In all cases, the confounding variable of whether PTSD symptoms were already present must be taken into account.

One study did find higher PTSD symptomatology in those who engaged in

domestic abuse, primarily on the hypothesis that PTSD was causal to the domestic abuse, but considering the idea that participating in the abuse might have
caused the PTSD (Dutton, 1995). It may be that the perpetration of additional
traumatic circumstances may more often exacerbate a previous condition than
actually cause a fresh disorder. Nevertheless, this mechanism will be of interest
for therapy and understanding of causation and prevention efforts.

Finally, there is an area of speculation—abuse that is done at a physical
distance. In the case of direct killing, distance can be provided in situations such
as the Nazi use of gas chambers or the air pilot's use of bombs. As discussed
in Chapter 2, it is not clear whether the absence of seeing the results of violence
one has perpetrated is actually protective against intrusive imagery. Some of
those who participate apparently use their imaginations. There are many types
of behavior that can be abusive to others but without the person who caused
them seeing the results: a landlord or landlady who saves money by leaving the
property in dangerous slum conditions; a factory owner who is callous to unsafe
working conditions which he or she arranged for; people who for the sake of
the money sell vicious weapons to brutal dictators in the knowledge that they
are likely to be used on political prisoners; sellers of known unsafe products;
overpricing of medicine so as to make it unavailable to desperately sick people.
This partial list shows a great variety, and items vary on how much the people
involved actually know or pay attention to the harm they are causing to others.
Just as the harm is far afield of their sight, it may be that posttrauma symptoms
are far away from these being etiological traumas. Alternative explanations are
readily available for symptoms such as deadened feelings (callousness), hypervigilance (legitimate fear of others' anger), sleep problems (worry), and a bad
temper. Intrusive thoughts of the victims—by dream, flashback, or unshakable
thoughts—might be another matter. In any event, having PTSD symptoms from
a different cause may have a role in contributing to the occurrence of such
behavior.

EXPERIMENTS THAT HARM THE SUBJECTS

In clandestine operations in Germany, America, and other places, harmful
experiments on human beings have caused major scandals. Among the famous
examples is the Tuskegee experiment in the United States, in which African
American men with syphilis were left untreated for decades for the purpose of
observing the course of the disease. Another example is the Nazi experiments
in their concentration camps, including Dr. Mengele's studies of twins. There
have been many others. In some cases, of course—as with Dr. Mengele—mental
disorders other than PTSD can be suspected and are worthy of investigation.
However, these experiments have had large numbers of people carrying them
out, and many have been more ordinary people. Does any form of PTSD symptomatology appear among them? Does it appear only when the results are
graphic?

Medical people have certainly become habituated to sights, sounds, and smells that are repulsive to others, and they must do so in order to be of help. This is ordinarily an adaptive attitude, with societal approval because of its benefits to individuals. Does this medical ability translate into situations in which the individuals do not benefit but, in fact, are harmed? Does an ability to be accustomed to pain and death as inevitable parts of medicine leave people inured when the medicine is injurious? This may be so at the time of the actual experiment, but is it so in the long term? Are there experimenters who are suffering, but do not say so because they believe their suffering to be peculiar, since no one else discusses it? In some clandestine cases, they cannot speak about their suffering because this would necessitate discussing the secret experiments.

Much more common now are experiments that harm animals. Does it make a difference that animals and not human beings are being injured or killed? Is there a natural repulsion to harming one's own kind that does not apply to other creatures, or does a graphic traumatic scene apply either way? Perhaps psychological consequences are lesser with animals than with humans, but are nevertheless present. In one case, an experimenter who decided to use real puppies in a Milgram-style study of obedience to authority reports that after the fact, he found himself still able to see the puppies clearly, a kind of memory he knew to be the kind that follows trauma (Charles Sheridan, personal communication). Herzog retains a middle-ground position on animal experimentation in an unpublished paper discussing the moral complexities, and reports his own experience: "My stomach turned queasy, I began to sweat, and my hands shook when I dropped it into the near-boiling water. . . . More shaky hands, a sweaty brow, a queasy stomach . . . my response was purely visceral, a physical nausea akin to the body's involuntary shudder in response to the odor of putrification."

A difficulty arises in studying this, however, in that the experimenters can view attempts to research their own reactions as an attack on their morality. Arluke (1991) did extensive interviews, and when he wanted to publish the results "one reviewer advised against using the term 'stress' because it suggested that some researchers were 'markedly' troubled by the use of animals . . . another reviewer advised 'toning' down the piece to avoid making researchers sound bothered by what they did." This illustrates the need to be scrupulously careful in designing and reporting research in this area in order to avoid being used as propaganda by opponents. It also illustrates the need to avoid ignoring good scientific data to please those who have the opposite political agenda. In all areas of researching PITS, the political implications complicate pure psychological research and thus underline the importance of rigorous standards.

KILLING OF ANIMALS

Euthanizing of animals in shelters has been reported as a trauma for staff in *Psychology Today*: "Shelter workers who have to euthanize animals as a regular part of their jobs suffer a wide range of distressing reactions, including grief, anger, nightmares and depression, according to a study I conducted with a fellow social worker. . . . [comments include] 'I have a lot of sleepless nights, a lot of crying' . . . 'I've had breakdowns in the euthanasia room because I feel so helpless'" (White, 1998). Of course, this group of people is different from many others, since they selected this form of employment because they love animals. They have a tendency to become attached to the animals in their care, which makes their reaction easier to understand.

Other kinds of violence that are massive against animals are the cruelties involved in factory farms and the killing done in slaughterhouses. Does the fact that these are merely animals prevent the psychological consequences that would accrue if people were to be treated this way? Does the fact that this kind of violence is done in massive numbers make it more of a psychological problem than violence to one or a few animals would? From the standpoint of research, a control group of other kinds of factory workers with similar demographics would be feasible.

Blood sports, such as hunting, provide another possible avenue of study. Hunting is normally done for relaxation (fishing, even more so) and would therefore make a peculiar candidate for a high-stress experience. Still, the exhilaration that often goes with the kill may have a place in the understanding of "addiction to trauma." Public exhibitions of bullfights, cockfights, and dogfights are another example.

In a report of the American television newsmagazine, *60 Minutes* (air date January 11, 1998), a Spanish bullfighter is reported as saying that he dreams of bullfighting every night—a possible posttrauma symptom. He identifies it as such by pointing out that, as a comparison, tennis players do not have the same problem, because the tennis player is not in danger of losing his or her life. This does complicate perpetration with risk to one's own life, but the risk is chosen. This bullfighter raises bulls himself, and when asked if it made him sad to think of those bulls dying in the ring, he said, "You know every—each bull that I—that I fight and kill him, he's a—he's a part of you for the rest of your life. You understand that?" This suggests other intrusive symptoms to go along with the dreams.

KILLING ON REQUEST

Finally, with human beings, there is the case where killing is requested: assisted suicide, active euthanasia by which an action takes a life, and passive euthanasia where it is inaction that causes the premature death by withdrawal of life-saving treatment. When this killing is involuntary or pressured, of course, it is not much different than ordinary killing, though the medical context can give it the same considerations as listed above under harmful human experiments. What about those cases in which the person being killed truly asks for and desires to be killed? Setting aside questions of bigotry against those with disabilities, possible pressures from family members with financial motivations, and traditional discriminations based on gender, race, or economic status, the case of someone asking to be killed may entail different psychological consequences than the majority of people who are clearly unwilling to die.

What kinds of consequences are accrued by the doctor or other person who assists? In the United States, Dr. Jack Kevorkian has been a famous example, and his obsession with death in art and otherwise could easily be a form of the intrusive imagery and the reenactment symptom. Still, Dr. Kevorkian is not the most typical case, and no diagnosis has been asked for or made.

Holland has the greatest numbers of doctors not only participating in euthanasia, but also willing to admit so to researchers, as shown in its governmental Remmelink Report. One book on Dutch euthanasia (clearly opposed to the practice) does find evidence of aftermath for the doctors. One doctor, when asked if he paid a price for his involvement, answered, "The price of any dubious act is doubt . . . I don't sleep for the week after" (Hendin, 1997, p. 52). Hendin remarks on this case: "That he felt his life had been changed by participating in the death of the woman tormented by memories of the concentration camp suggested that he might now be afflicted by disturbing memories of her and others whose lives he had ended . . . he seemed pleased if not relieved to be talking about euthanasia or consulting about it rather than still performing it" (p. 53). Of course, all this one example shows is that an opponent who is searching for anguish can find it. The evidence is only sufficient to suggest that the effort required for further research is warranted. Scientifically designed studies with large samples and control groups are necessary before conclusions are drawn.

PEOPLE IN HISTORY

The concept of PITS may be able to shed some light on historical events. For example, the Aztecs had massive human sacrifices on public display at the time the Spaniards arrived. If results of this included massive perpetration-induced traumatic stress, might this help in any explanation of subsequent events? What about other instances of human sacrifice, which were common in the ancient world?

The application to wars throughout history is obvious, but practices from cruel maintenance of slavery to those carrying out massacres to bloody purges in protection of dictatorships or monarchies would also apply. Kings and rulers who commonly engage in ordering and carrying out killing may have incidents in their histories that become more understandable when the concept of PITS is applied. The historians studying those particular problems may wish to take the concept into account and search for mention of symptoms. No diagnosis could be made, of course, but historians commonly conjecture that certain diseases were present at some level based on evidence of symptoms mentioned.

Hendin and Haas (1985) use this approach in a psychohistory article detailing especially two veterans of the American Civil War: Lewis Paine, a Southerner involved in the assassination plot of Abraham Lincoln, and Ambrose Bierce, a Northerner who went on to become a prominent author. Hendin and Haas are psychiatrists who have done extensive work with Vietnam veterans, and this article presents illustrations of examining historical data with the concept of PTSD in mind. Both examples given are men for whom killing in war included the traumatic circumstances that would have caused their PTSD. Hendin and Haas state their goal: "Although our familiarity with the symptomatology and manifestations of posttraumatic stress to some degree qualifies us for this undertaking, it is our hope that these initial efforts will stimulate professional historians to become familiar enough with posttraumatic stress to undertake additional study in this area" (p. 26). Since thousands of years of worldwide history includes abundant sources and unfortunately copious amounts of killing, this article on two veterans should be a bare beginning of what can be found by looking at the entire field with this concept.

Of course, the terminology in historical documents will be much different than modern psychological clinical terms. Terms to look for include nightmares, haunting, nerves and nervous breakdown, and sleep troubles; see Chapter 3 on executioners and the section on world literature in Chapter 8, as well as the Hendin and Haas (1985) article for more possibilities. Even a term like "bloodthirsty" can be linked to perpetration-induced trauma, as will be shown in Chapter 10.

REFERENCES

Arluke, A. (1991). Going into the closet with science: Information control among animal experimenters. *Journal of Contemporary Ethnography, 20*, 306–330.

Dutton, D.G. (1995). Trauma symptoms and PTSD-like profiles in perpetrators of intimate abuse. *Journal of Traumatic Stress, 8*, 299–316.

Fanon, F. (1968). *The wretched of the earth.* New York: Grove Press, Inc.

Haney, C. (2000). Reflections on the Stanford Prison experiment: Genesis, transformations, consequences. In T. Blass (Ed.), *Obedience to authority: Current perspectives on the Milgram paradigm* (pp. 193–237). Mahwah, NJ: Lawrence Erlbaum Associates.

Hendin, H. (1997). *Seduced by death: Doctors, patients, and the Dutch cure.* New York: W.W. Norton and Company.

Hendin, H., & Haas, A.P. (1985). Posttraumatic Stress Disorders in veterans of early America. *Psychohistory Review, 12*, 25–30.

Herzog, H. (n.d.). Human morality and animal research: Confessions and quandaries. Unpublished paper. Cullowhee, NC: Western Carolina University.

White, D. (1998). It's a dog's life. *Psychology Today,* November/December, 10.

Chapter 8

Implications for Psychology

THERAPY

Being a victim of circumstances beyond one's control has often been presumed as the necessary prerequisite to PTSD among therapists. One of the major implications of the existence of Perpetration-Inducted Traumatic Stress (PITS) is that it is necessary to include active participation in traumatic circumstances as another etiological mechanism. It is one that seems to lead to more severe aftermath, with some differences in pattern—not enough to establish it as a different phenomenon from PTSD, but differences with which therapists should be familiar.

Both Haley (1974) and Shatan (1978) have pointed out that when patients report having committed atrocities, the therapists have more trouble listening. Killing which does not fit the category of "atrocities" may well have the same problem. The very element of the diagnosis itself can be impacted: "there are many parallels in the experiences and behavior of those labeled as suffering from post-traumatic stress disorder and those with personality disorder label, although the two groups are perceived very differently by professionals. The major common factor, however, may be different manifestations of PTSD" (Hodge, 1997). Therapists who want to do the best work for their clients must have the knowledge that killing is a stressor with certain common features in its psychological aftermath (violent outbursts, intrusive imagery, perhaps a sense of disintegration).

Any differences in what constitutes effective treatment need to be understood. For example, Foa and Meadows (1997) note one treatment that might differ:

"In particular, PTSD sufferers whose traumatic memories are about being perpetrators rather than victims may not benefit from [Prolonged Exposure as a treatment] and perhaps will even deteriorate from such treatment" (p. 475). The article they cite is a set of six case studies which point out times when the flooding technique, involving intense reminders of the trauma for the purpose of desensitization, seemed to be counterproductive (Pitman et al., 1991). Participation in abusive violence was one of those times. On the other hand, Kruppa (1991) cites an individual case in which she used flooding therapy with a person who had committed a criminal homicide for the specific purpose of treating the symptom of flashbacks. The treatment was successful for that specific symptom, though it had no effect on the patient's symptom of remorse or disgust over the act. She also notes the risks of the therapy, including a greater possibility that the patient will drop out or have a violent incident in reaction. Both of these studies involve numbers too small for any conclusions. Possible differences for such techniques as eye-movement desensitization or pharmacological interventions require much more attention as well.

When therapists consider the implications of this idea, it is not uncommon that traditional religious concepts of dealing with wrongdoing arise. Foa and Meadows (1997), for example, suggest that when guilt is justified, "alternative strategies . . . [include] exploring ways of making reparations and bearing witness" (p. 475). Atonement, repentance and forgiveness, bearing witness, and reidentifying one's self as a different person than the one who did the killing (as in being "born again") have been suggested in many verbal discussions with therapists. These have been some of the responses of the human community in diverse cultures and through many historical periods to the common phenomenon of dealing with killing. They have remained because of extensive experience that they are, in fact, helpful.

CAUSATION

One of the clear implications for studying the causation of PTSD is that animal experiments have very limited application. Animals who kill are almost entirely predators for meat, engaging in self-defense, or have been subjected to circumstances that make them frenzied or out of control. They do not kill in the kind of social contexts that human beings do. Any PTSD symptoms that result from perpetration rather than victimization need to be studied in human beings living in social structures. It would be unworkable and unethical to reproduce this kind of stressor in the lab.

The construct of learned helplessness, observed in such experiments, has been applied to the biology of PTSD (e.g., van der Kolk et al., 1985). It may have some application to the concentration and memory problems, since in the multivariate analysis they entered as discriminators for the nonperpetrator groups. Concentration and memory problems can be more easily measured in the laboratory than is the case with other PTSD symptoms.

This has implications for determining the physical and psychological causality of individual symptoms. If perpetrators, who are more active in a trauma, are less inclined toward concentration or memory problems, than are the victims who are more passive during the event, then the search for the underlying causal mechanisms can be directed along more fruitful avenues.

Additionally, the multiple regression on concentration and memory problems as a factor showed that self-rated battle intensity was not associated. Whether or not the veteran had killed was negatively but only very weakly associated, as shown in Table A.4 of the Appendix. This also suggests that, while trauma may be necessary as a trigger, this particular set of problems requires other explanations.

One possibility, as mentioned above, is that the problems may be associated with having been in a situation of helplessness. Or the causation may be in reverse order: those who go into a combat situation with concentration and memory problems, or who are most inclined to have such problems immediately upon entering a high-stress combat situation, are less inclined to get into situations in which they will kill. This hypothesis is complicated by the possibility that those who do not kill include medics and people responsible for strategy, and such groups are not noted for concentration and memory problems going into a situation. Therefore, when trying to ascertain the causation, the characteristics of who fell into the different groups will need to be taken into account.

Again, this finding is based on self-report. One advantage of concentration or memory problems is that they are much easier to measure objectively. While there is really no other way to assess the content of dreams or the presence of feelings other than various means of self-report, many methods for assessing concentration or memory problems have been designed for the laboratory. This will allow for effective replication, or lack of replication, for this finding. If replicated, it will allow for using this finding as a foundation from which to expand.

Intrusive imagery, on the other hand, seems to be more prevalent and intense among those who were active in the trauma. This is possibly qualitatively different from the intrusive imagery of the passive victim, and the victim's intrusive imagery may come from a source of learned helplessness or a personality trait of timidity. Only future research focused on this question could ascertain whether the imagery is similar or markedly different. However, if there are similarities in what causes the imagery symptoms, the biological mechanisms should be searched for elsewhere.

Either way, knowledge of an active/passive distinction in the trauma, and its differing impacts on various symptoms, should be valuable in the search for causation. Due to the intense interest in the subject, there have been many theories and models of what causes various symptoms of PTSD or the disorder as a whole—behavioral, neurobiological, psychodynamic, and so on. They are not covered here; individual researchers will have different approaches and all of these approaches may have some insight to offer. The point here is that failure to make a distinction between perpetrators and victims or rescuers is likely to lead down more unproductive paths. Leaving out such an important element in the event or events is bound to interfere with a true understanding of the mechanisms leading to the condition.

DEFINITION

Van der Kolk and Fisler (1995) suggest as a provisional definition of trauma "the experience of an inescapable stressful event that overwhelms one's existing coping mechanisms" (p. 506). This defines trauma in a way that allows for only the passive victim, since the event is presumably escapable for a perpetrator. However, they say this in the context of pointing out how a trauma, by this definition, cannot be reproduced in the laboratory, and that traumatic memories cannot therefore be understood through experimental manipulations of normal subjects.

The definition of the stressor trauma also changed from the third revised edition of the *Diagnostic and Statistical Manual of Mental Disorders* (American Psychiatric Association, 1987), when it was to be "outside the range of ordinary experience." In the fourth edition, *DSM-IV*, the revised definition is: "(1) the person experienced, witnessed or was confronted with an event or events that involved actual or threatened death or serious injury, or a threat to the physical integrity of self or others; (2) the person's response involved intense fear, helplessness, or horror" (American Psychiatric Association, 1994).

One of the reasons for this change was that, unfortunately, too many traumatic experiences, such as child abuse and sexual abuse, are not outside the range of ordinary experience. It was not the lack of ordinariness that was the point. The committee formulating the definition wanted to exclude more common experiences such as grieving over deaths, divorce, and so on. They wanted to make clear that it was an extreme stressor. However, individuals vary greatly on what they perceive as extreme. Therefore, in *DSM-IV* (1994) the definition deliberately relies on subjective appraisal (van der Kolk, McFarlane, & Weisaeth, 1996, pp. 117–126).

Though the first part of the definition certainly seems aimed at passive victims, it is worded ambiguously enough that it could still cover perpetrators as well. The second part of the definition does include perpetrators who responded immediately with revulsion over what they had done. However, it leaves out those who already felt numb at the time of the event, and those who had thoroughly dehumanized the victims at that time. There are even those who feel a sense of exhilaration. In cases where the killing responds to danger, or where it was pre-planned, there can be a sense of relief that the situation is now over. The symptomatology of such perpetrators is thus left without a definition in *DSM-IV*, in spite of evidence that PTSD symptoms are prevalent and severe among such people.

Of course, there would have to be a large number of people who did react to the initial event with immediate revulsion or horror. Otherwise, we would have no reason to believe it was a trauma. That is why this point was first established in the chapters on the death penalty and abortion, and mentioned in the cases of war and Nazis. Nevertheless, its absence in specific individuals does not mean that they are protected from later PTSD symptoms.

However, it was not the intention of the committee who determined the definition to exclude this group. There is no reason to think that the idea that such a group exists occurred to them. This is a common blind spot.

The *ICD-10*—the psychiatric manual of diagnostic criteria of the World Health Organization—defines the causal mechanism for PTSD as "a stressful event or situation (of either brief or long duration) of an exceptionally threatening or catastrophic nature, which is likely to cause pervasive distress in almost anyone" (World Health Organization, 1992). The idea that perpetration could be included is not something that would be immediately obvious, but neither is it precluded by this definition.

If the definition of *DSM-IV* were strictly adhered to (and not that of the previous edition, *DSM-III-R*, or of the *ICD-10*), then a peculiar situation could arise. Suppose there were two men who both participated in the exact same massacre during a war, and years later, both men had the exact same PTSD symptoms. However, one man had reacted with revulsion and horror at the time, and the other with nonchalance, relief, gallows humor, or rage. By one strict definition, these two men with the same condition caused by the same circumstance could have one diagnosed with PTSD and the other not eligible for the diagnosis, based simply on their immediate reactions to the event. It may be, therefore, that more thought as to the nature of what defines a trauma is called for.

There has already been some work on the idea that those who are chronic rather than one-time victims, such as those suffering domestic abuses over the course of years, have some different patterns of symptomatology. This has been called "Complex" PTSD (Herman, 1992). Similarly, further work may suggest that Perpetration-Induced Traumatic Stress (PITS) is another subcategory of PTSD. Complex PTSD has not yet been accepted in the official psychiatric definitions, and further work on PITS may lead the committee who makes such decisions to believe it is simply another form with minor differences to be noted.

CLUSTERS AND FACTORS

While the international *ICD-10* definition of PTSD (see Chapter 1) is more in narrative form, the definition of the American Psychiatric Association in *DSM-IV* divides symptoms into clear clusters, with: "A" designating the need for a trauma to cause the disorder, "B" including symptoms of intrusive imagery, "C" including avoidance and numbing, and "D" including arousal and agitation symptoms. The method of determining this was committee agreement over how to divide the symptoms according to what seems reasonable (van der Kolk,

McFarlane, & Weisaeth, 1996). Alternative division schemes possess only the lack of official organizational authority, and nothing else to make them invalid. Several different ideas of how to divide the symptoms have been used.

Statistical divisions based on factor analysis of empirical data can at least provide further insight. There are only a few studies doing factor analyses of PTSD. Factor analysis is a sophisticated correlational technique that finds how well certain items coalesce with one another when a large number of people have answered the items. Once one has the figures for which items do go together, a theme usually emerges that can then provide a label for the factor. Factor analysis studies of PTSD symptoms can advance our understanding of posttraumatic stress reactions because distinct factors may correspond with distinct mechanisms. However, high intercorrelations among symptoms do also cause problems for the distinctiveness of factors in the analysis.

Laufer, Brett, and Gallops (1985a) looked at the symptom patterns and argued that instead of unitary diagnosis of the psychiatric manual, there should be a dual model: symptoms listed under reexperiencing or denial. That is, the symptom cluster listed under "B" criteria are reexperiencing, the cluster under "C" are avoidance and denial, and the miscellaneous symptoms listed under "D" all really belong under one or the other rather than being separated out and made miscellaneous. They argue that if the unitary model is closer to reality, then various kinds of stressors should lead to equal rates of the disorder on the basis of symptoms from each criterion category. However, if the two-dimensional model is more fitting, then different stressors are related to different types of symptoms. Accordingly, rates of denial versus reexperiencing symptoms should be different depending on what type of trauma was experienced, and the overlap between the two symptom types would be small. The authors found that the dual model picks up a lot more cases of PTSD, since people who did not make the full symptom pattern under the psychiatric diagnostic manual still had symptoms in one of the two dimensions. In another article (Laufer, Brett, & Gallops, 1985b), they further divided these two dimensions. Reexperiencing was divided into intrusive imagery and hyperarousal, and denial was divided into numbing and cognitive disruption.

In roughly a dozen factor analytic studies (those published are summarized in Taylor et al., 1998), differing solutions have been arrived at and no consensus seems to emerge. Different samples have been used, but most deal with clear victims of such things as hurricanes, car accidents, and rescue work. Those that deal with veterans do not make the distinction between killing and not killing. Only the Laufer et al. studies mentioned previously make that distinction. The official symptom clusters of *DSM-IV* (1994) are not consistently used, but researchers used their own ideas of sensible divisions rather than statistically derived ones.

As reported in the Appendix, I did a set factor analyses on the U.S. government data from the National Vietnam Veterans Readjustment Study. In all cases, in every list, a confirmatory factor analysis by limiting the factors to the number expected failed to find the clusters of the official definition of *DSM-IV* (1994). Intrusive imagery, which is Cluster B, does coalesce into its own factor, but other items frequently factor in with it. Avoidance and deadened feelings/alienation, which are in Cluster C, do not coalesce with each other. Cluster D is also not a factor. The factors are not consistent with the dual model scheme suggested above. They are not identical with other factor analyses of other groups in the literature, and they are not even identical within different groupings of the respondents in the NVVRS.

There are some findings that are clear-cut across different ways of measuring a factor analysis. Numbing, alienation, and deadened feelings do not go with avoidance, and do not go with intrusion. When the factors are limited in number in order to force larger factors together, temper practically always loads not with intrusive imagery or avoidance but with numbing, as detailed in Chapter 2. Concentration and memory problems in the NVVRS set of analyses always coalesced out as its own factor, was one of the later factors, and is usually not paid much attention in the factor analyses of other studies.

The factor structure of PTSD for those who said they killed was not meaningfully different from those who said they did not. The differences were of the level that the statistical quirks of individual samples are probably sufficient to account for them. Though there are variances in patterns such that an analysis can use factors to discriminate between the two groups, the symptom items do not coalesce differently. This serves as further empirical evidence to suggest that PITS may be best conceptualized as a form of PTSD, with the etiological trauma for PTSD defined in such a way as to allow for perpetration, rather than the nonparsimonious solution of seeing PITS as a separate phenomenon with a different cause but similar effects.

DANGER OF LEAVING OUT THE PERPETRATION VARIABLE

King et al. (1995) had done a structural equation model using several factors including "perceived threat" and "atrocities" as the labels for their model of causal variables for PTSD. I used their correlation matrix to isolate a simpler model. The path from perceived threat to PTSD was actually stronger than that of atrocities. Yet, when the intrusion/avoidance scores were removed, the path from perceived threat to PTSD weakened quite a bit and the path from atrocities to PTSD was slightly strengthened, making the two paths closer together. Both of these suggested that perhaps the intrusion/avoidance symptoms were lesser for the atrocities variable.

However, as discussed in Chapter 2 and shown in the tables of the Appendix, different statistical methods on the same data set simply do not back up this suggestion. Intrusive symptoms (nightmares, flashbacks, unwanted thoughts) are greater for those who said yes to killing than for those who said no. This is true as a whole and for individual items. The symptoms are greater for those directly involved in the killing or injuring of civilians and prisoners than for those who only saw—even if they had killed in other contexts. The intrusive imagery symptoms consistently appeared in the discriminant function analyses as major criteria for discriminating the perpetration groups from the nonperpetration groups. These symptoms also discriminated the greater perpetration group (directly involved in atrocities) from the lesser perpetration group (only saw atrocities, but said yes on the question of killing). The findings were more consistent with Glover's (1985) finding on the greater frequency of intrusive dreams associated with active participation in killing situations.

In the case of the structural equation model, researchers were looking for the overall contribution of various factors to PTSD. The study with discriminant function analysis was looking at the direct contribution of just one variable. The "atrocities" variable only applies to 41% of the entire set. Those who "only saw" and were "directly involved" altogether came to only 672 out of 1,638. The structural equation model researchers did a transformation of the data due to high skew, which came from the variable being almost 60% zeroes. The mean score they reported for "atrocities" actually came out as a small negative number.

The items of being superalert and watchful when there was no reason to be loaded as high for the perpetration groups in the discriminant analyses. As shown in Table A.8 in the Appendix, it entered at step 6. In contrast to ordinary experience, it is easy to account for this heightened sense of alertness in proximity to battle situations. The same feeling of intense watchfulness that in everyday life would be invalid would be seen as quite reasonable when in or near combat. This can readily be translated into "perceived threat." The concept of perceived threat may be so entrenched in the PTSD itself that it cannot be singled out as a separate phenomenon.

An initial comparison of the "directly involved" group with the "only saw" group turned out to be invalid as a measure of perpetration versus nonperpetration simply because the majority of those who "only saw" had also answered yes to the item on whether they had killed. An analogous process could apply to this question. Just as "only saw" had a majority of those who said they had killed, perhaps "perceived threat" did as well. It would stand to reason that those who killed may be disproportionately represented there. The path between perceived threat and atrocities was not significant. However, the atrocities variable covers only a minority of those who said they killed, since most scored zero—they did not report ever seeing such an incident. Therefore, the remainder of those who killed is covered under other categories. If those who said yes on killing are distinguished with more alertness and watchfulness, then those who killed can easily have higher scores of perceived threat.

The same applies to the "traditional combat" category. The correlation of the variable that authors labeled traditional combat with the score on the intrusive imagery cluster of symptoms is slightly higher than that for the "atrocities" category. This was the exception, since the correlation of traditional combat to other symptom clusters was lower. The first interpretation of this could be that more intense violence actually leads to less intrusive imagery than the form of violence covered by the label of traditional combat. However, if the majority of those who killed are actually in the traditional combat category, then it is not so surprising that intrusive imagery would more highly correlate with that category. If intrusive imagery is especially characteristic of those who kill, this is actually what would be expected.

The "atrocities" group, as defined by these researchers, is not a perpetration group, but rather one in which the perpetration veterans score higher, with a "two." The score of "one" is shared by those who had killed in other contexts and those who had not, further confusing the matter. The "perceived threat" group may similarly be made up of those who killed scoring higher and those who did not kill with lower scores on the measurements for perceived threat.

In short, comparing these two groups is not comparing a perpetration group to a nonperpetration group. Rather, it is comparing two groups in which there are perpetrators who tend to score higher and nonperpetrators who do not. The comparison is useless for answering the research questions regarding the effect of the act of killing on traumatic stress symptoms.

This is one example to illustrate the point that understanding the etiology of PTSD for veterans must include the variable of active killing, not just exposure to atrocities. Otherwise, this unnoticed variable can confuse the findings.

AREAS OF PSYCHOLOGY

Most of the study of PTSD is done under clinical psychology—counseling or psychiatric care, the areas for which a license is required to practice. Ramifications for social psychology are also integrated into the discussion in this and the next chapter. Aspects of biopsychology are covered in Chapter 10. Cognitive psychology can take an interest in and help understand the variations on concentration and memory problems; the intrusive imagery; and the impact of visual, auditory, olfactory, and tactile stimulation during the trauma on subsequent aftermath.

Only very preliminary work has been done in personality psychology. Strayer and Ellenhorn (1975), writing before the official definition of PTSD was established, found that the authoritarian personality difference had a positive effect on postwar adjustment. Their sample was small, their study was early, and no published follow-up research was found. Personality traits might have more impact under some conditions and less impact under others. Possible traits include introversion and extroversion, narcissism, paranoid tendencies, depression, psychoticism or the lesser Machiavellianism, aggression and hostility, and sensation seeking. Traits that precede the violent incident and personality changes after the event, as mentioned in the *ICD-10* definition of PTSD, must be better understood. There have been many studies relating personality traits to PTSD vulnerability, but the failure to make a distinction between victim and perpetrator etiologies has interfered here, as it has in other forms of PTSD research.

Health psychology is the area that most commonly deals with ordinary stress, so the related concept of posttrauma stress would naturally be of interest as well. There is a distinction between the two, in that PTSD has different additional characteristic symptoms, ordinary stress is ascertained rather than diagnosed, and the shattering of worldview is more clearly indicated in PTSD. PTSD requires some different forms of treatment, both in counseling and pharmacologically, and is not entirely the same in terms of physical components. On the other hand, many of the physical components are in common, such as with the catecholamines (epinephrine and norepinephrine, also known as adrenaline and noradrenaline), and there are circumstances in which ordinary stress and posttrauma stress can sensibly be put in the same category. PTSD is often seen as a severe form of stress, but it is not simply stress that is more severe. It is more complicated than that, and there are times when it is appropriate to clarify ordinary stress and posttrauma stress as being in different categories. In fact, the purpose of Criterion A in the *DSM-IV* definition of PTSD is precisely this—to distinguish the condition from ordinary stress.

However, health psychology is interested in the effects of behavior and mental attitudes on physical health. As with ordinary stress, there is reason to believe that PTSD (and therefore PITS) can be related to a higher number and greater severity of physical health problems (Litz et al., 1992). Such problems range from headaches to heart disease. Psychophysiological reactivity may also figure into research that health psychologists conduct on other matters, and should therefore be taken into account.

The varying perspectives within psychology can offer differing viewpoints within the study of Perpetration-Induced Traumatic Stress. This short discussion has only scratched the surface.

FORENSIC PSYCHOLOGY AND CRIME PREVENTION

It has been suggested several places in this book that an understanding of PITS, its prevention and treatment, can be a contribution to prevention of further violence. In the case of violence whose occurrence is decided on only by individuals and not policymakers, such as domestic abuse and street crime, there has been some investigation of the precise mechanisms by which PTSD symptoms could be a risk for that kind of violent behavior. The forensic literature, which deals with the legal ramifications, criminal defense, and prosecution, has some consideration of this.

Especially on point is an article called "A Classification of Psychological Factors Leading to Violent Behavior in Posttraumatic Stress Disorder" (Silva et al., 2001). The authors offer case studies to illustrate four categories of how PTSD symptoms can cause violent behavior:

The most mild is "Sleep Disturbance Associated Violence." The nightmares that are a symptom of the intrusive imagery cluster are frequently accompanied by physical thrashing around in the bed—kicking, slapping, and so forth. As is usual with dreams, the sleeper is unaware that this is occurring. This means that anyone in the same bed with the sleeper can be at the receiving end of blows without warning and with no intention by the sleeper. This does not often end up in court cases; however, it does often end up with separate beds.

One of the most obvious symptoms leading directly to violence, with a fair degree of frequency, is what Silva et al. call "Mood Liability Associated Violence." This is violence that results from the outbursts of anger, irritability, and hostility, which in *DSM-IV* is symptom D(2).

Another category is "Flashback Associated Violence." Specifically, this arises from a flashback-induced misidentification of others. Flashback experiences, just like the dreams of PTSD, can seem quite real. This is especially so since they are based on experiences that the person has actually had in the past. On occasion, the flashback can be severe enough that it leads to a loss of ordinary reality testing.

Silva et al. offer by way of illustration the case of Mr. A:

During some of these flashbacks he perceived the faces of others as changing into faces of his once Vietnamese foes. Mr. A would usually isolate himself during these frightening experiences as he was generally aware that these flashbacks represented an abnormal visual phenomenon. However, sometimes he would lose contact with reality and believed that the people whose faces changed into Vietnamese faces were actually enemy soldiers. On one occasion, he had just won several games of pool and in frustration the losing party verbally attacked Mr. A. At that point, Mr. A noted that the man's face had transformed into the face of a Vietnamese foe who was wearing the traditional black clothes of the Viet Cong. Mr. A stated that for several minutes he was convinced that he was dealing with a dangerous Viet Cong soldier and therefore attacked the man perceived as the enemy with his hands. . . . Only after the fight did Mr. A regain his ability to accurately identify the man he had attacked. Mr. A recalled that he had been drinking alcohol for several hours before the physical assault and remained intoxicated at the time of the attack. (Silva et al., 2001, p. 309)

Flashbacks are dissociative, but other forms of dissociation can also lead to confusion that contributes to violent events. Such dissociation can be involved in confusion between the individual's thoughts and the objective environment, as well as memory impairment. Even without a gross loss of reality testing, the lowered capacity to distinguish real threats from circumstances that others would not regard as threatening can be disabling when the goal is avoiding unnecessary violence.

Finally, there is the "Combat Addiction Violence." Combat addiction is defined as "a behavioral pattern involving aggression where the affected individual seeks to re-experience thoughts, feelings and actions related to previous combat experiences" (Silva et al., 2001, p. 313). The authors also call it "action-addiction" syndrome, which could make the concept apply more widely than just combat in war. Physically, only an adrenaline flow as a desirable outcome is suggested. These are reenactments pursued for pleasure, excitement, postaction calmness, or other mental states perceived as positive.

The case offered to illustrate this is of Mr. D, who would:

frequent Chinatown and other areas of the city with significant Asian populations. There, he would engage in numerous physical fights with those reminding him of his former Vietnamese enemy. He sought these physical confrontations in order to "feel alive." . . . After those fights, he would welcome the sense of calmness. As is the case for many Vietnam veterans with PTSD, he often had feelings of emptiness and numbness that contributed to a lack of meaning in his life. His engaging in frequent physical fights brought about a sense of excitement that he described as "being alive again." His repeated violent addictive behaviors resulted in decreases in anxiety, tension, and other negative emotions. (Silva et al., 2001, pp. 310, 313)

This phenomenon has also been called the repetition compulsion. Freud believed that as a reaction to trauma it was an attempt to master the event. The above quotation offers other reasoning. There has also been a suggestion of actual biochemical addiction in terms of the hormones released at times of high stress. This could also help account for the postfight calm. This idea will be covered in more detail in Chapter 10, in the section on addiction to trauma. Whatever the cause, a pattern of behavior that involves reenactment of violent events in later and entirely different circumstances could mean additional violent behavior.

In all four of these categories, there is reason to believe that the form of PTSD that comes from perpetration as its causative trauma could be a bigger problem than other forms of the disorder. The analysis of symptoms in the United States government data for veterans of its war in Vietnam, as discussed in Chapter 2, showed that symptom patterns differed. The biggest differences for those who said they killed, consistently across several ways of measuring and with large effect sizes, were the intrusive imagery and the angry outbursts. Both the thrashing-around dreams and the flashbacks, then, would be expected to be more intense in cases of PITS, along with the violence caused by anger and hostility. Dissociation as a whole, with its interference in understanding what is and is not threatening, is also higher in those who killed, even when battle intensity is controlled for, as is shown in Table A.4 in the Appendix. The action-addiction syndrome or repetition compulsion may be more likely to lead to violence if the events being reenacted were acts of violence.

Knowledge of prevention and treatment of PITS can therefore make a contribution to crime prevention efforts. The crime of domestic abuse would be of particular concern, since the kind of violent crimes that occur without planning and are due to anger, reenactment, and flashbacks can be readily inflicted on those people who are most frequently at hand.

THEORIES OF CAUSES OF VIOLENCE

The above discussion deals only with the kind of chaotic violence that is not planned even by the individuals who engage in it, much less by the social organizations that may have caused them to have killed or committed other extreme violence. There are many theories in psychology that deal with the psychological underpinnings of violence that is planned by groups. These theories can tell us something about what generates the events that cause PITS. Here we will discuss the role of PITS in being not just a result, but also a cause within these theories.

One category of psychological causes of violence is the attitude and thoughts held about the targets of the violence. Bandura et al. (1996) pull together a set of such reasoning that can be used to facilitate violence. The first mechanism is the cognitive transformation of the reprehensible conduct into good conduct— that is, changing how one thinks about it. This is done through moral justifications, making the conduct seem less consequential by comparing it to worse conduct, and euphemism. The second mechanism is displacing or diffusing the responsibility for the conduct or for its detrimental effects. This is otherwise known as "scapegoating." The third mechanism is to minimize, ignore, or distort those detrimental effects. The fourth is to dehumanize or blame the victim; an excellent documentation of the similarities in the language used to dehumanize various groups by characterizing them as garbage, parasites, nonpersons, diseases, and so forth can be found in the book *Dehumanizing the Vulnerable: When Word Games Take Lives* (Brennan, 1995).

All of these can help facilitate violence in a variety of situations, but the symptoms of PITS when present in leaders and/or a large portion of the population can also contribute to the use of these mechanisms. *DSM-IV* (American Psychiatric Association, 1994) symptom C(5) is a "feeling of detachment or estrangement from others," and symptom C(6) is a "restricted range of affect (e.g., unable to have loving feelings)." These symptoms can clearly exacerbate, or even on occasion initially cause, the practice of using dehumanizing language about the targets of violence along with euphemisms about the actions carried out against them. They certainly support minimizing or ignoring the effects of the actions. Those two symptoms along with symptom D(2), "irritability or outbursts of anger," render the occurrence of scapegoating more likely.

Another common phenomenon in the action of violence is to use thought processes about the action itself rather than the target. A person can separate himself or herself from the violence he or she is doing by a process called distancing. Physically, this can involve having the violence happen in a separate place where the person causing it does not see the results, as with Nazi doctors selecting who lives and who gets sent to the gas chamber, or as with soldiers pushing a button to bomb a location by airplane. Even when the violence is in close proximity, however, and the results are clearly visible, the human mind can do mental distancing. This can take the form of denying that the event is happening, even if it is right in front of the person who is causing it, or the perpetrator can assertively "not notice" the event by studiously looking the other way.

Any strategy that puts a mental distance between the doer and the deed must include avoidance. Most particularly, such strategies can be facilitated by the availability of the "numbing of general responsiveness" that helps define symptom cluster C of the *DSM-IV*. When PITS precedes the violent action, and includes this numbing, then its existence can help facilitate and therefore contribute to the cause of such action. Other aspects of the environment will also be necessary, but when those circumstances are there, the existence of PITS can mean that more violence will occur than would otherwise take place. PITS could also interfere with efforts of conflict resolution.

One of the oldest theories for psychological causes of violence is the Frustration-Aggression Hypothesis. This has turned out to be limited, in that much aggression is caused without any frustration, and frustration can exist in great amounts without any aggression ever taking place. The hypothesis is better at accounting for riots and lynch mobs than public policy. Still, riots and lynch mobs are group violence, and if members of the mob have PITS by virtue of having been in combat or a similar situation, then the symptom D(2) outbursts of anger can help spark group violence in the same way that it sparks individual crime. Massacres within wars, or other excessive use of violence which is not ordered and is unproductive to the goals of the military, can happen when numbers of those involved have this symptom.

One of the major sources of violence that has nothing to do with frustration or anger is the common habit of obedience to authority, even when that authority is destructive. This was famously illustrated through the much-replicated Milgram electric shock experiments (Milgram, 1974; Blass, 2000). The original idea in the 1960s was to first test Americans, who Milgram expected would generally not comply when an experimenter instructed them to continue giving higher levels of electric shocks to a "learner" (actually, a confederate of the experimenter). He would then run the same experiments in Germany, expecting greater compliance, as could be seen by the then fairly recent experience of the Nazis, in the hope of discovering what the difference was. However, they found solid majorities of compliance among the Americans, and already had their answer as to how the destructive obedience to authority could occur. This launched one of the major findings of social psychology: that even among people who had no animosity to the "learner," who expressed that they were suffering great tension, and who were clear that they preferred not to do this, compliance with demands of authority is quite high. No threats or promise of rewards were necessary.

This does help account for how people can get into PITS-causing situations without having suffered prior traumas or having any form of hatred or anger. Though it may be stressful, it is not necessary for there to be emotions against the target of the violence.

However, those people who already have PITS may to a certain extent be even more susceptible to destructive demands of authority. The estrangement from others, blocked emotions, and numbing take away one of the major resources available to cause noncompliance. Those who did not comply with the experiment most commonly cited the effect on the learner, which required a sensitivity to the learner that would probably be absent from someone in a state of numbness or detachment from others.

Noncompliance with the experimenter was also increased when a parallel experiment was run in the same vicinity and the participant in it refused to comply. This response to a role model would require a level of social coherence that could be absent in someone suffering from a sense of detachment or estrangement from others.

The question of why the authority expects violent behavior and gives the demands for compliance can also be influenced by the leaders suffering from PITS symptoms. The same symptoms that make compliance more likely also make the issuance of the orders in the first place more likely.

Finally, the psychological theory involving the connection of over-simplification of thinking to violence can have application here. This affects the ability to ascertain what is or is not a real threat. The same problems for individual crime can cause problems in large groups. Content analysis studies of the rhetoric of leaders as international crises occur and they move toward war have shown a marked lowering in scores for a construct called "integrative complexity" (Conway, Suedfeld, & Tetlock, 2001). This construct has two features: one is differentiation, which is the degree to which people see differences among aspects of or perspectives on a particular problem; and the other is integration, which is the degree to which people then relate those perspectives to each other within some coherent framework. The basic idea is that leaders who take an oversimplified, inflexible approach to any conflict that could lead to war are more likely to end up in war. Leaders who are more flexible, willing to compromise, able to understand the other side's perspectives, are less likely to get into a war.

Studies that have analyzed the content of public speeches and similar documents before various wars have shown that a drop in the integrative complexity scores is a good predictor of an outcome of war. In two-sided wars, the scores drop on both sides as they move to war. In one-sided wars (in which one nation attacks another), the scores drop on the attacking side but go up for the defending nation—defenders are hoping for a negotiated solution that avoids war. In revolutions within a country, analyzed as far back as that of Cromwell in England, the scores drop as the revolution is successfully taking over.

There are some laboratory studies in which people do simulations of international conflict that suggest mechanisms whereby low complexity may be a cause rather than just a symptom. Those who came into the situation with low scores did tend to move to more violent solutions within the same situations as compared to those who came in with high scores. They got frustrated more quickly and lacked the kind of negotiating skills that require integrative complexity.

Integration and dissociation are processes that go in opposite directions. Inasmuch as the mental process of integration of different perspectives is necessary to avoid moves toward war (or other violence), any sense of dissociation can interfere with this ability. Additionally, detachment or estrangement from others would reduce motivation to attempt the integration of differing perspectives.

Conway, Suedfeld, and Tetlock (2001) suggest that there is a change in the scores of content analysis of rhetoric leading up to wars because high levels of stress deplete the cognitive resources needed for complex thinking, group dynamics, and the characteristics of individual leaders. The arousal states, hypervigilance, sleep disturbances, and so on constitute a continuing level of stress for those who already suffer PITS. The associated dissociation states along with intrusive imagery can add further confusion as to what is indeed a threat and whether it can be dealt with in a negotiated way.

Group dynamics includes the "groupthink" model, whereby pressures for consensus within a group escalate and individuals therefore go along with group decisions they would regard as foolish if they were making the decision as individuals. Part of this process is that those individuals must lower the complexity of their thinking. Studies of those in historical situations classified as groupthink scenarios back this up. They also find that groups of individuals who are lower in complexity to begin with seem to be more likely to get into groupthink situations. This could be expected of many of those with PITS symptoms.

Of course, those who have a level of PITS symptoms so severe as to constitute a diagnosable disorder are not likely to be in leadership positions. If they are badly impaired, their contribution to additional group violence is more likely to be in being ordered rather than doing the ordering. However, only a portion of those who have the same perpetration-trauma experiences gets a full diagnosis of the disorder. People with less severe cases can be found in government leadership positions throughout history. Former United States Senator Robert Kerrey, for example, publicized his emotional aftermath to killing in Vietnam at the time the killing incident was in the media. Kings, dictators, prime ministers, and presidents along with cabinet ministers, legislators, and judges can similarly be drawn from combat veterans and police who have engaged in killing or torture. Political circumstances, past and present, have allowed PITS to have a psychological effect on decision making.

Much more study needs to be done to confirm whether it is true that having individuals with PITS can contribute to greater violence by groups, either at the level of policy or at the level of a large supply of individuals more likely to commit violence when policy has been decided. The discussion here has covered psychological mechanisms by which this might be done if it were the case, based on long-established work already done on the psychological causes of violence. The extent to which PITS fits into these other theories should be a rich and productive area of research.

REFERENCES

American Psychiatric Association. (1987). *Diagnostic and statistical manual of mental disorders* (3rd ed., revised). Washington, DC: Author.

————. (1994). *Diagnostic and statistical manual of mental disorders* (4th ed.). Washington, DC: Author.

Bandura, A., Barbanelli, C., Caprara, G.V., & Pastorelli, C. (1996). Mechanisms of moral disengagement in the exercise of moral agency. *Journal of Personality and Social Psychology, 71,* 364–374.

Blass, T. (2000). *Obedience to authority: Current perspectives on the Milgram paradigm.* Mahwah, NJ: Lawrence Erlbaum Associates.

Brennan, W. (1995). *Dehumanizing the vulnerable: When word games take lives.* Chicago: Loyola University Press.

Conway, L.G., Suedfeld, P., & Tetlock, P.E. (2001). Integrative complexity and political decisions that lead to war or peace. In D.J. Christie, R.V. Wagner, & D.D. Winter (Eds.), *Peace, conflict, and violence: Peace psychology for the 21st century.* Upper Saddle River, NJ: Prentice-Hall.

Foa, E.B., & Meadows, E.A. (1997). Psychosocial treatments for Posttraumatic Stress Disorder: A critical review. *Annual Review of Psychology, 48,* 449–480.

Glover, H. (1985). Guilt and aggression in Vietnam veterans. *American Journal of Social Psychiatry, 1,* 15–18.

Haley, S.A. (1974). When the patient reports atrocities. *Archives of General Psychiatry, 30,* 191–196.

Hendin, H., & Haas, A.P. (1984). *Wounds of war: The psychological aftermath of combat in Vietnam.* New York: Basic Books.

Herman, J.L. (1992). Complex PTSD: A syndrome in survivors of prolonged and repeated trauma. *Journal of Traumatic Stress, 5,* 377–391.

Hodge, J.E. (1997). Addiction to violence. In J.E. Hodge, M. McMurran, & C.R. Hollin (Eds.), *Addicted to crime?* New York: John Wiley & Sons.

King, D.W., King, L.A., Gudanowski, D.M., & Vreven, D.L. (1995). Alternative representations of war zone stressors: Relationships to Posttraumatic Stress Disorder in male and female Vietnam veterans. *Journal of Abnormal Psychology, 104,* 184–196.

Kruppa, I. (1991). The perpetrator suffers too. *The Psychologist, 4,* 401–403.

Laufer, R.S., Brett, E., & Gallops, M.S. (1985a). Symptom patterns associated with Posttraumatic Stress Disorder among Vietnam veterans exposed to war trauma. *American Journal of Psychiatry, 142,* 1304–1311.

————. (1985b). Dimensions of Posttraumatic Stress Disorder among Vietnam veterans. *Journal of Nervous and Mental Disease, 173,* 538–545.

Litz, B.T., Keane, T.M., Fisher, L., & Marx, B. (1992). Physical health complaints in combat-related Post-traumatic Stress Disorder: A preliminary report. *Journal of Traumatic Stress, 5,* 131–141.

Milgram, S. (1974). *Obedience to authority: An experimental view.* New York: Harper & Row.

Pitman, R.K., Altman, B., Greenwald, E., Longpre, R.E., Macklin, M.L., Poire, R.E., & Steketee, G.S. (1991). Psychiatric complications during flooding therapy for Post-traumatic Stress Disorder. *Journal of Clinical Psychiatry, 52,* 17–20.

Pollock, P.H. (1999). When the killer suffers: Post-traumatic stress reactions following homicide. *Legal and Criminological Psychology, 4,* 185–202.

Shatan, C. (1978). Stress disorders among Vietnam veterans: The emotional context of combat continues. In C.R. Figley (Ed.), *Stress disorders among Vietnam veterans: Theory, research, and treatment.* New York: Brunner/Mazel.

Shay, J. (1994). *Achilles in Vietnam: Combat trauma and the undoing of character*. Toronto: Maxwell MacMillan.

Silva, J.A., Derecho, D.V., Leong, G.B., Weinstock, R., & Ferrari, M.M. (2001). A classification of psychological factors leading to violent behavior in Posttraumatic Stress Disorder. *Journal of Forensic Sciences, 46*, 309–316.

Strayer, R., & Ellenhorn, L. (1975). Vietnam veterans: A study exploring adjustment patterns and attitudes. *Journal of Social Issues, 31*, 81–93.

Taylor, S., Koch, W.J., Kuch, K., Crockett, D.J., & Passey, G. (1998). The structure of posttraumatic stress symptoms. *Journal of Abnormal Psychology, 107*, 154–160.

van der Kolk, B.A., & Fisler, R. (1995). Dissociation and the fragmentary nature of traumatic memories: Overview and exploratory study. *Journal of Traumatic Stress, 8*, 505–525.

van der Kolk, B.A., Greenberg, M., Boyd, H., & Krystal, J. (1985). Inescapable shock, neurotransmitters, and addiction to trauma: Toward a psychobiology of posttraumatic stress. *Biological Psychiatry, 20*, 314–325.

van der Kolk, B.A., McFarlane, A.C., & Weisaeth, L. (Eds.). (1996). *Traumatic stress: The effects of overwhelming experience on mind, body, and society*. New York: Guilford Press.

World Health Organization. (1992). *International statistical classification of diseases and related health problems* (10th revision). Geneva, Switzerland.

Chapter 9

Social Implications

SOCIOLOGY

A guidebook to the official American Psychiatric Association's diagnostic manual says: "It is noteworthy that once Posttraumatic Stress Disorder occurs, its symptom pattern is remarkably uniform regardless of the individual's previous psychological history or cultural background" (Frances, First, & Pincus, 1995, p. 258). If the symptom pattern is consistent regardless of varying cultural circumstances, and if the extreme traumas that cause this symptom pattern are ones that occur throughout human history in different cultures, then human communities must have come up with adaptive mechanisms and group responses to this phenomenon. Accepting the dimension of perpetration as a trauma adds to this understanding, since it has also been common across varying cultures.

Studies of various ethnocultural groups would be necessary to ascertain the extent to which PTSD in general and PITS in particular is a culture-bound concept or is useful cross-culturally. The most comprehensive work on this is a volume entitled *Ethnocultural Aspects of Posttraumatic Stress Disorder* (Marsella et al., 1996). This work shows that PTSD has been diagnosed in a wide variety of cultures worldwide, from Southeast Asian refugees to Latin American disaster survivors to Navajo and Sioux veterans. The authors were unaware of any ethnocultural cohort in which it was absent, though of course prevalence rates and symptom patterns did vary. The idea of perpetration as a causal trauma mechanism, however, is not considered; such additional consideration could greatly improve cross-cultural studies.

Different understandings of social realities can be expected to provide variations in how trauma and reactions to it are perceived, manifested, and dealt with. Do different interpretations of reality result in different responses? Which forms of treatment are more relevant for diverse groups?

Since the latest version of the psychiatrist manual, *DSM-IV*, states as part of the definition of PTSD that there must have been a subjective reaction of "intense fear, helplessness, or horror," much of the perceptual differences between cultures can already be taken into account. There is a growing body of evidence that there is a biological basis for some of the symptoms, especially the flashbacks and arousal symptoms, so some of the aspects of PTSD are universal. There is less evidence for a biological basis of avoidant and numbing symptoms, suggesting that these may be even more susceptible to culture-specific influences.

The level to which expressions by participants concerning the original events or the later aftermath are encouraged or discouraged also varies across cultures and historical periods. Inasmuch as the absence of an ability to express memories or emotions can impact symptoms, this will be another source of variation in symptom pattern and severity across cultures.

In addition to these questions, the insights of sociological theories and concepts have much to add to the understanding of what PTSD is, how it is dealt with within groups, and what can be done about it. While psychologists have been most interested, especially those responsible for therapy with individual sufferers, PTSD cannot be fully understood without its social context. This is especially true with the differing social contexts of perpetration, such as approval and disapproval, or whether the violence is merely allowed or actually required. Some possibilities for application of sociological theories are discussed below.

DURKHEIM AND THE STUDY OF SUICIDE

In his book, *Suicide*, Emile Durkheim (1951) offered the idea of differing kinds of suicide. He classifies suicides of military personnel as "altruistic," which under his scheme is the opposite of egoistic. It comes from excessive attachment to the society (in this case, the military) and subsequent belittling of one's own importance. The suicide rate among soldiers ranged from 25% to 900% higher than civilians. In his usual fashion of considering and debunking alternative explanations first, Durkheim suggests that it cannot be disgust and lack of acclimation to military life, since the suicide rate was higher for those who had been in the military for several years than for newer people, and was greater for volunteers and reenlisted men. Military life was easier for officers, yet they had a higher rate of suicide, and elite troops with their intense renunciation of individual welfare had an especially high rate. To bolster his case of the rate being highest in those most integrated into military society, Durkheim pointed out that those with desk jobs, in the ambulance service, and so on— jobs with "less military character"—had a lower suicide rate (Durkheim, 1951, pp. 228–239).

There is another alternative explanation that Durkheim could not address, because the concept did not yet exist. If traumatizing events such as battles cause "battle fatigue," then those people who were most involved in battles would be most likely to suffer. Those are precisely the people he has indicated as having the higher suicide rate. If suicidal ideation is associated with PTSD, then this could be the actual social current causing these suicide rates, and the origin would fit again under the egoistic classification, or in an altruistic/egoistic complex.

The concept of "egoistic" suicide, which is committed by unintegrated individuals, could apply to those who do not necessarily go to the extreme of committing suicide but nevertheless suffer. The isolation and lack of common bonding is also ingrained in the concept of PTSD, since one of its criteria is a complaint of feeling detached or estranged from other people. As was stated by the psychiatrist to Vietnam veterans, "When a survivor of prolonged trauma loses all sense of meaningful personal narrative, this may result in a contaminated identity. 'I died in Vietnam' may express a current identity as a corpse. When the 'I' who died is understood to be the bearer of a civilized social morality, what remains may reflect a tainted, evil identity" (Shay, 1994, p. 170). Shay goes on to apply this to varying traumatized groups.

Durkheim declares that, "this type of suicide well deserves the name we have given it. Egoism is not merely a contributing factor in it; it is its generating cause. In this case the bond attaching man to life relaxes because that attaching him to society is itself slack" (Durkheim, 1951, pp. 214–215). With Durkheim's view that a decline in common morality can come about through a division of labor that excessively isolates individuals, how much more would be caused by events in which the detachment of individuals from others was not only situational, but traumatizing?

Durkheim lived at a time when suggesting that veterans had psychological repercussions from the discharge of their duties would have been impugning their bravery or patriotism. It was not until World War II that the conceptual development occurred, allowing the idea of "battle fatigue" to be a result of combat and not an insult to the combatants who suffered from it.

Durkheim also addressed how a clinician differs from a sociologist. This was applied to the study of suicide, but would also apply to a field like PTSD. According to Durkheim, the clinician

confronts exclusively particular cases, isolated from one another . . . [He] explains the act by one or the other of these psychopathic states. In a sense he is right; for if this person rather than his neighbors committed suicide, it is frequently for this reason. But . . . this motive does not cause . . . a definite number to kill themselves in each society in a definite period of time. The productive cause of the phenomenon naturally escapes the observer of individuals only; for it lies outside individuals. . . . Only certain ones are called . . . These are the ones who through circumstances have been nearer the pessimistic currents and who consequently have felt their influence more completely. (Durkheim, 1951, p. 323)

In the case of PTSD, epidemiological evidence shows that only a portion of people subjected to similar traumas actually get the disorder, and the study of those pessimistic currents is another part of coming to a full understanding of why certain people have a full diagnosis, others have symptoms at varying subclinical levels, and others show no signs of any problems at all.

MEAD AND SYMBOLIC INTERACTION

George Herbert Mead, in his theory of symbolic interactionism, dealt at length with the development of self as something that could happen only in relation to other selves, as an emergent of social interaction, a conversation of gestures that have meaning. The effect of trauma on this self is delineated by the psychiatrist from Vietnam: "Since the earliest studies of concentration camp survivors, it has been known that severe trauma shatters a sense of the meaningfulness of the self, of the world, and of the connection between the two. The same obliteration of meaning has subsequently been confirmed for rape victims, Hiroshima survivors, survivors of the Cambodian genocide, and Vietnam combat veterans" (Shay, 1994, p. 170).

In other words, one of the ways of viewing PTSD is that the normal significance and meaningfulness of acts, gestures, and symbols breaks down. The rules, the "organized set of responses" which make a "whole," as Mead (1967) says, are in disarray. Inasmuch as meaning corresponds to predicting likely behavior of others, some of the ability to do that has been impaired by the trauma, especially when the individual feels the trauma had an inherently unpredictable nature.

Mead (1967) refers to times when the "self does not enter" due to intense action, and gives as an illustration that "Tolstoi as an officer in the war gives an account of having pictures of his past experience in the midst of his most intense action" (p. 137). The intrusive symptom cluster is thus mentioned in passing as an experience wound up in outside activity in which the self as an object does not enter, in contrast with memory in which the self is the principal object.

Since Mead lectured in the 1920s and early 1930s, he was relying on unassociated observations rather than an organized set of knowledge about response to trauma. He did clearly address in a general way a dissociative aspect: "There is a certain technique, then, to which we subject ourselves in enduring suffering or any emotional situation, and which consists in partially separating one's self from the experience so that it is no longer the experience of the individual in question" (Mead, 1967, p. 170).

In the case of Perpetration-Induced Traumatic Stress, the meaning of the event is far different from victims or rescuers in traumatic situations. Feelings become much more complicated about what the event says about the self. This is another perspective on how an inability to talk to others about the experience could hinder the construction of self. An ability to talk to others about the killing activity when others approve, as in the activity of Homer and other bards singing the praises of previous warriors in the *Iliad*, might have a different effect.

Much of the historical societal responses, from Homer's itinerant poetry to the Sioux sweat lodge ceremony, can be seen as attempts to put meaning into the experience and restore some modicum of predictability to current, nontraumatic human interactions. Mead (1967) says: "The self . . . arises in the process of social experience and activity, that is, develops in the given individual as a result of his relations to that process as a whole and to other individuals within that process" (p. 135). If social interaction and greater reflexivity are key mechanisms for the original development of the self, they could also be mechanisms for the reestablishing of the self, which through the trauma feels itself to have "died."

The analysis of government data on Vietnam veterans (see Chapter 2) also showed that those who said they had killed had more of a sense of disintegration than those that did not. Perhaps the insights from Mead can help to explain this, or provide a starting point.

GOFFMAN AND MANAGEMENT OF STIGMA

Erving Goffman's 1963 book on how people deal with stigma relates to PTSD, especially if the trauma has a stigmatized origin. The war is now protested; the executioners are snubbed; past government torture is over and strongly condemned; crime has always been stigmatized. In the example of James Berry, whose case is used as an illustration for PITS in executioners in Chapter 3, Goffman notes that Berry concealed the tools of his trade: "his sense of isolation and being disliked by everyone he met probably explained the extraordinary episode when his wife and small son accompanied him to Ireland for an execution . . . no one would suppose that a man walking along holding the hand of a ten-year-old boy would be the executioner on his way to hang a murderer" (Atholl, 1956, pp. 88–89; cited in Goffman, 1963, p. 93). This form of "information management" is done by the "discreditable" people, who would be disgraced were information about them to be known.

Even if the source of trauma were unanimously socially designated as honorable or otherwise unstigmatized, all the insights that apply to those who have been mental patients would apply to those who had sought treatment. The techniques of either concealing the information or engaging in "disclosure etiquette" would apply.

Disclosure etiquette is "a formula whereby the individual admits his own failing in a matter of fact way, supporting the assumption that those present are above such concerns while preventing them from trapping themselves into showing that they are not" (Goffman, 1963, p. 101). If the trauma is of stigmatized origin, then the person may wait until those present make it clear to what extent they would condemn such a person before he or she says anything. If it is not of stigmatized origin, it still differs from those things that ought to be "above concern." The concern should be one of sympathy for someone having gone through the experience and its aftermath, so the discloser would need to be careful that the conditions for an appropriate response were met. After attempts to conceal, then, voluntary disclosure can be a phase of the "moral career," typically seen as a final one, more mature and well adjusted.

On the other hand, there are certainly many that do not reach that point, and Goffman (1963) points out a strategy for managing information about stigma that sounds like one of the symptoms of PTSD: "By declining or avoiding overtures of intimacy the individual can avoid the consequent obligation to divulge information. By keeping relationships distant he ensures that time will not have to be spent with the other; for . . . the more time that is spent with another the more chance of unanticipated events that disclose secrets" (p. 99). This is reminiscent of the symptom cluster, which includes efforts to avoid thoughts, feelings, or conversations associated with the trauma, and estrangement from others. The distinction between a trauma, a secret, and a stigma may not be as clear-cut in some cases as in others. In any event, a similar social dynamic applies.

MERTON AND LATENT FUNCTIONS

PTSD could be seen as an unintended consequence of war, executions, torture, the violent maintenance of slavery, and other deliberate infliction of extraordinary stressors. Not only the obvious intentions of participants, but the latent, inadvertent reverberations deserve attention. Any study of those institutions should include consideration of resultant PTSD to more fully understand the social dynamics involved.

Many of the ceremonies and other activities societies engage in after wars and other major traumas could have the stated, intended, manifest function of celebrating victory or memorializing the dead, but in fact also have the unstated, latent function of socially addressing the healing processes for individuals with PTSD and other repercussions from trauma. As with many other instances of applying the analysis of latent variables, this "clarifies the analysis of seemingly irrational social patterns" and "directs attention to theoretically fruitful fields of inquiry . . . [and] significant increments in sociological knowledge" (Merton, 1996, pp. 92–93).

Merton was interested in this as a sociological, not a moral concept. If political machines persisted, then they may be serving some function, and if we wish to get rid of them for moral reasons, we should understand those latent functions that are not adequately being fulfilled by other existing patterns and structures. Persistent patterns that perform positive functions need to be understood, and if they are to be replaced in any way, the need for the positive function should be understood in contemplating the replacement. If American veterans of the war in Vietnam came home without the outburst of enthusiasm that World War II veterans met, for example, an understanding that the ticker tape parades did more for the veterans than simply celebrate victory can be important. Those who find the celebration of war abhorrent still must find healing mechanisms for the veterans. Ignoring the latent function means ignoring the needs of the people who benefit from it. Ample numbers of World War II veterans still developed PTSD in spite of the warm reception they received upon returning home, but the contrast between the two sets of veterans is still instructive. Just as the political machine may have a "notable vitality," and rise like a phoenix from the ashes, the glory accorded to soldiers, which can impact willingness to participate in future wars, may have an important latent function for the soldiers of the past. All human beings like to be accorded glory, of course, but the meaning involved may not be something that veterans suffering from PTSD would be willing to let go of as easily as other people might.

BUREAUCRACY AND MODERNITY

Both the definition of what is wrong and the healing strategies used for PTSD by different cultures have fit into the pattern of rationalization that Max Weber held was increasing in human societies. As he put it, "One of the most important aspects of the process of 'rationalization' of action is the substitution for the unthinking acceptance of the ancient custom of deliberate adaptation to situations in terms of self-interest" (Weber, 1971, p. 57).

The response of modern bureaucracies to the phenomenon of PTSD also illustrates his work on this point. The American Psychiatric Association has clearly delineated criteria for a precise definition of what the disorder involves, complete with letters and numbers to specify individual symptoms and instructions on how many in each cluster must be present for a full diagnosis. This allows individuals to be classified as having it, having it only partially, or having some other form of anxiety. Previous cultures would only be interested in the fact that there was anxiety and that it needed healing; they would indiscriminately apply available healing strategies without regard to individual diagnoses.

Because in modern times an individual can be so defined, statistics can be and have been gathered. The official diagnostic manual includes not only what percentage of the population as a whole have PTSD, but also what percentage of specific at-risk subgroups have it. The precision and calculation at which bureaucracies excel, as Weber noted, is evident here.

Modernity is the optimistic perspective that emerged with the Enlightenment, the philosophy that human beings can take things into their own hands, make progress, continually understand things better, and continually do more with what we know. Sociological theorists have viewed this in both positive and negative ways.

To start with the negative, Zygmunt Bauman suggests that the Holocaust can be accounted as "a paradigm of modern bureaucratic rationality" (Bauman, 1989, p. 149). Similar forms of violence, torture, and war also fit this model. PTSD can make such bureaucratic actions more possible through its psychic numbing.

The symptom of numbing was important to keeping the formal rationality of the system in place, as Robert Jay Lifton discussed in a book on Nazi doctors at concentration camps: "In discussing patterns of diminished feeling, Ernst B. told me that it was the 'key' to understanding what happened in Auschwitz. In also pointing out that 'one could react like a normal human being in Auschwitz only for the first few hours,' he was talking about how anyone entering the place was almost immediately enveloped in a blanket of numbing" (Lifton, 1986, pp. 442–443).

Then again, those who believe that modernity has positive potential can point to the way PTSD is currently dealt with to bolster their case. The very concept of PTSD, after all, came about fairly recently, due largely to the modern ideas of rational and systematic observations followed by well-defined diagnoses and scientific treatment.

In accord with the modern idea of figuring out what the problems are and how to solve them, there is a bureaucracy attuned to efficiently delivering services to those who suffer from PTSD. The extensive data gathered by the United States government on the veterans of its war in Vietnam, for example, increases our understanding and may therefore help prevent problems in the future and mitigate them in the present. The Israeli government also gathers data on its soldiers, who are veterans of a series of wars and battles (Solomon, 1993). Widespread clinical therapy and scientific studies to find out which treatments are most effective are also a triumph of efficiency and "bureaucratic rationality." These are much more encouraging forms. The increased intensity of reflexivity and the reexamining of social practices which are features of modernity mean that PTSD can come about as a concept that describes a problem, and that it can be seen as a problem that can be solved.

POLITICAL SCIENCE AND PUBLIC POLICY

For people such as Nazis or those who carry out torture of political prisoners or other acts of massive violence, the question has been raised as to what the legal ramifications of findings of Perpetration-Induced Traumatic Stress (PITS) would have. American veterans of the war of the United States in Vietnam, for example, have used PTSD as a defense in trials for subsequent criminal behavior. PTSD, which results from being a victim of a trauma, can be regarded as a mental illness for defense in court. For practitioners of massive violence, this is already the case, as long as they suffered PTSD previous to their actions. Many Nazis, for example, may well have done so, due to combat in World War I.

However, an argument that the criminal act itself resulted in PTSD is not likely to have much legal impact. Injuries resulting from a crime are not normally a defense, as with a criminal who breaks his or her leg during the commission of a crime. The ramifications of the idea of Perpetration-Induced Traumatic Stress are primarily in the areas of prevention and therapy. Legal consequences for individuals are unlikely. As Hall and Hall (1987) say, to use PTSD as a defense in court cases, it has to be established that "the PTSD existed at the time of the violent crime and did not stem from it" (p. 49).

Other litigation, however, is a possibility. Jobs that require perpetration and therefore obligate workers to be at risk for a mental disorder, or for subclinical levels of a disorder, should at the very least include informed consent as a minimal ethical standard. Just as people involved in emergency rescue work require extra attention to possible posttrauma reactions, so might those involved in perpetration work such as executions. The legal case for avoiding a requirement to participate on the basis of conscience is strengthened with this additional consideration.

This information could add valuable insight into public policy debates over whether such socially sanctioned violence should be a public practice at all. Regarding the death penalty, for example, many of the arguments offered never take into account the effect of the executions on those who carry them out. It may be that even with this added information, there will be those who still favor the death penalty. Nevertheless, this information should be taken into account.

If the information about PITS is valid and if it applies to those who carry out executions, then the execution punishes far more than the condemned and his or her family and friends. It also punishes the people who had no part in the decision-making process, but who nevertheless are expected to carry out the sentence. If this is the case, many people in those countries that still practice the death penalty, or that might be debating reinstituting it, may change their minds on their view of public policy concerning it.

Grossman (1995) proposes a field of "killology," based on the recent precedents of new fields of "suicidology" and "sexology." He argues that facing up to what the act of killing really does to well-intentioned people is necessary to realistic social policies. Veterans are not helped if the real causes of their PTSD are assumed to be more benign or due to their individual predispositions. The same is true for other classes of socially sanctioned killers. Society as a whole has made the arrangements that caused this individual affliction. It is social forces that can heal it, and social forces that, with greater knowledge and understanding, can stop making those arrangements.

Taking more care that wars are not casual but extreme last resorts would be one point. This is already recommended on grounds of what war does to obvious victims, not just perpetrators. However, knowledge of the long-lasting aftermath for those sent into combat is certainly pertinent to decision making.

It can also be helpful to mitigate the damage when wars do happen. For example, the motive of revenge commonly arises among soldiers, and they can be strongly cautioned in their training that this can have lifelong consequences for them. Grossman, who is an army officer, relates that he advises soldiers and police officers during training that the close friends who died would want the sacrifice of their lives to mean that the lives of their partners or fellow soldiers should be full and rich. He suggests that they are actually throwing away the sacrifice of their friends' lives if they take revenge and thereby keep their own lives from being so full. The concept of PTSD being a consequence of killing may or may not impact killing in war that is seen as self-defensive or otherwise tragic but necessary, but the knowledge of PITS may help at least minimize killing outside of those contexts.

The move to believe that violence is necessary in certain instances may also be tempered by the knowledge of these additional consequences to those who carry out the policy. The casualty count cannot be known merely because the war, or other violent policy, has ended; it is yet to be ascertained, and will be borne by the society for years to come.

The technology of nonlethal weapons has received only a little attention. These are methods of controlling riots and similar outbreaks with techniques such as tasers, foam, nets, and so forth. These obviously have merits in terms of harming the targets less, and that is the primary reason they have been developed. If it is true, however, that the more lethal forms of crowd control have an effect not only on the targets but long-lasting psychological consequences for those given the duty to use them, then nonlethal technologies could also be seen as an issue of taking care of the needs of soldiers and police.

Finally, there is public policy concerning treatment. The need for recognition that PTSD can result from shooting someone is crucial for police officers, since there are bureaucratic and financial as well as treatment ramifications. When the bureaucracy for both police and veterans has an interest in saving money by not recognizing the taking of job-related violent action as being a traumatogenic stressor, it is crucial that they understand the evidence that it can be. The idea that men and women who take these jobs are "tough" and therefore are not really bothered by such things would not hold up under scientific scrutiny.

ARTISTIC LITERATURE

William Shakespeare wrote a passage in *Henry IV* in which a combat veteran's wife gives (in flowery Shakespearean language) what amounts to a list of PTSD symptoms for those who have been involved in combat. Shay (1994) gives the lines and explains how each fits in with PTSD criteria:

Henry IV, part I, act 2, scene 3, lines 40–62

    A combat veteran's wife is speaking:
    40 O, my good lord, why are you thus alone?
    41 For what offense have I this fortnight been
    42 A banish'd woman from my Harry's bed?
    43 Tell me, sweet lord, what is't that takes from thee
    44 Thy stomach, pleasure
    45 and thy golden sleep?
    46 Why dost thou bend thine eyes upon the earth,
    47 And start so often when thou sit'st alone?

48 Why has thou lost the fresh blood in thy cheeks,
49 And given my treasures and my rights of thee
50 To thick-eyed musing and cursed melancholy?
51 In thy faint slumbers I by thee have watch'd,
52 And heard thee murmur tales of iron wars,
53 Speak terms of manage to thy bounding steed,
54 Cry "Courage! to the field!" And thou has talk'd
55 Of sallies and retires, of trenches, tents,
56 Of palisades, frontiers, parapets,
57 Of prisoner's ransom, and of soldiers slain,
58 And all the currents of a heady fight.
59 Thy spirit within thee hath been so at war
60 And thus hath so bestirr'd thee in thy sleep.
61 That beads of sweat have stood upon thy brow,
62 Like bubbles in a late-disturbed stream;

Shay's explanation of symptoms by line:

40: social withdrawal and isolation
42: sexual dysfunction, reduced intimacy
44: somatic disturbances, loss of ability to experience pleasure
45: insomnia
46: depression
47: hyperactive startle reaction
48: peripheral vasoconstriction
49: loss of intimacy
50: depression
51: fragmented, vigilant sleep
52–59: traumatic dreams, reliving episodes of the trauma
60: fragmented sleep
61–62: night sweats, autonomic hyperactivity

As with any case of combat, killing is likely but cannot be assumed. Historically, most men engaged in combat have not killed (Grossman, 1995). For purposes of Perpetration-Induced Traumatic Stress, however, the most obvious candidate is Shakespeare's story of *Macbeth*, which clearly portrays a psychological response to having killed.

This has been noted by Bennet Simon in his forward to a book on posttraumatic nightmares (Lansky & Bley, 1995): "Finally, recall that the perpetrator can also experience the nightmarish and hallucinatory disturbances of sleep that are encapsulated in Macbeth's famous lines after he has slain the sleeping king, Duncan, 'Methought I heard a voice cry, Sleep no more! Macbeth does murder sleep' (2.2.49–50)." Further literary exposition of PITS can be seen in several places in act V. In scene I, Lady Macbeth, while sleepwalking, is reported to have been seeming to wash her hands for up to a quarter of an hour, and yet still finds a spot there, concluding "Here's the blood still. All the perfumes of Arabia will not sweeten this little hand."

Other lines of interest, all in act V:

Scene II

Others are speaking about Macbeth in his absence:
13 Some say he's mad. Others, that lesser hate him,
14 Do call it valiant fury. But for certain
15 He cannot buckle his distempered cause
16 Within the belt of rule. / Now does he feel
17 His secret murders sticking on his hands

Scene III

The doctor is reporting on the condition of Lady Macbeth:
36 Not so sick, my lord,
37 As she is troubled with thick-coming fancies
38 That keep her from her rest.

Scene V

Macbeth is speaking:
10 The time has been my senses would have cooled
11 To hear a night shriek, and my fell of hair
12 Would at a dismal treatise rouse and stir
13 As life were in't. I have supped full with horrors.
14 Direness, familiar to my slaughterous thoughts,
15 Cannot once start me

. . .

24 Life's but a walking shadow, a poor player
25 That struts and frets his hour upon the stage
26 And then is heard no more.
27 It is a tale full of sound and fury,
28 Signifying nothing.

The lines from scene II suggest the symptoms of explosive outbursts, rage, and temper, which have been found especially high in veterans who say they killed as opposed to those who do not (see Chapter 2). Line 17 also suggests the intrusive thoughts, though this is reported by someone else. The lines from scene III especially suggest intrusive imagery—"thick-coming fancies"—which interfere with sleep. The first lines above in scene V indicate a sense of numbness attached to a preceding preoccupation with horror—again, intrusive imagery. The last lines, 24–28, are an oft-quoted verbal outburst suggesting a sense of foreshortened future, the markedly diminished interest in significant activities, and restricted range of affect of Cluster C in the *DSM-IV* (American Psychiatric Association, 1994).

In ancient Greek literature, the *Iliad* is full of instances of PTSD, as one would expect from a war story that serves as a ballad of remembrance. Jonathan Shay, in his 1994 book entitled *Achilles in Vietnam*, uses this ancient work extensively as an analogy to American veterans of the war in Vietnam, showing the cross-cultural and cross-era nature of the condition.

Care must be taken in interpretations of literature. For example, several people have suggested PTSD symptoms in the *Epic of Gilgamesh* from ancient Babylonia. Indeed, the presence of the symptoms is plausible in the main character. Gilgamesh is depicted as having killed many times, so that if he had such symptoms, they could reasonably be regarded as perpetration-induced. However, Gilgamesh himself attributes the symptoms to grief over the death of his close friend, which had happened recently. There is no indication in the epic that the symptoms continued throughout his life. Such acute reactions are not the same as PTSD, and should not be confused with it. This kind of confusion is especially easy to make in the realm of literature, of course, in which characters are even less available than historical figures for clarifying questions. In any literature before the middle of the twentieth century, authors would have been without the conceptual framework of PTSD and would have left only hints rather than clear-cut expositions.

Turning to the literature of illegal single murder, several nineteenth-century authors dealt with this theme and showed literary exposition of PITS. For example, *The Marble Faun*, a novel by Nathaniel Hawthorne, details a sense of dissociation at the time of the murder and alienation and withdrawal symptoms afterward. For Edgar Allan Poe, the entire story "The Tell-Tale Heart" could be interpreted with this concept. From a different story, "The Imp of the Perverse," comes this, spoken by a man who murdered a man and inherited his estate:

there arrived at length an epoch, from which the pleasurable feeling grew, by scarcely perceptible gradations, into a haunting and harassing thought. It harassed because it haunted. I could scarcely get rid of it for an instant . . . At first, I made an effort to shake off this nightmare of the soul. I walked vigorously—faster—still faster at length I ran. I felt a maddening desire to shriek aloud. Every succeeding wave of thought overwhelmed me with new terror, for, alas! I well, too well understood that to *think*, in my situation, was to be lost. (Poe, 1845/1978)

Dostoevsky draws a similar theme in *Crime and Punishment*. He had been in prison in Siberia for five years, and accordingly had extensive contact with a number of those who had murdered. In his prison memoirs, *Notes from the House of the Dead*, he noted that, "almost all of the convicts raved and talked in their sleep." What they raved about normally had something to do with the violent past. The novel was intended to be one of psychological realism, and has been compared to *Macbeth*.

As for contemporary war stories, the works of Ernest Hemingway and Stephen Crane contain intimations of PTSD. Hendin and Haas (1985), for example, cite Crane's story, "The Sergeant's Private Madhouse," as a possibility. Such classics as *All Quiet on the Western Front* and *Catch-22* have portions that seem to be describing PTSD symptomatology. Those familiar with literature and with the concept of PITS can probably uncover further examples.

Hendin and Haas (1985) especially cite the works of Ambrose Bierce. They detail several pieces of historical evidence that Bierce suffered PTSD due to his experiences as a Union soldier in the American Civil War. Prominent among the evidence is his collection of short stories, *Tales of Soldiers and Civilians*, based primarily on his own experiences: "The realism of Bierce's many accounts of irrational, inescapable horrors and their striking degree of detail suggest that his own nightmares may have been the source of much of his fiction" (p. 28). This involved not merely graphic scenes, but killing. Hendin and Haas comment, "In several of Bierce's stories, the greatest threat to the bravest of soldiers . . . lies not in the external dangers they confront, but rather derives from the inevitable consequences of internal terror . . . The theme of solders and civilians being killed by the ghosts of those they have killed is a common one throughout his writing" (pp. 27–28).

The history of expressions of posttrauma symptoms in poetry is also interesting. The format of poetry seems to be favored almost entirely by combat veterans. A thorough library search, along with inquiries to a few organizations that represent them, failed to turn up any poetry written by the various other groups discussed in this book. The only poem with indications of processing PITS symptoms that did not come from combat referred to an experience of having killed two baby birds several years previously, and even this poem was found in a book of explicitly antiwar poetry that was otherwise written almost entirely by combat veterans.

In addition to being the first group in which PTSD was noticed and defined, combat veterans are by far the most numerous. Only a very small portion of the group is needed in order to include a good number of poems. It may be that the same portion of any other group would amount to less than one person, but for veterans, that portion can be dozens of people. Wars also bring intense interest by large numbers of people for both support and opposition, so the audience for poems would be great enough for poems to get published. It is certainly easier to find books of war poems than poems on executions.

The poetry of specific wars throughout the ages, before the twentieth century, has been almost entirely about the glories involved in that war. The poetry was often commissioned by the victors or otherwise intended to edify the rulers of the time. It may have also been helping people in the public to process their feelings about the war (Shay, 1994). Most importantly, however, the published poetry that we still have was rarely written by the combat veterans themselves.

One exception is George Gasciogne, who died in 1577. He participated in the wars of Holland against the Spaniards and was an ailing veteran for the rest of his life. He wrote, among many other things, a poem called *Dulce Bellem Inexpertis*. His poetry gave some indication of Posttraumatic Stress Disorder: "The broken sleepes, the dreadfull dreames, the woe / Which wonne with warre and cannot from him goe" (verse 40).

At around the beginning of the twentieth century, the phenomenon of combat veterans translating their experiences into poetry became relatively common. Several instances can be found from World War I and World War II. An upsurge of such poetry occurred among American Vietnam War veterans. Some of this mirrored the glories of past war poetry and involved bragging or fond memories of camaraderie or sarcastic put-downs of the enemy. Much of it, however, was quite negative about the experience. During and after the American war in Vietnam, several books full of such negative poetry were published. Critical remarks were made about the war experience itself and the decision-making process that led to the events, as well as expressions about the psychological aftermath to the veterans themselves. It appears that the composition of the poetry was one of the therapeutic methods these veterans used to deal with their experiences.

The PTSD symptom most prominent in poems is that of intrusive imagery—nightmares, flashbacks, unwanted thoughts that intrude and cannot be shaken. Of all the symptoms, this one lends itself best to expression in poetry. As mentioned in Chapter 2, intrusive imagery also loaded in a discriminant function analysis of United States government data on combat veterans as being more characteristic of the pattern of those who said they had killed in Vietnam compared to those who said they had not.

As an example, this rendition of intrusive imagery comes from a portion of one of the earliest poems, a British veteran of the Anglo-Boer War in 1899:

> I killed a man at Graspan
> I killed him fair in fight;
> And the Empires' poets and the Empire's priests
> Swear blind I acted right . . .
> But they can't stop the eyes of the man I killed
> From starin' into mine. (Van Wyk Smith, 1978, p. 152)

Another example of intrusive memory is a poem by a veteran of the American war in Vietnam for whom a thunderstorm serves as a reminder of participating in a napalm attack. He writes of seeing branches as wire and thunder as pounding mortar, and closing his eyes and seeing the girl running from her village. He tries to imagine her having wings and flying above the pain, but this does not work. Reality still intrudes, and "she is burned behind my eyes" (Weigl, 1985).

The subject of emotional numbing is not often portrayed in the format of poetry, but an example comes from Wilfred Owen, a British soldier who wrote poetry during World War I and died days before the end of the war. He observed the numbing in others. People who suffer from it themselves would by definition be disinclined to get the feeling down into words. In a poem called "Insensibility," Owen refers to those who cease feeling and use dullness to solve their situation (Owen, 1963).

The feeling of "detachment or estrangement from others," which is *DSM-IV* symptom C(5), is given artistic expression in a poem by Richard Levine, American veteran of the war in Vietnam. It is entitled "Nights in Shining Armor," and he refers to having a suit he cannot get off and will always have. He lowers his visor, his suit is haunted, and he has learned to sleep in it (Barry, 1981, p. 139).

Even the theme of a flashback-induced identification is covered in a poem by Charles Purcell. He expresses the fear of running amuck, running into the street shouting "Airborne all the way!" and shooting the milkman (Rottman, Barry, & Paquet, 1972).

Poetry does lend itself to a variety of themes, but as stated above, the most common theme by far in the poetry by combat veterans who are discussing their own aftermath is that of intrusive imagery, either in the form of dreams or in thoughts that cannot be shaken. Of the twenty-eight poems dealing with PTSD symptoms that I was able to find, twenty-three clearly dealt with this theme. Though the statistical studies do show that intrusive imagery is especially high in those who said they have killed, this alone may not account for this predominance. The nature of the medium, poetry, particularly lends itself to this motif.

Finally, moving from classics, which were written by keen observers of the human condition, and from those who have used artistic means to express their own feelings, there is the form of widespread art that has great influence on popular perceptions: motion pictures. Hollywood movies have treated PTSD in various ways. In the movie *Antz*, the term was used incorrectly in reference to a veteran who was acting in an erratic manner and making wild statements, but not engaged in behavior that fit with the definition of PTSD. This was a folk misdiagnosis. On the other hand, PTSD was never mentioned but clearly portrayed in *The Legend of Bagger Vance*, complete with one flashback where the young captain could hear the guns of the war.

There was a remark in the film *Almost Famous* that indicated a minor symptom of PTSD, which could be regarded as PITS since it involved a man who was in a hit-and run accident. In the scene, everyone is making confessions as their airplane is going down and apparently about to crash. One character mentions running away from the accident when the other was injured and says, "I see his face every day." That sounds like a possible expression of intrusive imagery. Similarly, an episode of the television series *Star Trek: Voyager* (broadcast the week of January 29, 2001) had a line from a man who had committed a murder. He expressed distress over still being able to see the sight and hear the sound of his victim.

The film *Saving Private Ryan* portrayed scenes during battle with sudden silence and slowness in the midst of battle. This is, of course, not a PTSD symptom, but was an artistic rendition of the sense of dissociation that has been associated with higher later levels of the symptomatology.

Fictional literature can deal with the phenomenon of PTSD and PITS in narrative form. Knowing about PITS can enrich the insight into literature. Conversely, fiction or poeticized narration of true events can provide illustrations and insight to psychology. World literature demonstrates how people in various places and throughout the ages have dealt with PITS, often in the absence of psychological definitions and procedures.

REFERENCES

American Psychiatric Association. (1994). *Diagnostic and statistical manual of mental disorders* (4th ed.). Washington, DC: Author.

Atholl, J. (1956). *The reluctant hangman: The story of James Berry, executioner 1884–1892*. London: John Long Limited.

Barry, J. (Ed.). (1981). *Peace is our profession*. Montclair, NJ: Faculty Press.

Bauman, Z. (1989). *Modernity and the Holocaust*. Ithaca, NY: Cornell University Press.

Durkheim, E. (1951). *Suicide: A study in sociology*. Glencoe, IL: Free Press.

Frances, A., First, M.B., & Pincus, H.A. (1995). *DSM-IV Guidebook*. Washington, DC: American Psychiatric Press.

Goffman, E. (1963). *Stigma: Notes on the management of spoiled identity*. Englewood Cliffs, NJ: Prentice-Hall.

Grossman, D. (1995). *On killing: The psychological cost of learning to kill in war and society*. Boston: Little, Brown and Company.

Hall, H.V., & Hall, F.L. (1987). Post-traumatic Stress Disorder as a legal defense in criminal trials. *American Journal of Forensic Psychology, 5*, 45–53.

Hendin, H., & Haas, A.P. (1985). Posttraumatic Stress Disorders in veterans of early America. *Psychohistory Review, 12*, 25–30.

Lansky, M.R., & Bley, C.R. (1995). *Posttraumatic nightmares: Psychodynamic explorations*. Hillsdale, NJ: The Analytic Press.

Lifton, R.J. (1986). *The Nazi doctors: Medical killing and the psychology of genocide*. New York: Basic Books.

Marsella, A.J., Friedman, M.J., Gerrity, E.T., & Scurfield, R.M. (1996). *Ethnocultural aspects of Posttraumatic Stress Disorder*. Washington, DC: American Psychological Association.

Mead, G.H. (1967). *Mind, self, and society*. Chicago: University of Chicago Press.

Merton, R.K. (1996). Manifest and latent functions (1949). In P. Sztompka (Ed.), *On social structure and science*. Chicago: University of Chicago Press.

Owen, W. (1963). Insensibility. In C.D. Lewis (Ed.), *The Collected Poems of Wilfred Owen* (pp. 37–38). Great Britain: Chatto & Windus, Ltd.

Poe, E.A. (1845/1978). The Imp of the Perverse. In T.O. Mabbot (Ed.), *Collected works of Edgar Allen Poe and sketches 1843–1849, vol. 3* (pp. 1224–1226). Cambridge, MA: Belknap Press of Harvard University Press.

Rottman, L., Barry, J., & Paquet, B.T. (Eds.). (1972). *Winning hearts and minds: War poems by Vietnam veterans*. New York: McGraw-Hill.

Shay, J. (1994). *Achilles in Vietnam: Combat trauma and the undoing of character*. Toronto: Maxwell MacMillan.

Solomon, Z. (1993). *Combat stress reaction: The enduring toll of war*. New York: Plenum Press.

Van Wyk Smith, M. (1978). *Drummer Hodge: The poetry of the Anglo-Boer War, 1988–1902*. Oxford: Clarendon Press.
Weber, M. (1971). *The interpretation of social reality*. New York: Scribner.
Weigl, B. (1985). *The monkey wars*. Atlanta: University of Georgia Press.

Chapter 10

Research Agenda

EXPANDING ON PREVIOUS FINDINGS

Various findings that require further research have been mentioned throughout this book. The essential case that PTSD is in fact a result of perpetration is still to be more firmly established. That it is present in certain groups and not in others needs much more clarification. The case was most strong in the group of combat veterans, since data included a large stratified random sample of veterans of a very large, long-lasting war. However, the data were cross-sectional, gathered at one point years after the war, employed self-report with no verification, and—most importantly—utilized questions not designed to actually look at whether or not PTSD can result from perpetration. In each other group, this book has simply offered a literature review upon which to base further investigation.

Matters of pattern and of implication also need extensive confirmation and expansion. There is a wide range of questions on rage, lifetime and current phases, concentration and memory problems, intrusive imagery, and a sense of personal disintegration. Do these vary across different types of groups, or with differing circumstances within groups? Do they have implications for therapy and other kinds of treatment? Are there implications for causation of symptoms? Have symptoms had social and historical impacts?

CONTEXT

Demographic variables such as gender, race, different ethnic groups, cultures, and subcultures may prove fruitful for future research. Physical, cultural, experiential, and role expectation differences could have profound influences on the psychological aftermath. The ages of the people, who could be at different developmental levels when the perpetration traumas occur, could also be a variable with profound implications. A very large portion of soldiers are in late adolescence, and in some parts of the world, some are even in early adolescence. Many soldiers are older, and clearly, police or those who carry out executions or torture are much more likely to be adults. Those who commit criminal homicide would fit the widest range of ages.

The circumstances and victims of the killing may be a major factor. Were anti-personnel weapons such as napalm or land mines involved? What was the level of risk to one's own life? Were the targets of killing personally threatening at the time, were they cowering, were they defiant, were they face-to-face? Were they familiar or unfamiliar, men or women or children? What was the emotion to the victim: hatred, disgust, apathy? What about the distance of the action, was it seen or only known about? What was the relational distance from the victim—family, friends, foreigners, animals? Are the killing events long since past, as with combat veterans, or are they continuing, as when it is included in a job?

On social support, what is the social acceptability of the violence—required, expected, allowed, tolerated, disapproved of, or outrage? Regarding social support, is it society as a whole, only a major portion of society with others protesting, only one's own social group, or entirely absent?

Various aspects of the meaning of the incident can be important. Did the action seem reasonable, necessary, or meaningless? What was the level of responsibility—was it a chosen activity, or something done just to follow orders? Is it reasonable to assume that if you did not do it, someone else would? Would you actually be in some sort of trouble (loss of job, jail) if you did not do it? Is it against your own moral code?

Had there been previous habituation or desensitization to killing? If so, did that help alleviate the aftermath, or make it worse, or not make much difference? Did successful departmentalizing or distancing take place? Was humor present (as in "gallows humor") and if so, what impact did it have? What was the level of denial?

Were people able to fully express their memories of the event to others, or were they strongly discouraged from even mentioning them? Were they able to discuss their emotional aftermath, or were they afraid of being seen as crazy, cowardly, or rude if they did? If they could discuss this, were they obligated to cast the events in positive terms? Were they instead obligated to cast them in negative terms? What impact does ability or inability to express these things have on symptoms?

Several studies with differing approaches will be required to answer these questions. Context alone offers a very lengthy research agenda.

The intensity of the killing is likely to be important. Since trauma has been noted to have a cumulative effect, with people more likely to suffer symptoms

after more than one trauma, an accumulation of killing could likewise be expected to make symptoms more severe. The data of the National Vietnam Veterans Readjustment Study (NVVRS), for example, was dichotomous. It only
allowed for dividing people into those who had killed as compared to those who
had not. If one man thinks he may out of fear have killed one enemy soldier
that was about to attack, and another knows he has killed in a fit of rage a
hundred soldiers who were retreating, the two are both counted in the same
group. Yet surely the numbers as well as the circumstances could be expected
to make a difference.

There are questions about the historical and cultural context. At the time of
the Trojan War, for example, people bragged about their exploits. The idea of
not being able to tell anyone about things done in the military did not apply to
them. This could be one of the major ways cultures, and therefore psychological
aftermath, differ.

GUILT AND COGNITIVE DISSONANCE

A justified guilt can be expected to be an important variable. Foa and Meadows (1997) address this directly:

a clear difference between veterans and most other trauma survivors is the level of
perpetration as well as victimization exhibited by the patient . . . the triggers for guilt and
shame in veterans are frequently quite rational. Thus, while challenging the guilt associated with being raped is clearly appropriate, the veteran who killed innocent civilians
might rightly resist attempts to challenge the justification for his guilt . . . alternative
strategies . . . [include] exploring ways of making reparations and bearing witness. (p.
475)

In this case, no distinction is made between those perpetrators who feel guilty
and those who do not.

There was only one item in the NVVRS that directly asked about guilt, and
it was very poorly worded. It was in the main set: "I have no guilt over things
done in the military." This negatively worded item would not be likely to get
the same results if it were positively worded and scored in reverse. It serves
more as an assertion of defense against an accusation, rather than as a statement
about feelings one is having. It also lends itself to assertive denial of the traumatic quality of actions, as might be expected by those who were active in
causing the event (Laufer, Gallops, & Frey-Wouters, 1984). Furthermore, it was
in the context of a list of positively worded symptoms, so people who were in
a response mode consistent with that context could easily miss the word "no"
and answer the opposite of what they intended.

Even so, all the perpetration groups did score higher on this item, which was
reverse-scored so that higher scores would indicate more guilt. However, the
effect size for the difference was small in all cases. In no case did it serve to

discriminate between groups. Statistically, there was no reason to pay much attention to it.

Other items in the NVVRS could also suggest guilt. For instance, the item on wondering why one survived when others did not suggests survival guilt. This is not the same as guilt over things done. In any event, the word "guilt" is not used, so it is not clear. Survival guilt could be a way to sublimate justified guilt, a natural accompaniment to justified guilt for which the veteran is in a state of denial. On the other hand, it could simply be an uncomfortable feeling that stands on its own and has nothing to do with guilt over actions.

Survival guilt was recognized as a symptom in the revised third edition of the *Diagnostic and Statistical Manual of Mental Disorders* (American Psychiatric Association, 1987), but was removed for the fourth edition, *DSM-IV* (1994). Guilt accompanying acts of aggression was never accounted as a symptom.

The item "certain things I did in military I can never tell anyone" might suggest possible guilt feelings, but again, it does not state so outright. It could simply be a response to how other people react. In the extensive symptom list of the clinical subset, one of the items assessed by psychiatrists was "guilt or shame—out of control expression of remorse." This is also ill suited as a measure of guilt, because it is deliberately designed to assess only a pathological extreme.

Guilt simply was not adequately covered in this data set. In future questionnaires and in-depth interviews, wording the questions on guilt in several different ways would be better. This could include such terminology as occasional "moral qualms," in order to get a fuller picture and use terminology that may arouse less defensiveness. This is all the more important in dealing with groups other than veterans, especially with those whose actions are controversial.

Guilt has been included in factor analyses with PTSD symptoms, and in those studies does come out as its own factor. Hovens et al. (1993) did an analysis of 967 Resistance veterans from World War II in the Netherlands, and found that survivor's guilt and guilt over people having suffered went into one of six factors. Silver and Iacono (1984) did include an item on feeling guilt over what one had done in Vietnam in its sample of 405 American veterans, and this factored together with an item on survivor's guilt and an item on grief.

In 1985, Glover published an article specifically addressing the point of guilt and aggression, discussing his years of clinical practice with American veterans of Vietnam. He divides those who killed into three categories:

men who willfully killed, whether on orders or on their own initiative, are frequently depressed, paranoid, and/or violence-prone. Individuals who are clearly *depressed* consciously struggle with feelings of guilt. They are also extremely inhibited in expressing any form of aggression. Veterans who deny feelings of guilt and are *paranoid* tend to be especially hostile and defensive when discussing Vietnam. . . . *Violence-prone* combat veterans . . . reveal their preoccupations with guilt when they are intoxicated, agitated, or depressed. Aggression serves a number of functions for them, including a defense against the feeling of guilt for having murdered civilians. (Glover, 1985, pp. 15–16, emphasis in original)

He also says that it is not necessarily the proximity to the act of killing which causes guilt, in that the two most guilt-ridden individuals were in supervisory roles with no direct combat experience.

Cognitive dissonance is a related concept. When there are two ideas a person must hold at once which are in conflict, this causes a tension that the person will seek to relieve in some way, in a variety of strategies. If the idea that one has killed is in conflict with one's moral code, the exercise of guilt keeps these two ideas from being in conflict. This serves as a different form of stress. Yet if guilt is not recognized, and one is not willing to acknowledge a conflict between the two ideas, but feels a conflict nevertheless, then efforts to bring the ideas out of dissonance will be practiced. The incident or incidents of killing are a fact and cannot be changed (except by denying the memory of them, which is one possible strategy). The previous moral code is an opinion, however, and amenable to change. A mental strategy of insisting that the action was justified and was in fact consonant with the moral code ensues. However, because this is a strategy for reduction of tension from cognitive dissonance, rather than a philosophically derived rationale, it is likely to be accompanied by excessive firmness in its advocacy—that is to say, belligerency. Such belligerency on behalf of justification of the action can impede healing. It can also complicate the social and political circumstances if practiced by large numbers of those engaged in socially sanctioned killing.

The role of a belligerent attitude of justification rather than guilt is much more complex in terms of research. Guilt, by definition, is admitted. A mental strategy of denying the discord of the action with the moral code, by definition, is not admitted. The proposal that this strategy even exists suggests a possible bias on the part of the researcher, in favor of the idea that the action was in fact not justified. Yet, the assertion that it does not exist is also a bias in favor of the idea that the action was justified. Once the research leaves categories such as "socially sanctioned" and enters categories about perceived moral justification, such complications are inevitable and unavoidable. If guilt is admitted, researchers can deal with the feelings of respondents without making their own judgments. If it is not admitted, its absence does not mean there are no unconscious feelings of guilt. The unconscious nature of the feelings is always a risky area for objective research.

MEANING

Another variable that is crucial to an understanding of the phenomenon is the role of meaning. Hendin and Haas (1984) suggest that ascribing significance to events is protective against PTSD. Shay (1994) also looked at the role of meaning in promoting PTSD: "Since the earliest studies . . . it has been known that severe trauma shatters a sense of the meaningfulness of the self, of the world, and of the connection between the two. The same obliteration of meaning has subsequently been confirmed for rape victims, Hiroshima survivors, survivors of the Cambodian genocide, and Vietnam combat veterans" (p. 170).

The fact that the person presumably had more control in the situation than does a passive victim does not necessarily add meaningfulness. In fact, meaningfulness may be more broken down because the event or events break down people's images of themselves. Perhaps Janoff-Bullman's (1985) observations about the "shattered assumptions" of PTSD sufferers do not only apply to passive victims. Having participated in violence not previously contemplated may also shatter previous assumptions. This is supported by the finding that the factor of personal disintegration in the extensive list of the clinical subset was such a strong discriminator on the side of those who said they had killed.

Antonovsky (1979) is a medical sociologist who has contributed the concept of "sense of coherence" to the psychology of stress. Briefly, he holds that people find it necessary to derive orderliness from an environment, to see meaningfulness, manageability, and comprehensibility. This sense of coherence is a resource that makes it easier to handle stressors. If the act of killing makes a person less able to have a sense of coherence (or the lack of such a sense makes a person more likely to kill in a combat situation), then that would be another theoretical reason why the act could have an influence on getting PTSD and on its pattern. While many theorists have posited a need for a sense of control as a resistance resource to stress, the sense of coherence is not the same as being in control. For example, if a mother takes a child to the doctor, she is no longer in control, because the doctor is. She is nevertheless calm because *things* are in control. In the same way, having control by virtue of regulating one's own actions may not be enough when one feels the situation is out of control. This may well be the normal case in active killing or injuring situations.

Direct questions can be asked on the differing interpretations of meaning in the experience of veterans in future research. Whether by questionnaire or in-depth interview, this could help clarify its role.

BIOLOGY

Biopsychology is also a rich area for investigation with the concept of PITS. In the hormonal and other biochemical phenomena, PTSD can be distinguished from the general stress response. The unusual hormonal profile in PTSD has the overall balance shifted towards low cortisol levels, continuously high levels of epinephrine and norepinephrine—also known as adrenaline and noradrenaline (the catecholamines)—a high norepinephrine/cortisol ratio, high testosterone levels, and high total thyroxine (T4) levels in the face of lower free T4 levels. The abnormally low cortisol levels are not due to exhaustion of surges of cortisol, which are common to the stress response, since those upsurges can still occur when stresses are introduced. This is an oversimplified summary in a very complicated area. This profile is still being explored.

Differences in whether the trauma was inflicted upon a helpless victim, rescuer, or was perpetration-induced have not been considered in many, if any, studies. Those studies on rape victims are likely to be a population that is entirely victims of trauma, but the majority of studies are done on combat-related PTSD. The two different types are therefore simply mixed in together. There could be biochemical differences that should be taken into account. For example, there has been some work on an association of testosterone with aggression; the role of testosterone may be one thing that differs. The area of understanding biochemical components of PTSD is still in its early stages, but the distinction of a perpetration-induced etiology may be crucial to its further development.

The role of endogenous opioids is also important, especially with the theory of addiction to trauma (see section covering this below). One literature review has found lower plasma b-endorphin levels in PTSD patients and other evidence of chronic baseline opiate depletion (Southwick, Yehuda, & Morgan, 1995). This is consistent with a theory that some symptoms are related to withdrawal symptoms and with efforts to provoke a stressor to increase endogenous opiate release. When the trauma is related to perpetration, the intrusive imagery, reexperiencing, and reenactment are likely to be as well, and this can make a difference to take into account.

Similarly, the role of dopamine release in the brain needs further exploration. Koepp et al. (1998) found that Positron Emission Tomography (PET) scans showed endogenous dopamine release during "goal-directed" video games, thus establishing that the chemical reaction can be behaviorally induced. A large portion of video games are not merely goal-directed but have as a goal the simulated killing of humans or fictitious aliens, about as close to studying the body's chemical reactions to perpetration as the laboratory will ethically allow. Dopamine would also have an effect that could lead to a sense of pleasure at the activity, and therefore possibly become addictive.

It has been found that there are possible brain differences in those who have PTSD. A smaller volume in the right hippocampus has been noted (Bremner et al., 1995). Investigation with longitudinal studies is currently ongoing to try to determine whether this results from the effects of biochemical and neurological components of PTSD, or whether people with this feature are more predisposed to get PTSD upon exposure to trauma. The hippocampus is associated with memory. Investigations have also focused on the amygdala, associated with the hippocampus and with stress, and on Broca's area, which deals with language. Language processing or lack of processing can have something to do with intrusive imagery or numbing. The area of brain differences is of course quite complicated, and the studies range from Magnetic Resonance Imaging (MRI) measures of brain parts, to Positron Emission Tomography (PET) scans, which look at the activity of the brain while events such as reminders of the trauma are occurring, to other measures of psychophysiological response in the brain.

Further study may show that there is actually little or no biological difference between those who are victims and those who are perpetrators in the traumatic circumstances. Even that would be an interesting finding, since the absence of a difference would deviate from an assumption that perpetration means control in the situation and therefore precludes it from being a trauma. Biological similarities would bolster the case that PITS is a form of PTSD, not an entirely separate phenomenon nor a nonexistent entity. It might also be found that, as with the symptom patterns found in veterans and discussed in Chapter 2, the biological patterns will be mostly the same but with some differences that can somewhat make a distinction between the two types. We should be familiar with these differences for therapeutic pharmacological interventions and for understanding of causation.

PERSONALITY

Johnson (1995), an army psychologist writing in the journal *Military Medicine*, proposed that the narcissistic personality is one character structure likely to heighten sensitivity to trauma. The grandiosity, hypersensitivity to the evaluation of others, lack of empathy, and fragility of self-concept associated with narcissism might lead to greater vulnerability. In extreme cases, the boundary between reality and fantasy becomes thin, creating a greater risk for dissociation, and thus for PTSD. Studies of the military population have suggested narcissistic personality features to be common in military outpatients, and even more prominent in the "special mission groups" that are at greatest risk for combat-related trauma. Enlistees in the military include a self-selection bias that attracts narcissists, with attention to appearance, tangible rewards, and public displays of reinforcement. Johnson provides little evidence for this speculation, but does illustrate the potential mechanisms with a single case study.

However, when a study was done administering the Millon Clinical Multiaxial Inventory (MCMI) to ninety-two outpatient veterans confirmed with a diagnosis of PTSD, it found the narcissistic score averaged 38.01, when a base rate of 75 is required to say that a personality feature is likely to be present (Hyer et al., 1992). In a later study administering the same test to 256 veterans with confirmed PTSD, they decided to remove the narcissistic scale from the analysis before the clustering procedure due to consistently low scores (Hyer et al., 1994). Less than 5% had a score above 60. Similarly, in a sample of 148 veterans, Sherwood, Funari, and Piekarski (1990) found that no veteran with PTSD scored above 85 on the narcissistic factor.

These findings were almost confirmed by Piekarski and Sherwood (1993). On the MCMI administered to 250 male inpatient Vietnam veterans, they statistically clustered the sample into four groups, three of which were well below the necessary base rate score to regard the narcissistic (or the related histrionic) variable as substantial. The one exception, the fourth group, was labeled "Nonstress-Aggressive." This group of thirty-nine people had a mean score of

77.5. Most interestingly, this group as a whole scored below the cutoff point for PTSD on a paper-and-pencil test. Of this group, the authors report that they "scored significantly lower than the other groups on the Anxiety and Dysthymic scales of the Millon . . . [they] also scored significantly higher on drug abuse. Thus, the Nonstress Aggressive group, despite being exposed to levels of combat comparable to the other groups, did not seem to have developed [PTSD]. Rather, they manifested an antisocial adjustment with substance abuse." This later refinement of their earlier work bears much more probing, particularly if a difference between perpetration-induced and passive-victim PTSD is being studied.

In contrast with Johnson (1995), these studies suggest that narcissism is actually protective against PTSD, leading instead to different undesirable consequences such as substance abuse. However, the rules for being designated PTSD treat it as a whole. It is also possible that there are different patterns of symptoms that are not picked up by overall scores.

Barnard, Hankins, and Robbins (1992) studied a group of fifty-two hospitalized sex offenders. They found the narcissistic personality to be prominent, and especially associated with antisocial traits. They divided the personality types into three different clusters, with Cluster B including histrionic, antisocial, and borderline as well as narcissistic scores. Of the sample, 19% were narcissistic, and 71% were at least one of the Cluster B types. "Subjects endorsed Cluster B traits indicative of pathological narcissism at 1.4 times the rate for Cluster A traits and 1.7 times the rate for Cluster C traits" (p. 412). The authors conclude: "This set of vulnerabilities, behavioral predispositions, attitudes, and beliefs, themselves a product of past trauma, may be some of the elements within the individual which enhance their tendency to indulge in sexually deviant/violent behavior in the present. The sex offenders in the current study appeared to be a significantly traumatized group of men by any standard" (p. 413).

In this case, Barnard, Hankins, and Robbins are finding the narcissistic personality to be the result of trauma, and causal of later perpetration-induced trauma. Whether this personality type did as Johnson proposed and heightened their sensitivity to even minor trauma cannot be ascertained. Whether the perpetration-induced trauma had any consequences for these men was not separated out from the previous traumas they had endured.

In addition to narcissism, much more can be done on two types of personality that could reasonably be associated with perpetration-induced trauma: authoritarianism and Machiavellianism. The only mention found of authoritarianism was in a fairly old article (Strayer & Ellenhorn, 1975), which found that a good portion of forty recently returned veterans did have such a personality, but they did not report what portion that was. High scores on the California F Scale were more likely to be high in participation in atrocities, yet unlike other such men, they had less guilt and depression and better adjustment. Since this study predates the publishing of criteria for PTSD, the concept was not applied, and so the findings are rather primitive by more current standards.

No studies relating Machiavellianism to PTSD were found. There has been some suggestion that this personality trait is a more mild, socially widespread version of what in extreme clinical cases would be psychoticism or antisocial personality (McHoskey, Worzel, & Szyarto, 1998). This could relate it to some of the studies, including antisocial personality as cited above. There are long-used twenty-item scales (the Mach IV and the Mach V; see Christie & Geis, 1970) that have been widely utilized and allow for standardized comparisons across groups.

DREAMS

Since intrusive imagery, and therefore nightmares, are symptoms that seem to be especially strong in perpetration-induced trauma, a question arises as to whether the form and content of such dreams differs between the passive victim and the perpetrator. The form and content of the experience itself differs, especially in variables such as level of control, and it would stand to reason that a symptom dealing so strongly with content could possibly be affected. If there were not much difference, that also would be interesting information.

Repetitive and frequent nightmares come essentially in two types: lifelong sufferers and posttrauma sufferers. Hartmann (1996) has studied extensively the differences over the years, and he concludes that the lifelong sufferers of nightmares have thin boundaries, a weak ability to differentiate things, and a tendency for things to merge into one another. The posttrauma dreams, by contrast, have stronger than usual boundaries, thicker than average "character armor, solid defenses," so that they would "encapsulate" their experience and "attempt to keep it walled off, separate from the rest of life" (p. 112). The sense in which it is walled off is that it is separated from other memories. Unfortunately, under certain conditions it is suddenly and involuntarily replayed. His conclusion comes from both content analysis of dreams and personality tests given to the two different types of nightmare sufferers. Sleep laboratory work along with personality tests by van der Kolk et al. (1984) have also found this distinction. Bearden (1994) provides a good overview of the studies that show the differences in the two categories.

Theories about the physiological and psychological nature of posttrauma dreams are still in a state of development. Ross et al. (1989) argue that flashbacks are actually the same thing as dreams that break in during waking hours. Conversely, Hartmann (1996) argues that posttrauma nightmares are not really dreams at all, but biochemically and conceptually, they are memory intrusions into dreams.

Bearden (1994), on the other hand, looked at the three categories of what induces nightmares—an external agent (drugs), an internal psychological state of particular vulnerability, and an identifiable traumatic event. She notes, "One common thread that links the three categories is that they all involve an increased REM-pressure . . . any sort of 'hyper-reactivity' of the nervous system would have this effect." Bearden concludes, "it is therefore possible that this hyper-reactive condition is the fundamental, underlying basis for all nightmares, whether induced by drugs, schizophrenic vulnerability, or traumatic experience" (p. 149).

Most of the studies that have looked at the phenomenon have been sleep laboratory studies with small numbers of participants, small or absent control groups, and widely varying findings (Greenberg, Pearlman, & Gampel, 1972; Lavie & Hertz, 1979; Lavie et al., 1979; Hefez, Metz, & Lavie, 1987; van der Kolk et al., 1984; Dagan, Lavie, & Bleich, 1991; Ross et al., 1994). It is the nature of sleep laboratories to expend a great deal of resources on the intensive study of each individual, so while this approach can yield a great deal of useful data, it has its limitations.

Great resources are also spent in direct individual or group therapy, of course, but this occurs whether or not it is additionally used for research. Glover reports several dreams explicitly linked to having killed in Vietnam based on his clinical experience working with American veterans of that war. Some of these do seem to be the eidetic dreams, that is, replays of the original event. Several other forms that are more like the normal metaphorical use of dreams also occur. In a summary of his clinical work, Glover (1985) says:

Men who suffer with guilt because they killed out of error or fear frequently dream of the incident, hoping somehow to undo the event. Those who willfully killed, but now suffer misgivings and conflict, frequently dream of seeing themselves killed in battle. Sometimes the veterans dream of being unable to defend themselves because they have a faulty weapon or because they are physically unable to respond. (p. 17)

Glover here notes both kinds of dreams—the replays and the metaphorical—and they are differentiated by the kind of killing, whether essentially accidental or willful. He wrote this as the concept of PTSD was developing but was not yet in the official definitions for psychiatry. No quantitative work has been found differentiating the types of dream content between even victim and perpetrator, much less accidental versus willful perpetration. His additional observation that it is those who feel guilty who have the dreams in which they are killed is also a distinction that deserves more exploration. This is difficult to study, since feelings of guilt can be unconscious but come out later in group therapy discussion as, for example, related by Lifton (1990, pp. 427–429).

Working with veterans in groups, Lifton also found that those who had killed reported being killed in their dreams. One veteran said:

I was riding on some kind of vehicle—a bus, I think—down Fifth Avenue. Somehow it turned into a military truck—and the truck got bigger and bigger, until it reached an enormous size. I was a soldier on the truck—and I fell off . . . and was killed. [In another dream] I was riding on a subway—underground—and somehow [along the course of the ride] I seemed to turn into a solider in uniform . . . There was a lot of confusion and then there was a battle with the police . . . in which I was killed. (Lifton, 1990, p. 427)

Another veteran reported that an enemy soldier who had shot him in the leg and whom he had apparently killed kept showing up vividly in a recurrent dream, with a face as clear as it had been in the original incident. This dream seemed to be a replay of the event, except that in the dream, the veteran himself was killed by his antagonist (p. 429).

Something similar is disclosed in the case of the police officer who was diagnosed with PTSD resulting from his having shot someone, as reported on television and discussed in Chapter 5. The content of his dreams as told to reporter Kotbe was that "over and over, in his dreams, Sal faced a man with a knife. In one dream, he faced him alone. In another, alone and unarmed. And in the worst of all, alone, stark naked and terrified" (*Dateline*, 2000).

The dream content of those who killed is reported to take additional forms. Glover (1988) cites a case in which the veteran "frequently hears the voices of the Vietnamese women and children he killed, accusing him (in English) of killing them or demanding of him the explanation of why he killed them. The voices warn him that bad things will happen to himself and his family" (p. 70). Lifton (1990) recounts a veteran offering this dream: "I was arguing with myself. Then there were two separate selves, and one of them finally shot the other, so that I shot myself" (p. 429). This mythological motif of the double, whereby the personality splits in two, is one that Lifton develops in various places, including his book on the Nazi doctors at Auschwitz. In this case, the veteran is killer and killed at the same time, killed in his dream, but killed by himself.

Forms of dreams in groups other than veterans have also been reported throughout this book. The motif of being a victim of the violence one is perpetrating was also noted, for example, by Craig Haney as he worked on the Stanford Prison Experiment (see Chapter 7). The same motif, plus that of being accused by those killed is also reported by Sallie Tisdale in her abortion clinic work, as reported in Chapter 6. The extent to which motifs apply or vary across the different kinds of groups could make a fascinating study.

While Glover and Lifton both attribute the dreams about being killed to a sense of guilt, a sense of deserving, there are alternative explanations to be considered. Both authors report veterans objecting to the guilt interpretation, but do not regard the objection as sufficient to show that guilt is not the reason, especially considering later discussion with the same veterans. Another possibility, however, has to do with the psychology of distinguishing the self from that which is not the self. All of us learn to do this as babies—when we choose to move our fingers, they move, and when we choose to move someone else's fingers, they do not, and so we learn through the course of time to distinguish the self from the not-self. This clear-cut distinction becomes blurred when we imagine being someone else or get absorbed in a story or in a task; it becomes nonexistent when we go to sleep. It is common in a dream state of mind for images to mingle together the self and not-self. When an act of killing takes place, the difference is quite conspicuous between the self who is doing it and the not-self who is killed. It may become a more blurred distinction in a dreaming state of mind—even one with strong boundaries walling off the memory of the event from other parts of the mind.

An investigation of dreams in the various groups that included only therapy clients would, of course, be badly skewed. Also skewed would be dreams reported in the literature, which are likely to be less eidetic and more interesting than the average. Quantitative methods for studying dreams in general are still being developed. Asking individuals to keep dream diaries, of course, can be helpful, especially when working psychologically with that individual. Another technique is doing a random sample of dream reports from specified populations, where each individual is asked to write out his or her most recent dream. A sample of 100 is regarded as a minimum for this technique, and there is a standardized quantitative method for comparing content (Domhoff, 1996). Esposito et al. (1999) have reported a beginning in developing a dream rating instrument specifically for PTSD-style dreams, drawn from the dream analysis literature and tested on eighteen veterans. More clear-cut knowledge of eidetic dreams and of the motifs common to those who killed, once better developed, could also help in studying the dreams and thereby coming up with quantitative assessments of prevalence and distinctions by kind of killing. This information can, in turn, provide more knowledge about causation of symptoms and how to improve therapy.

SOCIOLOGICAL QUESTIONS

There are research questions that are especially pertinent from a sociological point of view. In addition to ethnocultural differences and theoretical considerations, as discussed in the last chapter, there are other questions of what it does to the group. From large institutions to small groups that deal directly with the individual, the social context needs more exploration.

The role of large institutions in causing people to engage in killing is obvious when that killing is socially approved. What about the converse—what effect does massive PTSD within a violent institution have on the institutions, as well as the society that creates them? Would symptoms lead to higher levels of physically injurious accidents? How well can such institutions be maintained in the face of massive PTSD among participants? What happens when the institution is not maintained? What happens when it is? Around the world, combat veterans are treated differently with varying levels of support for their psychological needs, and these differences may well have an impact on the society as a whole. Other institutions will vary even more, since carrying out executions will have a markedly different social context than being a police officer put in dangerous situations, which is different from working in a slaughterhouse.

The social aspects of treatment are another area of study. What varying arrangements have been made? For example, an argument has been made that a major function of the Sioux sweat lodge ceremony was to help combat veterans readjust after war (Silver & Wilson, 1988). What is the role of social support groups, in what different ways are they manifested, and to what extent do they accomplish their purposes? How do social institutions foster helpful programs? How could it be better done? Are there ways that the social institutions are making the problem worse, and are there ways to address this?

ADDICTION TO TRAUMA: THE THRILL OF THE KILL

There is a prominent paradox regarding stress symptoms from perpetration that has been noted in several studies: there is often a sense of thrill, of exhilaration, that accompanies the act. The opposite of horror is the actual reaction. Furthermore, this thrill can be addictive.

Grossman characterizes the exhilaration as a common stage in the killing process. He quotes a Rhodesian veteran:

Combat addiction . . . is caused when . . . the body releases a large amount of adrenaline into your system and you get what is referred to as a "combat high." This combat high is like getting an injection of morphine—you float around, laughing, joking, having a great time, totally oblivious to the dangers around you. . . . Problems arise when you begin to want another fix of combat, and another, and another, and, before you know it, you're hooked. As with heroin or cocaine addiction, combat addiction will surely get you killed. And like any addict, you get desperate and will do anything to get your fix. (Grossman, 1995, pp. 234–237)

Many of the examples Grossman offers involve fighter pilots. He does not know whether they actually experience this thrill sensation more frequently, but they may be more willing to talk about it since descriptions of downed aircraft may be more tolerable in polite company than more graphic descriptions of face-to-face killing.

Solursh (1988) reports on interviews with twenty-two combat veterans, which showed that prominent in nineteen of them was a "clear history of combat, killing and flashback or nightmare recall as excitatory, similar to an adrenergic 'rush.'" He quotes a case study, a combat veteran who says: "It's hard to duplicate this high with drugs, except the only drug I know is cocaine, that would reproduce this high for you, the same type of high of killing." He gives more detail in a second paper (Solursh, 1989).

As these were selected to be men with chronic PTSD, it is clear that this "rush" is not protective against PTSD and may well be connected to its aggravation. Solursh suggests the possibility that the intrusive imagery symptoms of nightmares and flashbacks may in fact be accompanied by this "rush," thereby contributing to symptom maintenance and complicating treatment. He reports the symptoms to be especially strong when respondents were answering with regard to demands of the workplace or authorities under whom they felt powerless. The reenactment is a mental assertion of power. Thus, the exciting nature of the original event gets repeated in the benefit of excitement in the recall.

However, as is common with "highs," there is a letdown period afterward, when powerlessness and frustration returns.

Nadelson (1992) reports on five case studies of combat veterans who had an "attachment to killing." He similarly finds analogies to a high from drugs made among these men. He also offers an operant conditioning model to explain the symptom maintenance. It is an effort to achieve psychological control as well as to reproduce the sense of a high. Wikler (1980) also was told through interviews with veterans that there were soldiers who were referred to as the "killer types," those who "seemed to enjoy their work, getting 'kicks' or 'highs' from killing" (p. 98).

There is a possible biological explanation for this "rush." Stress situations, especially highly traumatic ones, can lead to endogenous opioid analgesia (van der Kolk et al., 1985; Southwick, Yehuda, & Morgan, 1995) and related complicated biochemical reactions. In other words, during high stress, the brain naturally releases opioids, which in the world of artificial drugs is related to morphine, heroin, and cocaine. The veterans' use of those specific drugs as analogies to the high they feel is not coincidental. There is a hypothesis of an actual biochemical connection. Studies are still in preliminary stages (for a review, see Southwick, Yehuda, & Morgan, 1995).

This leads to the irony that a reaction of a sense of thrill can still be seen as a reaction to trauma. Those brain-produced opioids are an adaptation for those in danger, because they relieve extreme pain. It is becoming addicted which is not adaptive. In historical terms, it may offer some insight into the term "blood-thirsty."

This has been noted in passing in several other sources, but the research is still at a very primitive stage. The concept can be applied across other groups besides combat veterans. For example, some of those involved in occupations that include killing may in fact be ensnared in a situation which is not easy for them to leave, in the same way that it is difficult for an addict to stop taking drugs, and for the same reason.

It also sheds new light on the thrill associated with blood sports such as cockfights, bullfights, and hunting. As Grossman (1995) says in this context, "What hunter or marksman has not felt a thrill of pleasure and satisfaction upon dropping his target?" (p. 234). Hunting and similar activities can even be a continual socially accepted means of reexperiencing the trauma of killing as a substitute for flashbacks, nightmares, and other intrusive thoughts.

The Spanish bullfighter interviewed by *60 Minutes* (air date January 11, 1998) persists in plying his trade in spite of the danger involved (his father was killed) and the objections of his family. This suggests the possibility of addiction. From the same report, an American bullfighter in Spain is quoted as saying:

When you come out of this experience and—you appreciate everything you have around you; the skies look bluer, the birds sound better, the food tastes better . . . I mean, if I could tell you what it was, maybe we could bottle it and sell it and save a lot of people—

you know, if we could bottle the adrenaline, if we could bottle that feeling a matador has after a fight and sell—and it'll be wonderful—manic—manic depressants and people. Be a wonderful thing.

Is there a resemblance between this statement and others made about those times when the feeling is in fact put in a bottle, a syringe, or a powder?

If there are people who have an addiction, either biochemical or behavioral, which causes continuing activity or continuing mental reenactment of the trauma—that is, intrusive imagery—then therapy needs to be altered accordingly. As one discussion of this aspect put it, "a therapeutic approach based on the assumption that the PTSD symptomatology was aversive the veterans would be unlikely to be successful" (Hodge, 1997, p. 96). Since there are definitely times when the symptoms are aversive, a clear distinction would need to be made. Nor does the lack of aversion mean that the symptoms require no treatment, as with any addiction. The dangers to other people are also a major concern in failing to treat someone with an addiction to violence, if the idea of such an addiction turns out to have merit after further research.

All of this is still in the realm of speculation. The interviews with combat veterans show that there is possibly a phenomenon that requires much more attention. Prevalence is not established even for the veterans, much less for other groups. Explanations, theories, and models also require much more development. This is obviously a crucial area for understanding causation of symptoms, therapy needs for sufferers, and public policy implications for prevention of further violence.

REFERENCES

American Psychiatric Association. (1987). *Diagnostic and statistical manual of mental disorders* (3rd ed., revised). Washington, DC: Author.

———. (1994). *Diagnostic and statistical manual of mental disorders* (4th ed.). Washington, DC: Author.

Antonovsky, A. (1979). *Health, stress, and coping.* San Francisco: Jossey-Bass.

Barnard, G.W., Hankins, G.C., & Robbins, L. (1992). Prior life trauma, post-traumatic stress symptoms, sexual disorders, and character traits in sex offenders: An exploratory study. *Journal of Traumatic Stress, 5,* 393–420.

Bearden, C. (1994). The nightmare: Biological and psychological origins. *Dreaming Journal of the Association for the Study of Dreams, 4,* 139–152.

Bremner, J.D., Randall, P., Scott, T.M., Bronen, R.A., Seibyl, J.P., Southwick, S.M., Delaney, R.C., McCarthy, G., Gharney, D.S., & Innis, R.B. (1995). MRI-based measurement of hippocampal volume in patients with combat-related Posttraumatic Stress Disorder. *American Journal of Psychiatry, 152,* 973–981.

Christie, R., & Geis, F. (1970). *Studies in Machiavellianism.* New York: Academic Press.

Dagan, Y., Lavie, P., & Bleich, A. (1991). Elevated awakening thresholds in sleep state 3–4 in war-related Post-traumatic Stress Disorder. *Biological Psychiatry, 30,* 618–622.

Dateline NBC. (2000). *NYPD Blues* (transcript). December 26. Livingston, NJ: Burrelle's Information Services.

Domhoff, G.W. (1996). *Finding meaning in dreams: A quantitative approach.* New York: Plenum Press.

Esposito, K., Benitez, A., Barza, L., & Mellman, T. (1999). Evaluation of dream content in combat-related PTSD. *Journal of Traumatic Stress, 132,* 681–687.

Foa, E.B., & Meadows, E.A. (1997). Psychosocial treatments for Posttraumatic Stress Disorder: A critical review. *Annual Review of Psychology, 48,* 449–480.

Glover, H. (1985). Guilt and aggression in Vietnam veterans. *American Journal of Social Psychiatry, 1,* 15–18.

———. (1988). Four syndromes of Post-traumatic Stress Disorder: Stressors and conflicts of the traumatized with special focus on the Vietnam combat veteran. *Journal of Traumatic Stress, 1,* 57–78.

Greenberg, R., Pearlman, C.A., & Gampel, D. (1972). War neuroses and the adaptive function of REM sleep. *British Journal of Medical Psychology, 45,* 27–33.

Grossman, D. (1995). *On killing: The psychological cost of learning to kill in war and society.* Boston: Little, Brown and Company.

Hartmann, E. (1996). Who develops PTSD nightmares and who doesn't. In D. Barrett (Ed.), *Trauma and dreams* (pp. 100–113). Cambridge, MA: Harvard University Press.

Hefez, A., Metz, L., & Lavie, P. (1987). Long-term effects of extreme situational stress on sleep and dreaming. *American Journal of Psychiatry, 144,* 344–347.

Hendin, H., & Haas, A.P. (1984). *Wounds of war: The psychological aftermath of combat in Vietnam.* New York: Basic Books.

Hodge, J.E. (1997). Addiction to violence. In J.E. Hodge, M. McMurran, & C.R. Hollin (Eds.), *Addicted to crime?* New York: John Wiley & Sons.

Hovens, J.E., Falger, P.R.J., Op De Velde, W., Meijer, P., De Groen, J.H.M., & Van Duijn, H. (1993). A self-rating scale for the assessment of Posttraumatic Stress Disorder in Dutch Resistance veterans of World War II. *Journal of Clinical Psychology, 49,* 196–203.

Hyer, L., Davis, H., Albrecht, W., Boudewyns, P., & Woods, G. (1994). Cluster analysis of MCMI and MCMI-II on chronic PTSD victims. *Journal of Clinical Psychology, 50,* 502–515.

Hyer, L., Davis, H., Woods, G., Albrecht, J.W., & Boudewyns, P. (1992). Relationship between the Millon Clinical Multiaxial Inventory and the Millon II value of scales for aggressive and self-defeating personalities in Posttraumatic Stress Disorder. *Psychological Reports, 71,* 867–879.

Janoff-Bulman, R. (1985). The aftermath of victimization: Rebuilding shattered assumptions. In C. Figley (Ed.), *Trauma and its wake: The study and treatment of Post-traumatic Stress Disorder* (pp. 14–35). New York: Brunner/Mazel.

Johnson, B. (1995). Narcissistic personality as a mediating variable in manifestations of Post-traumatic Stress Disorder. *Military Medicine, 160,* 40–41.

Koepp, M.J., Gunn, R.N., Lawrence, A.D., Cunningham, V.J., Dagher, A., Jones, T., Brooks, D.J., Bench, C.J., & Grasby, P.M. (1998). Evidence for striatal dopamine release during a video game. *Nature, 393,* 266–268.

Laufer, R.S., Gallops, M.S., & Frey-Wouters, E. (1984). War stress and trauma: The Vietnam veteran experience. *Journal of Health and Social Behavior, 25,* 65–85.

Lavie, P., Hefez, A., Halperin, G., & Enoch, D. (1979). Long-term effects of traumatic war-related events on sleep. *American Journal of Psychiatry, 236,* 175–178.

Lavie, P., & Hertz, G. (1979). Increased sleep motility and respiration rates in combat neurotic patients. *Biological Psychiatry 14,* 983–987.

Lifton, R.J. (1990). Adult dreaming: Frontiers of form. In R.A. Neminoff & C.A. Colarusso (Eds.), *New dimensions in adult development* (pp. 419–442). New York: Basic Books.

Marmar, C.R., Weiss, D.S., Metzler, T.J., & Delucchi, K. (1996). Characteristics of emergency services personnel related to peritraumatic dissociation during critical incident exposure. *American Journal of Psychiatry, 153,* 94–102.

Marmar, C.R., Weiss, D.S., Schlenger, W.E., Fairbank, J.A., Jordan, B.K., Kulka, R.A., & Hough, R.L. (1994). Peritraumatic dissociation and posttraumatic stress in male Vietnam theater veterans. *American Journal of Psychiatry, 151,* 902–907.

McHoskey, J.W., Worzel, W., & Szyarto, C. (1998). Machiavellianism and psychopathy. *Journal of Personality and Social Psychology, 74,* 192–210.

Nadelson, T.N. (1992). Attachment to killing. *Journal of the American Academy of Psychoanalysis, 20,* 130–141.

Piekarski, A.M., & Sherwood, R. (1993). Personality subgroups in an inpatient Vietnam veteran treatment program. *Psychological Reports, 72,* 667–674.

Pollock, P.H. (1999). When the killer suffers: Post-traumatic stress reactions following homicide. *Legal and Criminological Psychology, 4,* 185–202.

Ross, R.J., Ball, W.A., Dinges, D.F., Kribbs, N.B., Norrison, A.R., Silver, S.M., & Mulvaney, F.D. (1994). Rapid eye movement sleep disturbance in Posttraumatic Stress Disorder. *Biological Psychiatry, 35,* 195–202.

Ross, R.J., Ball, W.A., Sullivan, K.A., & Caroff, S.N. (1989). Sleep disturbance as a hallmark of Posttraumatic Stress Disorder. *American Journal of Psychiatry, 146,* 697–707.

Shay, J. (1994). *Achilles in Vietnam: Combat trauma and the undoing of character.* Toronto: Maxwell MacMillan.

Sherwood, R., Funari, D.J., & Piekarski, A.M. (1990). Adapted character styles of Vietnam veterans with Posttraumatic Stress Disorder. *Psychological Reports, 66,* 623–631.

Silver, S.M., & Iacono, C.U. (1984). Factor-analytic support for DSM-III's Posttraumatic Stress Disorder for Vietnam veterans. *Journal of Clinical Psychology, 40,* 5–14.

Silver, S.M., & Wilson, J.P. (1988). Native American healing and purification rituals for war stress. In J.P. Wilson, Z. Harl, & B. Kahana (Eds.), *Human adaptation to extreme stress: From the Holocaust to Vietnam.* New York: Plenum Press.

Solursh, L. (1988). Combat addiction: Post-traumatic Stress Disorder re-explored. *Psychiatric Journal of the University of Ottawa, 13,* 17–20.

————. (1989). Combat addiction: Overview of implications in symptom maintenance and treatment planning. *Journal of Traumatic Stress, 2,* 451–462.

Southwick, S.M., Yehuda, R., & Morgan, C.A. (1995). Clinical studies of neurotransmitter alterations in Post-traumatic Stress Disorder. In M.J. Friedman, D.S. Charney, & A.Y. Deutch (Eds.), *Neurobiological and clinical consequences of stress* (pp. 335–350). Philadelphia: Lippincott-Raven.

Strayer, R., & Ellenhorn, L. (1975). Vietnam veterans: A study exploring adjustment patterns and attitudes. *Journal of Social Issues, 31,* 81–93.

van der Kolk, B.A., Blitz, R., Burr, W., Sherry, S., & Hartmann, E. (1984). Nightmares and trauma: A comparison of nightmares after combat with lifelong nightmares in veterans. *American Journal of Psychiatry, 141*, 187–190.

van der Kolk, B.A., & Fisler, R. (1995). Dissociation and the fragmentary nature of traumatic memories: Overview and exploratory study. *Journal of Traumatic Stress, 8*, 505–525.

van der Kolk, B.A., Greenberg, M., Boyd, H., & Krystal, J. (1985). Inescapable shock, neurotransmitters, and addiction to trauma: Toward a psychobiology of posttraumatic stress. *Biological Psychiatry, 20*, 314–325.

Wikler, N. (1980). Hidden injuries of war. In C.R. Figley, & S. Leventman (Eds.), *Strangers at home: Vietnam veterans since the war* (pp. 87–106). Philadelphia: Brunner/Mazel.

Chapter 11

Technical Aspects of Research

CONFOUNDING VARIABLES: PRIOR TRAUMA, STIGMA, AND CONTROVERSY

The largest and most confounding variable is the extent to which traumatization preceded, and perhaps even caused, the act of killing. Posttrauma symptoms, especially rage and numbing, can themselves be causal in acts of violence. The converse then follows: of those who commit violence, a disproportionate number may well have suffered prior traumatization compared to the general public.

For criminal homicides, Pollock (1999) looks at this directly by ascertaining a group that did not experience previous traumatization and therefore does not have this as a confounding variable. For Vietnam veterans, an article looking at premilitary factors found no personality or traumatic predecessors for those who engaged in "abusive violence" (Hiley-Young et al., 1995). It was the level of combat that most predicted engagement in such behavior. Especially when killing is socially sanctioned or even socially obligatory, there will be a set of people for whom prior traumatization is not an issue.

However, because there will also be those for which prior traumatization is a confounding issue, leaving this group out will lead to only partial understanding. Some studies on PTSD have tried to eliminate the confounding variable of alcohol abuse by removing those suffering such abuse from the experiments. While this does give more details about what is attributable only to the PTSD, it gains an understanding only of those without alcoholism. Since substance abuse problems are commonly associated with PTSD, a major portion of the population has simply remained unstudied. Similarly, the role of prior traumatization may confound the results, but it is also a necessary variable to take into account.

Even ascertaining that no prior traumatization has occurred can be a problem. Those soldiers who have no traumatization prior to the war do have the combat itself. Executioners may have other traumatic circumstances in prison work. Traumatization such as child abuse is not always remembered or reported, and a self-image of machismo may further block the reporting of previous stresses.

Another complication is those who are known to have a personality disposition that in certain circumstances inclines toward killing: the psychotic. Pollock (1999) suggests that this is protective against PTSD; it is, of course, another form of disorder. Grossman (1995) also suggests that the psychopath or sociopath is a category that is orthogonal to PTSD development. How prevalent this personality predisposition is varies by group, but a situation in which killing is expected may attract a disproportionate number.

Another major problem in research is that many of the groups of socially sanctioned killing are, in fact, not entirely socially sanctioned. While veterans of most wars are regarded by their societies as heroes, there are some wars from which veterans have been stigmatized. Stigmatization has also been present for hangmen in Europe, for those who carry out executions or abortions, and for those involved in animal research (Arluke, 1991). Stigmatization complicates the assessment of PTSD in terms of offering alternative explanations for some behavior, especially if actual violence against respondents has upon occasion been threatened. Controversy also makes potential respondents much more suspicious of researchers and their intentions.

On any controversial issue, opponents might have reason to find one way rather than another. Proponents have reason to find the converse. Advocates of each side have purposes of their own propaganda.

In many cases, controversial issues can be handled by having a research team that includes people who have differing opinions on the issue. This adds perspective, helps avoid unwarranted conclusions, and contributes to the validity of the findings. It is crucial that more in-depth studies be done with rigorous scientific standards. In the highly likely event that researchers involved have a pre-established bias, a team approach with a balance of researchers who have opposite biases would lead to greater confidence in the validity of results.

This may or may not help with the respondents, however, depending on the situation. For different groups and different individuals, advocates on their own side may be more acceptable or may bring even more suspicion, while opponents may be utterly unacceptable or more interesting. Compared to psychological research as a whole, which is already very complicated, the presence of social and political controversy complicates the research in this area tremendously.

METHODOLOGIES

The term "Posttraumatic Stress Disorder" is used as a very specifically defined disorder, with a diagnosis that is dichotomous. Therapists can use this disorder to get insurance compensation for their work. Veterans can receive monetary benefits for having a service-related disorder, which they would not be eligible for if their mental disorder were not combat related. They therefore often have a strong interest in getting the diagnosis. Much of the work has accordingly been aimed at figuring out who does *not* have PTSD. Under these conditions, several different kinds of assessment are used on one individual—psychiatric interviews, psychometric scales, and psychophysiological reactivity. Those individuals who do in fact have aftereffects of battle, but not enough to constitute a diagnosis for the disorder, are then treated no differently than those who currently have none.

This dichotomy is not helpful for other uses. When contrasting groups, for example—either demographic groups, or a target group with a control group—a continuum of severity may be more beneficial. The same is true of designing prevention or treatment efforts, or trying to determine what causes the condition.

For ascertaining levels of the condition in individuals and populations, the methodologies available and discussed in the literature are: interviews; direct self-report scales; indirect scales including the MMPI, MCMI, and Rorschach (discussed below); and psychophysiological reactivity. Added here will be gleaned information from written materials, used as a qualitative technique.

The psychiatric interview is generally considered the gold standard against which other methods are judged. This is a qualitative technique requiring expert interviewers who often have further training for the specific study in order to try to standardize the assessments between different interviewers as much as possible. It has the advantage of going into depth, probing for information that the respondent might otherwise not think of with just a simple statement on a self-report instrument. It can be used to clarify the subject's verbal reports so that ambiguous interpretations are more likely to be avoided. It provides more detailed information for determining the best treatment options, tailored to this specific individual.

Interviews can lead to case study documentation, which then becomes qualitative data that gives texture to the condition, as well as a better understanding of what it is like and what meaning it has to those who suffer. The qualitative data also gives more of an indication of the rich variety of experience that is entailed in the symptoms. A quantitative scale that gives a summary statement covering a wide assortment of experience misses the richness and details of individual differences within that experience. All of these advantages of the psychiatric interview are also true for qualitative interviews done by people who may not have psychiatric or therapeutic expertise. This is not often found in the literature, but will sometimes be used in books to illustrate points about specific types of trauma victims.

Disadvantages include the potential for the interviewer to subconsciously interpret according to preconceived stereotypes or treat people differently such that comparisons are not valid. The method is also very cumbersome and time-consuming, and so can only be done in studies with either very small samples or very large budgets.

Some work on concurrent biochemical possibilities is also being done on catecholamines, testosterone, endorphins, and other hormones, but this is not yet conclusive and not being considered as part of ascertaining whether the condition exists. Similarly, there is a suggestion that there may be changes in the brain, most notably a shrinkage in the hippocampus, but the longitudinal studies to establish causal direction are currently still in progress. These biological manifestations are important for understanding the condition. Research including the distinction of perpetrator rather than victim or rescuer may lead to some interesting findings as to whether biological underpinnings vary or are similar. For the purpose of ascertaining the existence of the condition, however, psychophysiological reactivity is currently the only biologically based technique.

The psychophysiological reactivity technique consists of hooking the subject up to monitors for such things as heart rate, blood pressure, and galvanic skin response. The subject sits in a chair, a base rate is taken, and he or she is then subjected to reminders of the trauma. Various forms are used: videotape, scripts detailing their own specific trauma, or recorded sounds associated with the trauma. The level of upsurge or lack of upsurge in the stress measures is then recorded, with a sharp rise indicating presence of reactivity associated with PTSD. This technique is used in the United States for veterans seeking benefits and sometimes by courts when it is essential to the litigation. It is very expensive, time-consuming, and by definition causes great anxiety to the subject. The studies backing up the use of the technique have been done with low numbers of subjects and have used a dichotomy of diagnosis so that those who have subthreshold PTSD are often in the group contrasted with those who have a full-blown case. One study (Orr & Pitman, 1993) found that four out of sixteen subjects instructed to fake a reaction were able to do so. Yet, that study concluded that it could not be faked well since only a quarter could do it, and the United States Veterans Administration has been satisfied to use this technique in clinical work.

Two comprehensive scales commonly given out have been used in assessing PTSD: the Minnesota Multiphasic Personality Inventory (MMPI), which is usually for the general population; and the Millon Clinical Multiaxial Inventory (MCMI), more often used in clinical populations. In the case of the MMPI, the items most resembling PTSD symptoms were pulled out and tests show concurrent validity with other PTSD measures. There is therefore a specific PTSD subscale in the MMPI. The MCMI also has a profile that seems to fit the "traumatic personality" (Hyer, Woods, & Boudewyns, 1991).

However, neither test was designed for this purpose, and both are poor for actually determining the PTSD status of individuals. Their advantage is that people may have already taken them in the past for other reasons, and this gives the possibility of finding data previous to the trauma that can provide insight on predisposing factors or previous posttrauma symptomatology.

In the case of the MMPI, there is an F Scale, which is normally interpreted as a validity or "lie" scale, for people wishing to "fake bad." People with PTSD tend to have elevated scores on this. In the cases when people have been through intensive evaluation, there was no reason outside the F score elevation to regard them as false cases. Orr et al. (1990) found the elevated F Scale was correlated with physiological reactivity, which is much more difficult to fake. Furthermore, the elevation of the scores averaged 76.1 in their sample among those who had PTSD, whereas those instructed to dissimulate got scores over 100. While the scores were much elevated over population norms, they were not as high as those who were known to actually lie.

Most importantly, the items on the F Scale frequently have face validity as indicators of PTSD. Examples include: "I have nightmares every few nights," "I believe my sins are unpardonable," and "I am never happier than when alone" (Orr et al., 1990, p. 333). Far from indicating lying, these are in fact indicating PTSD symptoms. An elevation in scores would therefore not be surprising.

The Rorschach, as a projective test, provides some unique perspectives on PTSD. One of the earliest studies (van der Kolk & Ducey, 1989) compared thirteen Vietnam veterans with PTSD to eleven matched for combat experience without PTSD. This was actually part of an effort to gain insight on the nature of the posttrauma nightmares. Results showed the unmodified reliving of traumatic material and the biphasic cognitive processing (a cycling of intrusion and avoidance) common to PTSD. Specifically, there was extensive use of unstructured color, a high number of inanimate movement responses, and a striking absence of integrated whole location/developmental quality responses. Those with PTSD had a higher proportion of color to movement scores, a heavy emphasis on conventional at the expense of sharp and accurate perception, and a high proportion of vague and formless categories. There was a disorganizing impact of the trauma in men for whom psychotic thinking had not been found in extensive interviews. There were very few human movement responses. All in all, the Rorschach confirmed the clinical impression that people with severe PTSD are unable to modulate their affective experience. They either respond with an intensity only appropriate to the traumatic situation itself, or they barely react at all.

Levin (1993) had similar findings. She tested six specific hypotheses: (1) disorganized thinking and troubled relationships would be shown by the human movement responses (M) having poor form quality and low numbers; (2) a disorder of affect would be shown with unstructured or severely constricted color; (3) there would be a disordered Affective ratio (Afr), with either over- or underresponsiveness; (4) feelings of helplessness would show up in an elevation of inanimate movement responses; (5) there would be a positive finding on the Hypervigilance Index (HVI); and (6) concrete trauma-related material would appear, because of the unintegrated reliving of the events. Essentially, the hypotheses were confirmed. She also did a table of Rorschach variables that corresponded with the specific diagnostic symptoms of PTSD.

The twenty-seven subjects were people known to have PTSD, but having been through different types of trauma—rapes and other violent assaults and major accidents. This has the advantage of being a different population from the veterans who are so commonly studied, but it introduces an even greater lack of homogeneity in the etiological trauma. With such a small sample size, finer distinctions in symptom pattern or characterological pattern would not be picked up.

In a book from the American Psychological Association detailing the various tests available for PTSD, Briere (1997) summarized the findings on the Rorschach. He pointed out that there are three scenarios—psychotic, personality disordered, and posttraumatic—which have enough similarities that the tester should be aware of the ways to distinguish them.

The test alone is by no means diagnostic. It can provide insight for individual patients, and may be used at appropriate times for secondary analysis. For example, as detailed in Chapter 4, two sets of Nazis—sixteen war criminals tried at Nuremburg, and about 200 Danish collaborators—had Rorschachs done, which can be analyzed with this in mind. A study of those individual Danish Rorschachs, which, instead of taking an average of the whole group divided those who committed violent acts from those who did not, might be a constructive approach.

Scales designed especially for the purpose of measuring PTSD have become prominent in recent years, and as one would expect, vary widely in their validity and applicability. The Mississippi Combat Scale is common, but only usable with combat veterans. The Impact of Events Scale is usable with more populations, but only if they have a specific event in mind as being traumatic. Other scales have been designed for those who have or previously had chronic traumas, such as victims of recurring abuse.

The most common form is a symptom checklist, and these have been through several generations. Psychometric issues to address include how to deal with those people who by personality are disinclined to admit having problems, or those inclined to complain about having too many. These are people who are either under- or oversensitized to their symptoms, or who have a characteristic way of answering when asked about them by strangers. Both stoicism and negative affectivity—tendencies to complain too little or too much—can cause problems in a scalar assessment in which no further probing occurs. Further, people who simply give inconsistent answers or who are paying little attention to what they are filling out need to be differentiated. Accordingly, scales that include validity subscales are an improvement over the old symptom checklists. Through massive empirical testing, items have been found which most people would admit to, and other items that hardly anyone admits to. They include items asked in sets of two different ways in order to catch the inconsistent. High scorers on these subscales can then be treated appropriately in the statistical analysis. More experience with the use of scalar measurements is ongoing and refinements are still improving the use of this technique (Briere, 1997).

Scales have several advantages as a method: they allow for standardization and are therefore useful when seeking comparisons; they can be adapted to different cultures or to different educational levels; and they can be improved and refined for the entire research community. Scales can be used more extensively with larger numbers of people at less cost in time and other resources. This allows for answering quantitative questions like prevalence or comparisons between different populations. For initial screening of an entire population, such as those in the hospital or those entering shelters, scales are an excellent method to determine who might benefit from more extensive assessment. They are considerably less burdensome for participants, and relatively easy to score and statistically analyze. They more easily allow for replication. Finally, short scales for PTSD can be included with a battery of scales for other constructs, or included in surveys, even when the posttrauma construct is tangential to the research question.

The disadvantages of scales include that they treat people like numbers, and therefore lose information about meaning and variety of experience. Misinterpretation of an item by the participant or a clerical mistake in answering can go unnoticed. They are quite simplistic and do not allow for clarification and nuance.

There are times when the disadvantages can be addressed by having the scales supplement other methods. Conversely, other techniques can sometimes be improved when answers on standardized scales are included.

It is with scales that the difference between a dichotomy and a continuum becomes most clear. A cutoff point for the purpose of making a dichotomy can lead to a situation where a person with a score of 25 is treated differently from a person with a score of 27. This is the mistake of treating a continuous scale as if it were a nominal scale.

A numerical value for a continuous scale is another of the advantages of psychometric scales, but care should be taken that this does not become overly artificial. The same person could come out higher than someone else on one scale but lower than someone else on another. The numbers imposed on reality provide insight that cannot be obtained any other way, but can also obscure other insights if not treated with care.

Many people are unavailable for interaction, but have left behind diaries and other writings that go into how they feel. No diagnosis can be made under conditions in which no probing and response can be done, but diagnosis is not necessary when the research question is historical or sociological, rather than being tailored to treatment or compensation for individuals. The PTSD symptoms are then used as a theme in qualitative analysis with no expectation of a quantitative result. Since this technique does not allow for precluding individuals as not having PTSD, prevalence among groups could not be ascertained. However, this method can unearth evidence of PTSD symptomatology in people long dead. Historical methodology is helpful in finding the original sources. The idea is that if the symptoms are in fact strong and widespread, then documentary evidence should occasionally surface.

That evidence will be in a different vocabulary from that which psychiatrists use. Individuals express their own experience in their own words, and with few exceptions no professional intervenes to ascertain the extent to which the lay terms fit the professional nomenclature. People will use terms such as "haunting," "weighing on my mind constantly," or "try as I might, I could not separate myself from the horribleness of it all," for intrusive imagery. "Waking dreams," "hallucinations," or "visions" could well be what we now call flashbacks. People can detail sleep problems and troubled dreams. They can speak of hearing their heart pounding at reminders of the trauma, which is an indication of physiological reactivity. They can give indications of avoidant or hypervigilant behavior. An intimation of a "nervous breakdown" or other problems with "nerves" indicates a need for closer inspection of the passage in which it is stated.

If somewhere in the range of 20% of the Einsatzgruppen (Nazi soldiers) had acute reactions and were treated by the best army psychiatrists, as Lifton (1986) indicates, then a set of psychiatric case notes may be possible to find. They could then be analyzed, both qualitatively and quantitatively. A more thorough study of the writings of Nazis and a look at the original transcripts of interviews with them with this analytical tool in mind should also be revealing.

Examples of this historical approach can be found in Chapter 3 on executioners and Chapter 4 on the Nazis. Hendin and Haas (1985) also use it in discussing two cases of earlier veterans.

One method for PTSD assessment that might make some sense is asking other people in the person's life to verify symptoms. Self-report may be essential for such symptoms as dream content, but other members of a household may know about sleep disturbances. They may be in a better position to report on things like concentration problems or explosive outbursts over minor things. Other psychological constructs, such as humor, are tested this way. This is more frequent in social psychology and apparently is less likely to occur to the clinical-minded. The method has its logistical problems, but interviewers and scale designers should be able to address this.

Stress up to the level of trauma happens rarely in laboratory experiments. One example that approaches that level is Milgram's shock experiment, in which authority figures kept telling participants to give higher and higher shocks to hidden actors even through the sound of pleas to stop. This was intended to be a test of obedience to authority, but it had a highly stressful effect on the participants, clearly visible in their behavior (Milgram, 1974). Since giving the shocks caused the stress, it can be identified as perpetration-induced. However, this experiment helped inspire the need for institutional review boards to certify the ethics of experiments. Later debriefing indicated that participants did not have long-lasting negative effects, but of course they were finally told that they had never actually shocked anybody. Another example is the Stanford Prison experiment, which realistically set up a mock prison situation with college students playing either prisoners or guards. The level of trauma got high enough that the experiment, which was supposed to last two weeks, lasted six days. Experiments using animal models, which by their nature are cruel, are still used for conceptual applications, but if Janoff-Bulman (1985) is correct that trauma goes beyond stress into questions of meaning and shattered assumptions about the world, these are of limited if any use.

This is an overview of methodologies currently used. Along with the above suggestions on areas that need to be addressed, many aspects can be covered. Both experienced researchers and creative people unencumbered by previous assumptions are likely to come up with a wide variety of possibilities that will add tremendously to our understanding of this phenomenon.

PROSPECTIVE STUDIES

Clearly, prospective studies are necessary to establish what personality traits or other predisposing factors might make an individual more vulnerable to PTSD and to PITS. Unfortunately, most studies are retrospective. The authors often suggest that the traits they found in people who already have PTSD may well have been predisposing ones, but they almost always admit that the causation may be the other way, or that there may be a circular dependence with PTSD intensifying preexisting personality traits, which then intensify the PTSD symptoms. As long as studies are retrospective, there is simply no way to know.

Two studies do take a prospective approach. Schnurr, Friedman, and Rosenberg (1993) had MMPI scores on 131 Vietnam-era veterans that were administered to Dartmouth College classes in 1967 and 1968. Noncombat veterans numbered thirty-eight, and fifty-six served in combat but did not have PTSD. Additionally, thirteen combat veterans had only symptoms of PTSD, fourteen had subthreshold PTSD, and ten had full PTSD.

There was no difference between MMPI scores for combat and noncombat veterans. Combat veterans with any lifetime PTSD symptoms had higher scores than the comparison combat subjects on hypochondriasis, psychopathic deviate, masculinity-femininity, and paranoia. The effect sizes were moderate, amounting to half of a standard deviation difference. Only two scales were able to enter a stepwise regression to predict PTSD: psychopathic deviate and masculinity-femininity. These two correctly classified 73.1% of the cases, but 60.2% correct would be expected by chance.

Dividing PTSD into full, subthreshold, and only-symptoms led to other findings. Before the participation in war, the MMPI shows that the Social Introversion scale scores are 50.3 for noncombat veterans, 49.4 for combat veterans without PTSD, 58.3 for those with symptoms only, 42.9 for subthreshold PTSD, and 50.4 for those with a full PTSD diagnosis. Thus, the men with full PTSD were not much different from normal. The subthreshold participants were lower than anyone else on introversion. Those who had some symptoms but not others were highest on introversion. In logistical regression, social introversion was the only factor that entered to predict differences between the three levels of PTSD.

A similar pattern occurred on depression. The symptoms-only group scored higher in college on depression than those with more severe PTSD as well as the non-PTSD controls.

Paranoia showed a small difference in scores, with full PTSD subjects having an effect size of .36, compared with subthreshold PTSD and those with any of all three levels of PTSD having an effect size of .50, compared to those without PTSD. Scores were 55.4 for noncombat veterans, 56.2 for comparison combat veterans, 60.7 for some symptoms, 59.3 for subthreshold, and 62.3 for full PTSD.

One of the things that became clear in this study is the utility of using sub-diagnostic reactions to trauma. Since scores differed on various factors and did not follow an upward line to greater severity on several important dimensions, causation·is more complex than is allowed by the analysis, which lumps various categories together.

Lee et al. (1995) conducted another prospective study, in which men who attended Harvard and became veterans of World War II were tested while at Harvard and periodically ever since. Unfortunately, though the authors mention the importance of studying personality factors prospectively, there is little on personality before the war. Primarily, "mature" defenses, by their definition, are found to be associated with less PTSD, and "immature" defenses are found to be associated with more PTSD, but these along with trait neuroticism are as-sessed after the war. The effect size was not large in any event.

In both studies, the variable of whether or not the veterans had killed during combat was not considered. Other groups besides combat veterans could also be tested, but of course there are ethical considerations in testing people in the knowledge that they will later kill. This would be impossible with such groups as those who commit criminal homicide and problematic in groups that will commit genocide. Police officers who shoot in the line of duty, however, can have had previous psychological tests as a matter of course in entering their profession. People who are going to engage in executions or provide abortions can be identified in advance, at least after they are already selected for the tasks. In all cases, there may already be data on psychological tests such as the MMPI, MCMI, or even the Meyers-Briggs test that were taken before the activity. As with the Dartmouth students who later went to Vietnam, they can be studied afterward, when it is known who fits into the target group and who into the control group.

DISTINGUISHING PTSD FROM STRESS

Unlike histories of the concept of posttraumatic stress, which tend to start with Janet and Freud and continue through Kardiner's study of World War II veterans and on through the psychiatric or clinical psychology tradition, a history of the concept of stress more commonly begins with Cannon and Selye and is most prominent in the field of health psychology. Cannon proposed a "fight or flight" response and first used the engineering term, "stress." Selye independently coined the term after extensive experiments with rats, and proposed a "General Adaptation Syndrome," basically a consistent set of physiological responses, no matter what the stressor was. Later work showed that psychological factors do have an influence. Being comforted by a mother, for example, lowers the physiological stress response.

Psychological factors impacting stress include predictability and control (Sapolsky, 1994). If these two factors had the same influence on posttrauma symptoms, then active participation in causing traumatic circumstances should mean that symptoms are less severe. Perpetration-Induced Traumatic Stress would then be either nonexistent or at least less severe than other forms of PTSD. As shown in previous chapters, however, the current evidence seems to be that it is more severe. If the same factors that tend to lower stress do not have the same effect when the stressor is at traumatic levels, then the aftereffects may have similarities but not be exactly the same thing. They differ not only in degree, but also in kind.

Much of the literature on stress emphasizes its impact on physical health, either directly through physiological mechanisms, or indirectly through influencing behavior that leads to bad outcomes, such as consumption of tobacco or alcohol. Studies dealing with the question of direct impact of stress on physical health therefore statistically control for these behavioral mediators. Such studies have shown long-term impact on coronary disease, diabetes, osteoporosis, infectious disease, the gastrointestinal and reproductive systems, and even growth (Sapolsky, 1994). In other words, the reduction of excessive stress is sought in order to avoid physical symptoms. In fact, there is no desire to eliminate stress completely. Some muscle tension is necessary to stand up rather than lie down, and small amounts of stress that can be handled can actually lead to better performance or greater perseverance. A single instance of below trauma-level stress is not likely to cause health problems, as would excessive amounts of stress. With PTSD symptoms, however, one event is sufficient to cause years of problems. While stress is reduced because of what it can lead to, with posttrauma reactions, it is not what the symptoms can lead to but the symptoms themselves that are the problem.

The physiology of the stress response includes an immediate and long-term health impact of glucocorticoids (the predominant one of which is cortisol), epinephrin and norepinephrin (which are the same as adrenaline and noradrenaline, and will sometimes be referred to by the class to which they belong, catecholamines), adrenocorticotropic hormone (ACTH), corticotrophin releasing factor (CRF), and endorphines, among others. The hormone profile for Posttraumatic Stress Disorder has similarities, but is not exactly the same. Most notably, cortisol levels may actually be much lower than normal rather than much higher.

Most importantly, stress responses are more likely to happen in episodes, depending on the presence or absence of a stressor. A hormone profile of a PTSD patient can show effects without a stressor present. The stress response is likely to have been present at the time of the initial trauma, at the time it was an episode, but the biochemistry of PTSD is more chronic and constant over time.

PROBLEMS OF DISTINCTIONS

Suppose there are two people with the exact same PTSD-style symptomatology, but one has had a traumatic event that can account for it, and the second has not. The second person must make one up, appropriate someone else's, or reinterpret an actual event as being more traumatic than it seemed at the time. All of these things have been done, and in the diagnostic criteria they explicitly mean that the problem is something other than PTSD. In that event, are there people who would actually be in the same condition, but because they *do* have an event that can reasonably be interpreted as traumatic in their past, they do not need to select one of the alternative strategies?

Does that mean that the time direction for PTSD does not flow from the event to the symptoms, but actually in the other direction? The presence of the disorder colors the interpretation of the event—especially in the delayed reaction cases. This is the argument made in a book called *The Harmony of Illusions: Inventing Posttraumatic Stress Disorder* (Young, 1995).

As a counterargument, a case could be made that the memory of a traumatic event does qualitatively change a condition over what it would be in the absence of the event. The finding of a dose-response reaction to events, with greater severity or number of traumas leading to more severe symptom patterns and greater prevalence, suggests at least that there is something causative about the traumatic event. This assumes that the dose-response findings, which are among the most robust in PTSD causation, are not spurious due to altered memories of events colored by the PTSD itself. All people have numerous events in their lives and features of their social environment that can impact their current behavior and feelings, so the situation is always complicated from an empirical point of view.

Young is a sociological ethnographer, someone whose work is primarily in direct and qualitative observations of social situations. He is strongly skeptical of empiricism. The "harmony of illusions" comes from a quotation indicating a scientist's belief that infectious diseases do not classify nearly as easily in reality as they have been made to do in the lab.

The tendency of human beings, especially scholars, to impose more order on reality that reality allows is both a problem and a benefit. It is something we should be aware of and cautious about, but it also allows for insights otherwise unavailable. As David Funder, personality psychologist, put it in Funder's Fourth Law: "There are only two kinds of data. The first kind is Terrible Data: data that are ambiguous, potentially misleading, incomplete, and imprecise. The second kind is No Data. Unfortunately, there is no third kind, anywhere in the world" (Funder, 1997, pp. 32–33).

There are unclear boundaries between stress (defined in its various ways) and, for example, anger or hostility. Much of the findings on the Type A personality were originally attributed to stress, but others argued the proper attribution was really to a personality type of constant hostility. Stress because a hoped-for event did not happen is different from stress caused from an event that did happen, which in turn is different from stress caused by constant noise or a barrage of minor irritations. The experimental stress brought by speaking in front of a group is different from stress that could not ethically be manipulated in an experiment, and people have entirely different attitudes about how stressful it is to speak in front a group. Individual differences in experience, meaning, reaction, and social interaction all make stress a very complex subject. The same is true of anxiety and depression. Classifications, which are used in order to get a handle on these subjects, are successful in doing so, but information on individual differences is necessarily lost in the process.

Thus, some people would categorize PTSD as a form of stress, and it does use the term "stress" in its name. Others would categorize PTSD and stress as being related but different phenomena. Others would question the utility of either construct. Even those people, however, like Young (1995), admit that when scholars are trying to communicate with other scholars about their work, there is a *lingua franca* which all must use in order to communicate with one another. At the same time, of course, since they are scholars, there will be plenty of disagreements and alternative perspectives and analyses. Given that the truth in most of social science is complex, and all of it is practiced by people rather than machines, this is to be expected.

REFERENCES

Arluke, A. (1991). Going into the closet with science: Information control among animal experimenters. *Journal of Contemporary Ethnography, 20*, 306–330.

Briere, J. (1997). *Psychological assessment of adult posttraumatic states*. Washington, DC: American Psychological Association.

Funder, D.C. (1997). *The personality puzzle*. New York: W.W. Norton & Co.

Grossman, D. (1995). *On killing: The psychological cost of learning to kill in war and society*. Boston: Little, Brown and Company.

Hendin, H., & Haas, A.P. (1985). Posttraumatic Stress Disorders in veterans of early America. *Psychohistory Review, 12*, 25–30.

Hiley-Young, B., Blake, D.D., Abueg, F.R., Rozynko, V., & Dusman, F.D. (1995). War zone violence in Vietnam: An examination of premilitary, military, and postmilitary factors in PTSD in-patients. *Journal of Traumatic Stress, 8*, 125–140.

Hyer, L., Woods, G., & Boudewyns, P. (1991). A three-tier evaluation among chronic veterans. *Journal of Traumatic Stress, 4*, 165–194.

Janoff-Bulman, R. (1985). The aftermath of victimization: Rebuilding shattered assumptions. In C. Figley (Ed.), *Trauma and its wake: The study and treatment of Posttraumatic Stress Disorder* (pp. 14–35). New York: Brunner/Mazel.

Lee, K.A., Vaillant, G.E., Torrey, W.C., & Elder, G.H. (1995). A 50-year prospective study of the psychological sequelae of World War II combat. *American Journal of Psychiatry, 152,* 516–522.

Levin, P. (1993). Assessing Posttraumatic Stress Disorder with the Rorschach projective technique. In J.P. Wilson, & B. Raphael (Eds.), *International handbook of traumatic stress syndromes* (pp. 189–200). New York: Plenum Press.

Lifton, R.J. (1986). *The Nazi doctors: Medical killing and the psychology of genocide.* New York: Basic Books.

Milgram, S. (1974). *Obedience to authority: An experimental view.* New York: Harper & Row.

Orr, S.P., Claiborn, J.M., Altman, B., Forgue, D.F., de Jong, J.B., & Pitman, R.K. (1990). Psychometric profile of Posttraumatic Stress Disorder, anxious and healthy Vietnam veterans: Correlations with psychophysiologic responses. *Journal of Consulting and Clinical Psychology, 3,* 329–335.

Orr, S.P., & Pitman R.K. (1993). Psychophysiologic assessment of attempts to simulate Posttraumatic Stress Disorder. *Biological Psychiatry, 33,* 127–129.

Pollock, P.H. (1999). When the killer suffers: Post-traumatic stress reactions following homicide. *Legal and Criminological Psychology, 4,* 185–202.

Sapolsky, R.M. (1994). *Why zebras don't get ulcers: A guide to stress, stress-related diseases, and coping.* New York: W.H. Freeman and Company.

Schnurr, P.P., Friedman, M.J., & Rosenberg, S.D. (1993). Preliminary MMPI scores as predictors of combat-related PTSD symptoms. *American Journal of Psychiatry, 150,* 479–483.

van der Kolk, B.A., & Ducey, C.P. (1989). The psychological processing of traumatic experience: Rorschach patterns in PTSD. *Journal of Traumatic Stress, 2,* 259–274.

Young, A. (1995). *The harmony of illusions: Inventing Posttraumatic Stress Disorder.* New Jersey: Princeton University Press.

Zillmer, E.A., Harrower, M., Ritzler, B.A., & Archer, R.P. (1995). *The quest for the Nazi personality: A psychological investigation of Nazi war criminals.* Hillsdale, NJ: Lawrence Erlbaum Associates.

Chapter 12

Conclusion

WHY IS THE CONCEPT OF PITS NOT ALREADY WIDESPREAD?

A natural question is why there appear to have been blind spots in various parts of the literature regarding perpetration as an etiological (causal) trauma for PTSD. The construct of PTSD has been applied widely, expanded from soldiers to crime victims and concentration camp survivors and even survivors of life-threatening accidents, disasters, and heart attacks. The discussion preceding the official definition in the *Diagnostic and Statistical Manual of Mental Disorders* (*DSM-IV*) states that the condition is more severe when the causal trauma is of human origin. Vicarious traumatization of those who must deal with those who have been traumatized, through therapy or legal proceedings, has been covered. Emergency personnel and rescue workers whose job it is to assist people in traumatic circumstances have been studied. A proposal has been made that those who suffer continual traumatizations, as with those who endure domestic abuse for several years, have a complex form of PTSD that requires separate or additional consideration (Herman, 1992). Interest in PTSD has been extensive, with theories, models, and variations offered in vast array.

Several years ago, when I first approached the subject of how the human mind responds to the act of killing, I knew that "battle fatigue" was called "Posttraumatic Stress Disorder" in the psychological literature. I therefore assumed that this is what I would need to study. It was an assumption derived from the bias of my background as a Quaker pacifist, in a similar tradition to that of Jane Addams. While I was making the same kind of assumption she did in her observation of World War I soldiers (see Chapter 1), I found upon delving into the literature that other people were not doing so. Even in the case of veterans, people were primarily thinking of the risks of combat and the stresses of seeing friends killed as being the traumas causing the problems. There was fear from the dangers of being shot at and grief from seeing the results of others being shot, but little consideration of the act of shooting as being traumatic. On the few occasions when active perpetration did come up, it was usually looking at the extremes of "abusive violence" or "atrocities," not killing as a whole. My discussions with other researchers active in the field of PTSD studies verified that etiological perpetration was receiving very little attention. If it did not occur to researchers in the case of veterans, it certainly did not occur to them for other groups.

There have been at least four major blind spots that have kept this from being considered. In the case of veterans, one is the sympathy for the veteran and denial that he has any reason to suffer psychological consequences. Studies on the second-most-studied group after Americans, Israeli soldiers, have explicitly avoided the idea that soldiers have done anything for which to feel guilt (Solomon, 1993). The belief is that all PTSD symptoms must relate to what the enemy did, not what the soldier did.

Related to this is the possibility that the nation which sends the soldiers into combat has responsibility for them, and that responsibility will feel much more like guilt if the activities necessary to combat have such an aftermath. Citizens and political leaders prefer to think that any long-lasting repercussions are the fault of the enemy. Fear is an easier explanation for PTSD symptoms. It is not necessary to be a pacifist to reach these conclusions. Grossman (1995) is an army lieutenant colonel: "Fear is a specific yet brief and fleeting emotion that lies within the individual, but guilt is often long term and can belong to the society as a whole. When we are faced with hard questions and the difficult task of introspection, it is very easy to avoid the truth and give the socially acceptable answers that war literature, Hollywood films, and scientific literature tell us we should give" (pp. 53–54).

The nature of controversy is a third reason, since it is often the case that these practices are controversial. People on the side of advocating a particular practice may be defensive about the idea that people in that practice may be suffering PTSD symptoms. They see it as an unfair and propagandistic attack on the practice. Opponents may not think of PITS because it does not occur to them that those engaged in the practice may warrant any sympathy. Many veterans returning to the United States from Vietnam, for example, faced hostility as "baby killers" from opponents of the war. Yet, when the idea of PTSD was coalescing as a psychiatric diagnosis, many pro-war groups regarded this as a propaganda ploy by those opposed to the war. If this were so with PTSD, it would have been all the more true with the idea of killing as the trauma that could cause it. This underscores the importance in scientific study of including advocates of both sides in research teams to achieve greatest credibility in results.

Finally, there are those for whom people in general currently have no sympathy at all—people who commit criminal homicide, Nazis, slave-catchers, torturers, those practicing genocide, and so on. These people are seen as villains. Much work is done on what causes people to become this way, but much less on the psychological consequences to them. Acknowledging the "villains" as having pain does not occur to many, who fear that such acknowledgment offers the "villains" more sympathy than they deserve.

Another problem that does not classify as a blind spot but still helps to explain how the phenomenon can be widespread and yet not widely known has to do with the lack of expression of the experiences from those who have symptoms. Once soldiers come home from war, it has commonly been the case that discussing horrors they have seen—much less participated in—is discouraged by their friends and families, nor do other veterans encourage it. There are few occasions to bring up one's own problems with nightmares, flashbacks, deadened emotions, hyperarousal, temper outbursts, and so on. If they do not break down to the level of a disorder that requires hospitalization, there would be a strong motivation not to bring them up. They are seen as private. There is a fear of judgment by other people, which would be more intense when the trauma arose from killing than it would be when one was a helpless victim of the trauma. There is also a worry that the experiences show one to be crazy. As long as the symptoms are generally absent from conversation and the war portrayals of novels and motion pictures, then the very absence makes some veterans think that their experiences are peculiar. They avoid talking about it themselves, which of course contributes to the absence of it being discussed. The same is true of groups other than combat veterans that may engage in socially approved killing. All these social considerations are compounded by the fact that one of the very symptoms of the condition is avoidance of reminders of the trauma—*DSM-IV* symptoms C(1) and (2).

There is also the level to which those suffering are unwilling to admit that there are problems, even to themselves. Some will forthrightly defend their own original actions, and this discounts the possibility of aftermath for those actions specifically. Some wish to maintain a self-image that precludes either that they even did the actions in the first place or that they have any problems afterward. There are also those as identified by Glover (1985):

The experience of having wielded considerable fire power in the Vietnam War has had a major impact on the lives of these men, [giving] exhilaration and sense of power. . . . Among this group of veterans are those who openly regard civilian life with contempt and think of it as being mundane and inconsequential. Not surprisingly, these individuals are most unlikely to come to the attention of psychiatrists except in acute situational crises. (p. 17)

These are men with an impatience toward solving problems because from their view, problems got solved quickly with firepower, a view formed during late adolescence at a highly formative time of their lives. They do not see their explosive temper when they do not get their way as anything other than justified, and would resent the suggestion that it is a "symptom" that flows from their experience. For the defensive, those maintaining a self-image, and for the contemptuous, the very definition by others of their feelings as being anything other than normal would be met with hostility.

ARGUMENTS AGAINST PITS AS A FORM OF PTSD

There are several ideas about the causation of PTSD that preclude the possibility that killing could be a causal stressor. Some have applied the model of learned helplessness from animal experiments (e.g., van der Kolk et al., 1985). Others have suggested the personality trait of "timidity" as a temperamental predisposing factor (Varela & Matchinsky, 1995). Yet others have advanced various opinions to the effect that a lack of control during the situation is a necessary feature of the causation. Janoff-Bulman (1985) talks about rebuilding shattered assumptions in the aftermath of victimization as a major component of PTSD. All four of these concepts—learned helplessness, timidity, lack of control, and a shattered worldview—are somewhat similar and have long been associated with greater stress. The thesis of shattered assumptions has been advanced as one of the major qualitative differences between ordinary stress and posttrauma stress.

All of these factors could be in force in some forms of PTSD, and could provide explanatory power. Any of them could also eliminate the concept of perpetration-induced traumatic stress if they are all that is needed to explain the occurrence of PTSD. As one skeptic of PTSD put it in regard to learned helplessness, "The model of inescapable shock seems likewise problematic in those cases where men were the authors of their etiological events—the perpetrators of violence rather than its victims" (Young, 1995, p. 283). Those who believe in such models would make predictions contrary to those necessary to establish wartime killing as a trauma that can cause PTSD.

The very concept of PTSD is questioned in Young's 1995 book, called *The Harmony of Illusions: Inventing Posttraumatic Stress Disorder*. It is not the reality of PTSD he questions (since it is very real to those who fit under its definition), but its nature and origin. Young believes PTSD arose as a glued-together historical product, not a timeless disorder with an intrinsic unity. He believes it is not something that exists and was discovered, but that PTSD was invented.

The concept of perpetrator-induced traumatic stress causes him to question the foundations of PTSD. Referring to changes in the criteria for a trauma that could cause the condition, he says, "The revised classification excludes no one who has been diagnosed with PTSD under the previous rules. For example, veterans who were traumatized by the deaths and grievous injuries that they inflicted without remorse are still covered by the diagnosis" (Young, 1995, p.

289). It seems obvious to him that the possibility of perpetration as an etiological mechanism casts doubt on the validity of the concept of PTSD itself.

Young is interested in the "validity" of the concept, not its usefulness. He does finally say that the official symptom lists of PTSD are now a *lingua franca* among psychiatrists and psychologists so that any scholarly work will have to utilize them. I argue that any time reality is put into categories, we are at the same time clarifying what those in the category have in common yet obscuring how they differ. Especially in a subject like psychology, which deals with individual human beings, differences abound. Categorization and definition will always either fit well or fit poorly, rather than being true or false. The same is true for defining the common cold.

RESPONSES TO THE CONCEPT OF PITS

At a conference of the Association of Genocide Scholars, I gave a paper on the Nazis, an earlier version of Chapter 4. One response at lunch later was, "So the Nazi killers had nightmares? Good!" This form of vindictiveness may well have occurred to others as well. In a softer and more scholarly way of putting it, philosophical implications of this theory include the knowledge that a large portion of Nazis and other direct perpetrators of genocide do not escape their actions with impunity. Often they are never caught, and in many situations it is impractical to try them all legally. Nevertheless, the natural psychological consequences of their own actions indicate that they do not all escape punishment for those actions.

Some people see this as justice. The harshness of it is a good thing, because they view those who kill as monsters who deserve the aftermath. Others look at the same information and object to it for fear that it provides too much sympathy to those who kill. They believe that it is misplaced sympathy, which should be reserved for victims. Yet others suggest that sympathy is not misplaced; that is, while the victims deserve all the assistance we can offer, we should be more understanding of the perpetrators, and see their need for therapy and healing.

I have had several occasions where the subject of PITS came up as being a major interest of mine, and I was approached afterward by veterans to receive more details. The more information I give them seems to be something that comports with their personal experience, as indicated by their conversation and facial expressions. They are grateful, because the conclusion they draw is that they are in fact having a normal response, that symptoms they had not told others for fear of appearing crazy were in fact typical and prevalent responses to the circumstances they had undergone. Even if their symptoms were mild enough that they did not seek therapy and could not be said to have a disorder, it was a relief for them to have the knowledge of natural, explainable, common psychological consequence.

Another common reaction is to say that if people who have killed suffer such an aftermath, and the killing is seen as justified, necessary, or beneficial in some way, then those who risk getting PITS from doing it are especially heroic and especially to be admired. As indicated in Chapter 4, this was Himmler's attitude after he was sickened by watching the shooting work of Nazi murder squads of Eastern Europe. Those who believe the death penalty is necessary, or who sympathize with police officers who have shot someone in the line of duty, could make the same case.

Investigation of the various ways people in the general population respond to the repercussions and philosophical implication of the concept of PITS could make another interesting set of studies. People are likely to think differently when the concept applies to their veteran compatriots—especially to their own friends and family—than they are when applying to far-off massacres that make no sense to them. They will have a different opinion of those engaged in practices of which they approve, such as specific wars or executions, than those engaged in practices of which they disapprove. Just as the differences in proximity, relationship, nature of experience, and visibility of trauma can impact PITS itself, it is to be expected that there are many variables impacting how people respond to the concept and what conclusions they draw from it.

A FAMOUS CASE IN THE NEWS: SENATOR KERREY

In the spring of 2001, an incident was publicized that serves to illustrate varying reactions to the concept of negative psychological reaction to the act of killing. Former United States Senator Robert Kerrey was a combat veteran of the American war in Vietnam, and it became known that there had been an incident in which he was involved in killing several civilians, including children and elderly people. This story arose in an article in the *New York Times Magazine* dated April 29, and was closely followed by a report including an on-camera interview with Kerrey on the television news program *60 Minutes*.

This is an example where the symptoms do not rise to the level of a disorder. According to the *DSM-IV* (American Psychiatric Association, 1994) definition of PTSD, for the condition the be a disorder, the "disturbance causes clinically significant distress or impairment in social, occupational, or other important areas of functioning." Kerrey became a Nebraska state governor and a United States senator, so a diagnosis of dysfunction would unlikely be justified. Still, there is some evidence that workaholism is associated with PITS, in that immersion in work is a way to crowd out the intrusive memories and other problems. One study of men who had fought in World War II showed that those with more PTSD symptoms were more likely to be listed in *Who's Who of America* (Lee et al., 1995). In some cases, there is actually a delay before symptoms become severe. In many more cases, symptoms never do become severe enough to be a disorder. If the disorder is the extreme form that clinicians deal with, then less extreme forms that are dealt with by individuals without recourse to therapists can be expected to exist. If this follows the pattern of many psychological conditions, the less extreme forms may be more prevalent.

Pertinent portions of the *New York Times Magazine* article are quoted below. The symptoms involving intrusive imagery, especially dreams, are clearly in evidence:

Senator Bob Kerrey's hands trembled slightly as he began to read six pages of documents that had just been handed to him. It was late 1998; the papers were nearly 30 years old. On the face of it, they were routine "after action" combat reports of the sort filed by the thousands during the Vietnam War. But Kerrey knew the pages held a personal secret—of an event so traumatic that he says it once prompted fleeting thoughts of suicide.

Pulling the documents within inches of his eyes, he read intently about this time as a member of the Navy Seals and about a mission in 1969 that somehow went horribly wrong. As an inexperienced, 25-year-old lieutenant, Kerrey led a commando team on a raid of an isolated peasant hamlet called Thanh Phong in Vietnam's eastern Mekong Delta. While witnesses and official records give varying accounts of exactly what happened, one thing is certain: around midnight on February 26, 1969, Kerrey and his men killed at least 13 unarmed women and children. The operation was brutal; for months afterward, Kerrey says, he feared going to sleep because of the terrible nightmares that haunted him.

The restless nights are mostly behind him now, his dreams about Vietnam more reflective. One of those, which he says recurs frequently, is about an uncle who disappeared in action during World War II. "In my dream I am about to leave for Vietnam," Kerrey wrote in an e-mail message last December. "He warns me that the greatest danger of war is not losing your life but the taking of others, and that human savagery is a very slippery slope."

Kerrey—who left the Senate in January and is now president of the New School University in New York—says he has spent the last three decades wondering if he could have done something different that night in Thanh Phong. "It's far more than guilt," he said that morning in 1998. "It's the shame. You can never, can never get away from it. It darkens your day. I thought dying for your country was the worst thing that could happen to you, and I don't think it is. I think killing for your country can be a lot worse. Because that's the memory that haunts." (Vistica, 2001)

Responses from both the Right and the Left showed a disdain for the personal suffering that Kerrey mentions. Their comments serve as an illustration of some of the complications that arise in dealing with this theory in the complexities of the real world.

John Leo, a conservative columnist for *U. S. News & World Report*, put it this way:

No journalist is better than Mickey Kaus at cutting quickly to the heart of an issue. Here is his opening comment . . . on his kausfiles Web site: "There is already entirely too much respectful attention being paid to the moral and psychological agony of Bob Kerrey and to the 'healing' process. . . . The question is what happened to the people who haven't had the luxury of agonizing for 32 years because they've been dead. Kerrey's agony is a distraction."

Exactly. Ex-Sen. Bob Kerrey undoubtedly feeling a lot of stress after finally admitting that his squad killed a lot of unarmed women and children during a Vietnam raid. . . . But his feelings are not the issue here. In an Oprahfied culture, important moral and political issues are always in danger of being obscured by huge clouds of media-created empathy. . . .

The Kerrey case is already a classic example of a serious moral issue propelled before the public almost entirely in psychological and therapeutic terms . . . An *Omaha World-Herald* account begins: "Bob Kerrey is confronting another wound from Vietnam, one that left him with no physical scars." "We should all recognize the agony that Bob has gone through," said the trustees of Manhattan's New School University, whose new president is Bob Kerrey.

The ex-senator kept issuing statements that encouraged a close focus on his psychological struggle. "Now I can talk about it. It feels better already," Kerrey told the *Los Angeles Times*. . . .

Stripped of psychologizing, the central issue is clear: Was this a war crime? . . . No more psychology, please. There are real issues to deal with. (Leo, 2001)

On the other side of the political spectrum, Adolph L. Reed Jr. is a professor at the New School University. As just mentioned, Kerrey had recently become university president. Reed wrote in *The Progressive*, a magazine that gives a forum to radicals whose antiwar sentiments commonly include scorn for pro-war liberals:

On reading the details of the Thanh Phong massacre and the feeble attempts by liberal "healers" to sanitize its heinousness with ambiguity and psychobabble, I found myself charged with the same outrage that I felt during the Vietnam War. The calls to write off the atrocity—and, by implication, the many other ones like it—to the nature of a confusing, unconventional war and to commiserate with Bob Kerrey's suffering are offensive to any decent human sensibility. They resurface, albeit in candy-coating, the jingoistic arrogance that only American lives and suffering count. (Reed, 2001)

The irony of the latter quotation is that when PTSD was first being officially defined and receiving government endorsement, groups such as the Veterans of Foreign Wars argued that it was nothing more than an antiwar propaganda ploy. The idea that killing in war would lead to psychological aftermath did seem more obvious to peace activists such as Jane Addams during World War I, as detailed in Chapter 1. The possible use of the concept of PITS as an antiwar propaganda ploy does not occur to Reed, who sees in it instead a way to "commiserate with the suffering" of a powerful senator and thereby excuse him from behavior Reed opposes.

John Leo is writing in a fashion typical for him. He has long had a concern that people claim victimhood as a way out of personal responsibility. He has often been critical of basing moral judgments on feelings, and frequently offered examples of how poorly he believes this works as a criterion. He says of Kerrey that "his occasional admissions that something horrific occurred are also expressed in the language of feelings: 'To describe it as an atrocity, I would say, is pretty close to being right, because that's how it felt'" (Leo, 2001). Leo asserts that whether something is an atrocity or not is based on the facts, not on the feelings.

However, responses to a specific case may be far different from responses to the concept in general. Reed had attended a gathering at his university—of which Kerrey had recently become president—and was disturbed by the tone of the discussion, which from his point of view was insufficiently aware of the injustice of the war itself. Leo's long-standing criticism of using emotions as a moral barometer is reflected in his understanding of the case. Both men saw this as a case of spinning a story, a powerful politician trying to get sympathy he did not deserve.

In all cases, the concept that these were PTSD symptoms never came up. PTSD was not mentioned in the articles by Vistica, Leo, and Reed, any of the newspaper quotations, or the *60 Minutes* report. Words such as "haunting," "suffering," and "agony" were used. The details only look like symptoms of subclinical level PTSD to someone familiar with the area.

Many news outlets were sympathetic to the agony, and people such as Leo and Reed responded critically in a manner consistent with previous views. Knowing what kind of response there might be if people did have the concept of PITS and understood its possible ramifications awaits societal conditions in which this is the case. Does it matter whether we are talking about a powerful ex-senator who was contemplating a run for United States president, rather than about an unemployed draftee? Does the knowledge that even a veteran who goes on to become a powerful senator can have some of these effects say anything about how prevalent the problem is? It does suggest that we cannot assume that PITS symptoms are absent in people who for years showed no public signs of them.

All of this illustrates that the philosophical implications can be very complex. From a scientific point of view, PITS can exist and be studied without reference to whether this increases sympathy for the sufferer, whether people are happy to know that the person who did the action at least suffers in this way, or whether people are angry at the suggestion that it even matters if a killer suffers. Whether the perpetrator understood the violence to be justified or not, whether the society understood it to be justified or not, whether or not it was even understood to be violence, are, from the point of view of scientific psychology, merely variables that can be measured and studied for impact. Members of the public, journalists, and ethicists are likely to have strong opinions on such points and are not accustomed to treating them as measurable variables. A variety of perspectives is therefore likely.

THE POSITIVE PERSPECTIVE

It may seem odd to suggest that there is anything positive about PITS. It seems entirely to be a problem that causes individuals and societies vast amounts of suffering. However, there are two points to make about it, given the knowledge that vast amounts of violence have been an integral part of the human condition for millennia.

In every study of any kind of disorder, of course, the positive point of the study is prevention of the disorder or its subclinical levels of suffering. Understanding PITS, however, may have a role to play in the prevention of violence. Violence has often been observed to operate in a cycle, and the understanding that "violence begets violence" is of long standing. The concept of PITS helps us to understand one of the reasons why this is so. The National Vietnam Veteran Readjustment Study, for example, found that combat veterans with PTSD reported an average of 13.3 acts of violence for the preceding year compared to 3.5 acts for those without PTSD (Kulka et al., 1990). Further research can offer a variety of options for interventions to prevent the cycle or the escalation of violence. If we understand this phenomenon better, there may be various methods of intervention, including therapy, public policy, and education, which can become available or more effective.

For those who already suffer from the aftermath, therapy and healing may be necessary for national reconciliation efforts and for prevention of further problems. If posttrauma symptoms make them more likely to perpetrate again, in the form of domestic abuse, street crime, or further participation in the original combat, massacre, or torture activity, then therapy of those individuals may not merely be good for them, but for prevention efforts for society as well. Public policy can take PITS into account and not treat those who are expected to carry out killing as unfeeling automata or as people simply doing unpleasant jobs. As for education, part of the ideology of genocide, torture, or massacres is that those who carry them out benefit from the activity. Efforts at arranging punishment through political means have been used to counter this idea. It may help to add education on how perpetrators do not escape with impunity even if political arrangements are inadequate.

The second positive point is what this says about humanity. The idea of Perpetration-Induced Traumatic Stress suggests that the human mind, contrary to certain political ideologies, is not well suited for killing. When studying the depths of depravity to which human beings are capable of succumbing, this is more heartening information.

REFERENCES

American Psychiatric Association. (1994). *Diagnostic and statistical manual of mental disorders* (4th ed.). Washington, DC: Author.

Glover, H. (1985). Guilt and aggression in Vietnam veterans. *American Journal of Social Psychiatry, 1*, 15–18.

Grossman, D. (1995). *On killing: The psychological cost of learning to kill in war and society.* Boston: Little, Brown and Company.

Herman, J.L. (1992). Complex PTSD: A syndrome in survivors of prolonged and repeated trauma. *Journal of Traumatic Stress, 5*, 377–391.

Janoff-Bulman, R. (1985). The aftermath of victimization: Rebuilding shattered assumptions. In C. Figley (Ed.), *Trauma and its wake: The study and treatment of Posttraumatic Stress Disorder* (pp. 14–35). New York: Brunner/Mazel.

Kulka, R.A., Schlenger, W.E., Fairbank, J.A., Hough, R.L., Jordan, B.K., Marmar, C.R., & Weiss, D.S. (1990). *Trauma and the Vietnam War generation: Report on the findings from the National Vietnam Veterans Readjustment Study.* New York: Brunner/Mazel.

Lee, K.A., Vaillant, G.E., Torrey, W.C., & Elder, G.H. (1995). A 50-year prospective study of the psychological sequelae of World War II combat. *American Journal of Psychiatry, 152*, 516–522.

Leo, J. (2001). Kerrey Agonistes: Is the ex-senator baring his soul and spinning his story? *U. S. News & World Report*, May 7.

Reed, A.L. (2001). Bob Kerrey, an American shame. *The Progressive*, June 16.

Solomon, Z. (1993). *Combat stress reaction: The enduring toll of war.* New York: Plenum Press.

van der Kolk, B.A., Greenberg, M., Boyd, H., & Krystal, J. (1985). Inescapable shock, neurotransmitters, and addiction to trauma: Toward a psychobiology of posttraumatic stress. *Biological Psychiatry, 20*, 314–325.

Varela, R.E., & Matchinsky D.J. (1995). Posttraumatic Stress Disorder: Physiological vulnerability and temperament. Unpublished manuscript, Emporia State University, Kansas.

Vistica, G.L. (2001). What happened in Thanh Phong. *New York Times Magazine*, April 29, 50–57, 66, 68, 133.

Young, A. (1995). *The harmony of illusions: Inventing Posttraumatic Stress Disorder.* Princeton: Princeton University Press.

Appendix: Statistics from the National Vietnam Veterans Readjustment Study

All tables here are generated by the author's work on the data from the National Vietnam Veterans Readjustment Study, a United States government-commissioned survey of a stratified random sample of Vietnam-era veterans, done in the 1980s. This data comes from the 1,638 theater veterans, that is, veterans who were actually in Vietnam.

GROUP LABELS AND STATISTICS

The groups are labeled this way:

No-Kill those who answered no, they did not kill in combat in Vietnam OR answered that they "only saw" killing of civilians

Kill those who answered yes, they did kill or thought they killed someone in Vietnam OR that they were "directly involved" in killing of civilians (or prisoners, or women, children and old people).

This appendix is primarily intended for those who are familiar with statistics and interested in checking the numbers. Those who are a little less familiar but still curious on numbers need to know:

- p value measures whether or not a different mean score between two groups is due to chance or is instead statistically significant. It is accounted as not due to chance if below .05.

- "Cohen's d" is a measure of effect size, of how large the difference is. As a rule of thumb, .2 is small, .5 is moderate, and .8 is large. If the difference is not statistically significant, then the effect size is normally not applicable. The size is based on a formula involving the standard deviation, so a value of 1.0 would indicate that the mean averages are one pooled standard deviation apart.

• The use of "n" indicates the number of people in the designated group.

SEVERITY

Table A.1
Overall Mean Scores on PTSD

	Kill mean (n)	No-Kill mean (n)	p value	Cohen's d
Did you kill?	93.4 (621)	71.9 (932)	.000	.97
Exposure to killing civilians	105.6 (272)	79.4 (157)	.000	.86

Note: Measurement for PTSD is the score on the Mississippi Scale plus four items, given to all participants.

BATTLE INTENSITY

Table A.2
PTSD Scores by Self-Rated Battle Intensity

Self-rated level of battle intensity	No-Kill mean (n)	Kill mean (n)	p value	Cohen's d
Almost none	66.47 (175)	73.67 (6)	.250	.48
Light	70.62 (507)	85.53 (118)	.000	.82
Moderate	77.87 (191)	91.04 (284)	.000	.57
Heavy	80.25 (59)	101.35 (212)	.000	.75

Table A.3
Multiple Regressions of Battle Intensity and Killing on PTSD Score

Source	Intensity Beta	Kill Beta	F value	p value	R-Square
Main Set	+.24	+.30	225.27	.00	.225
Clinical Subset	+.28	+.17	28.79	.00	.161
MMPI Subset	+.21	+.15	15.33	.00	.103

Main Set = the entire group, with PTSD measured by the Mississippi Scale plus four items
Clinical Subset = a group of 340 which were pulled out for extensive psychiatric interviews, with PTSD measured by diagnosis of symptoms by the psychiatrists
MMPI Subset = a group of 294 who took the Minnesota Multiphasic Personality Inventory, with PTSD measured by the MMPI subscale on PTSD.
The three different groups were used to cross-validate with different kinds of measurement. In all cases, it is clear that once self-rated memory of battle intensity is controlled, killing adds additional explanation for PTSD scores.

Table A.4
Multiple Regressions of Battle Intensity and Killing on Factors of the PTSD Score

Factor	Intensity Beta	Kill Beta	F value	p value	R-Square
intrusion	+.28	+.28	240.87	.00	.237
alienation	+.06	+.19	30.23	.00	.049
suicidality	+.06	*	5.35	.00	.003
temper	*	+.18	52.86	.00	.033
concentration	*	−.06	6.52	.01	.004
sleep problems	+.15	+.13	48.48	.00	.059

Additional items, an associated but separate scale other than PTSD:

dissociation	+.15	+.46	32.67	.00	.178

*Did not enter

For an explanation of factors, see the section on factor analysis, below. The dissociation scale was derived by adding items CF14A through CF14H, dealing with dissociation both at the time of event (event unknown) and currently.

MINNESOTA MULTIPHASIC PERSONALITY INVENTORY

Table A.5
Comparison of MMPI Subscales

MMPI Subscale	Kill (n = 130)	No-Kill (n = 156)	p value	Cohen's d
SI-Social Introversion	54.20	53.49	.534	N/A
PA-Paranoia	60.54	56.45	.003	.36
D-Depression	60.57	56.69	.038	.25
L-Lie	51.43	51.36	.000	N/A
F-Infrequency	62.00	54.37	.000	.60
K-Defensiveness	53.79	58.49	.000	.47
HS-Hypochondriasis	61.22	55.25	.000	.49
HY-Hysteria	60.68	56.94	.003	.36
PD-Psychopathic Deviate	64.11	60.07	.003	.36
MF-Masculinity-Femininity	57.86	52.78	.000	.52
PT-Psychasthenia	61.42	55.62	.000	.46
SC-Schizophrenia	66.54	57.10	.000	.57
MA-Hypmania	60.67	54.41	.000	.52

SUBSTANCE ABUSE DIFFERENCES

Table A.6
Substance Abuse

	Kill mean (n)	No-Kill (n)	*p* value	Cohen's d
Cannabis	1.35 (153)	1.17 (175)	.009	.29
Opioid	1.16 (152)	1.03 (175)	.002	.34
Alcohol	1.90 (157)	1.49 (174)	.000	.45

Note: These were all done in the clinical subset of 340, who were pulled out for more extensive
psychiatric interviews. Scores are based on the psychiatrist's assessment and could range
from 1 to 3.

RACIAL DIFFERENCES

Table A.7
PTSD Scores by Race

	Black mean (n)	White mean (n)	*p* value	Cohen's d
Did you kill?	96.7 (163)	91.4 (469)	.029	.2
Exposure to killing civilians	107.1 (69)	103.2 (180)	.322	–

PATTERN DIFFERENCES: RESULTS OF DISCRIMINANT FUNCTION ANALYSIS

In summary, Discriminant Function Analysis showed:

YES ON KILLING:
Especially high:
   violent outbursts
   intrusive symptoms
Also high:
   hyperarousal
   alienation
   survivor guilt
   sense of disintegration.
NO ON KILLING:
High:
   concentration problems
   memory problems.

Table A.8
Discriminant Function Analysis for Entire Group

		Predicted No-Kill	Predicted Kill
Group No-Kill	n = 953	749 (78.6%)	204 (21.4%)
Group Kill	n = 625	195 (32.4%)	430 (68.8%)

Percent of group correctly classified: 74.71%

Centroids:
Group 1 (No-Kill):   −.54265
Group 2 (Kill):   +.81440

Step	Item	Function Coefficient
1	certain things did in military never tell	+.46
2	if pushed too far, likely become violent	+.32
3	have nightmares of military experience	+.35
4	have cried for no good reason	−.27
5	wonder why alive when others died in military	+.30
6	feel superalert—on guard most of time	+.17
7	had more close friends before military	+.15
8	have trouble concentrating on tasks	−.12
9	lately feel like killing myself	−.11

Note: Centroids are similar to mean averages, but a more complicated calculation for the entire group. A positive function coefficient means that the item loads on the group that has the positive centroid, and a negative function coefficient means that it loads on the group with the negative centroid. In this case, items in steps 4, 8, and 9 are more characteristic of the No-Kill group, and the remaining items are as a matter of pattern more characteristic of the Kill group.

Table A.9
Discriminant Function Analysis for Entire Group, "Directly Involved" Removed

In this analysis, those "Directly Involved" in atrocities were removed from the Kill group. This presumably leaves those who killed in more traditional-combat scenarios.

		Predicted No-Kill	Predicted Kill
Group No-Kill	n = 920	699 (76.0%)	221 (24.0%)
Group Kill	n = 395	128 (32.4%)	267 (67.6%)

Percent of group correctly classified: 73.46%

Centroids
Group 1 (No-Kill):   −.35341
Group 2 (Kill):   +.80843

Table A.9 (continued)

Step	Item	Function Coefficient
1	certain things did in military never tell	+.42
2	if pushed too far, likely become violent	+.34
3	have nightmares of military experience	+.35
4	have cried for no good reason	−.33
5	wonder why alive when others died	+.30
6	feel superalert—on guard most of time	+.23
7	memory as good as ever, reversed	−.18
8	had more close friends before military	+.19
9	lately feel like killing myself	−.15

Note: The analysis was almost the same as in Table A.8. The same items loaded, except that a reverse-scored statement that "memory was as good as ever" replaced "trouble concentrating on tasks" and came seventh in order. Coefficients were very close. See note at end of Table A.8 on interpreting centroids and coefficients.

Table A.10
Discriminant Function Analysis for Exposure to Non-combatant Killing

The group that said they had never killed but did see non-combatants killed are compared here with those who said they were "directly involved" in such killing. Both were subjected to the same kind of trauma, with the difference being witnessing versus participating. Those who killed in other contexts are not included, in order to make a clear-cut distinction. The item "certain things did in military never tell" was removed; it is not clearly a PTSD symptom and overpowered the analysis.

		Predicted Only Saw	Predicted Involved
Group Saw	n = 153	121 (79.1%)	32 (20.9%)
Group Involved	n = 269	71 (26.4%)	198 (73.6%)

Percent of group correctly classified: 75.59%

Centroids:
Group 1 (Saw):   −78691
Group 2 (Involved):   +.44711

Step	Item	Function Coefficient
1	have nightmares of military experience	+.28
2	if pushed too far, likely become violent	+.36
3	times when used alcohol, drugs to sleep	+30
4	feel comfortable when in a crowd (reverse)	+.26
5	have trouble concentrating on tasks	−34
6	stay away from things remind me of military	+.27
7	feel superalert—on guard most of time	+.22

See note at end of Table A.8 on how to interpret centroids and coefficients.

Table A.11
Discriminant Function Analysis for Killing of Different Kinds

In this set, both groups answered yes on killing and both were exposed to non-combatant killing. The comparison is between those who only saw the non-combatant killing and those who were directly involved in it, according to self-report.

		Predicted Saw	Predicted Involved
Group Saw	n = 225	139 (61.8%)	86 (38.2%)
Group Inv	n = 234	69 (29.5%)	165 (71.5%)

Percent of group correctly classified: 66.23%

Centroids:
Group 1 (Saw):   −.42301
Group 2 (Involved):   +.41188

Step	Item	Function Coefficient
1	dreams so real waken in sweat & stay awake	+.52
2	certain things did in military never tell	+.65

In the following set, the groups are the same as for above. Both are shown because the difference is instructive, as discussed in Chapter 2. The item "certain things did in military never tell" was removed because it is not clearly a PTSD symptom and overpowered the analysis.

		Predicted Saw	Predicted Involved
Group Saw	n = 225	163 (72.4%)	62 (27.6%)
Group Inv	n = 271	115 (42.4%)	156 (57.6%)

Percent of group correctly classified: 64.31%

Centroids:
Group 1 (Saw):   −.36393
Group 2 (Involved):   +.30603

Step	Item	Function Coefficient
1	dreams so real waken in sweat & stay awake	+.59
2	certain sit make me feel back in military	+.34
3	unexpected noises make me jump	+.33

Table A.12
Discriminant Function Analysis Comparing Lifetime vs. Current

These two analyses are on different items from the same people, who were drawn from a subset of the whole group and given psychiatric interviews. The first shows a report of lifetime symptoms, and the second lists those symptoms that were currently being suffered at the time of the interview. This was done to test an observation of deteriorating intrusive imagery. As discussed in Chapter 2, this way of measuring it did not confirm the observation.

Table A.12 (continued)

Life-time symptoms:

		Predicted No-Kill	Predicted Kill
Group No-Kill	n = 148	105 (70.9%)	43 (29.1%)
Group Kill	n = 146	49 (33.6%)	97 (66.4%)

Percent of group correctly classified: 68.71%

Centroids:
Group 1:   −.53007
Group 2:   +.52623

Step	Item	Function Coefficient
1	jumpy, startled by sudden noises	+.45
2	act/feel you're back at that time	+.45
3	wonder why you survived, others didn't	+.40
4	avoid things that remind you of event	−.47
5	watchful even when no reason to be	+.40

Current symptoms:

		Predicted No-Kill	Predicted Kill
Group No-Kill	n = 151	100 (66.2%)	51 (33.8%)
Group Kill	n = 147	53 (36.1%)	94 (63.9%)

Percent of group correctly classified: 65.10%

Centroids:
Group 1:   −.40548
Group 2:   +.41148

Step	Item	Function Coefficient
1	wonder why you survived, others didn't	+.48
2	jumpy, startled by sudden noises	+.53
3	act/feel you're back at that time	+.41

FACTOR ANALYSIS

An exploratory analysis was done in various ways; below is only the result of the factors in the main set, the entire group. The orthogonal rotation was used since there is high inter-correlation between the items.

The first factor analysis of the Mississippi Scale plus four items, using the entire sample of 1,638, had an excellent KMO of .97. It specified six factors, with only sixteen or 2.0% of the correlations being different by more than .05 from the originals. The oblique rotation failed, but the orthogonal rotation yielded strong loadings on all six factors. The AIC table showed all items high, so that there was no need to delete any item; this is not surprising with the KMO already so high. In short, there was an excellent factor solution on the first run, and no need to modify it for improvements on a second run.

The first factor was labeled "intrusion/avoidance/hyperarousal," using the same terms that are ordinarily utilized in discussing PTSD symptomatology. Intrusion symptoms are ordinarily in Cluster B, avoidance part of Cluster C, and hyperarousal one of the items in Cluster D. The items that loaded are: if reminded of military become distressed, have nightmares of military experiences that happened, wonder why alive when others died, certain situations make me feel back in military, dreams so real I waken in sweat and stay awake, daydreams very real and frightening, have cried for no good reason, frightened by urges, unexpected noises make me jump, certain things did in military never tell, times when use alcohol or drugs to sleep, afraid to go to sleep at night, stay away from things remind me of military, feel things happened in military reoccurring, feel superalert—on guard most of time, and when reminded of military get anxious/panicky.

The second factor was labeled "alienation/deadened feelings." These are part of Cluster C. The items were: had more close friends before military than now, able to get emotionally close to others (reverse-scored), seems as if I have no feelings, don't laugh/cry at same things others do, still enjoy doing things used to do (reverse-scored), enjoy company of others (reverse-scored), no one understands how I feel, feel comfortable when in a crowd (reverse-scored), and hard time expressing feelings to people.

The third factor was labeled "suicidality." It included these items: think of X in military, wish I were dead; lately feel like killing myself; and I feel like I cannot go on. Suicidality is not actually part of the official definition, but is often associated with PTSD.

The fourth factor was labeled "temper." Its items were: if pushed too far, likely become violent; people who know me best are afraid of me; easygoing even-tempered person (reverse-scored); and lose cool and explode over minor things.

The fifth factor involved concentration and memory problems. Items loading highest here were: have trouble concentrating on tasks, memory is as good as ever (reverse-scored), and not able to remember things from military.

Finally, the sixth factor's theme was a little harder to label, but still had four items that loaded highest on it, involving sleep problems and trouble keeping a job: no guilt over things done in military (reverse-scored), fall and stay asleep/wake only with alarm (reverse-scored), easy to keep job since separated from military (reverse-scored), and fall asleep easily at night (reverse-scored).

There were no substantial differences in how the factors came out when a separate factor analysis was run for those who said they killed and another for those who said they did not. Discriminant function analyses using the factors rather than individual items were consistent with the findings for individual items. All factors loaded on the side of those who killed, with the exception of concentration and memory problems, which entered on the side of those who said they did not. Multiple regressions using the factors as dependent variables so that the effect of battle intensity could be separated out from the variable of killing are shown in Table A.4.

Bibliography

American Psychiatric Association. (1987). *Diagnostic and statistical manual of mental disorders* (3rd ed., revised). Washington, DC: Author.

———. (1994). *Diagnostic and statistical manual of mental disorders* (4th ed.). Washington, DC: Author.

Antonovsky, A. (1979). *Health, stress, and coping.* San Francisco: Jossey-Bass Publishers.

Arluke, A. (1991). Going into the closet with science: Information control among animal experimenters. *Journal of Contemporary Ethnography, 20,* 306–330.

Atholl, J. (1954). *Shadow of the gallows.* London: John Long Limited.

———. (1956). *The reluctant hangman: The story of James Berry, executioner 1884–1892.* London: John Long Limited.

Bandura, A., Barbanelli, C., Caprara, G.V., & Pastorelli, C. (1996). Mechanisms of moral disengagement in the exercise of moral agency. *Journal of Personality and Social Psychology, 71,* 364–374.

Barnard, G.W., Hankins, G.C., & Robbins, L. (1992). Prior life trauma, post-traumatic stress symptoms, sexual disorders, and character traits in sex offenders: An exploratory study. *Journal of Traumatic Stress, 5,* 393–420.

Barry, J. (Ed.). (1981). *Peace is our profession.* Montclair, NJ: Faculty Press.

Bauman, Z. (1989). *Modernity and the Holocaust.* Ithaca, NY: Cornell University Press.

Bearden, C. (1994). The nightmare: Biological and psychological origins. *Dreaming Journal of the Association for the Study of Dreams, 4,* 139–152.

Beckham, J.C., Feldman, M.E., & Kirby, A.C. (1998). Atrocities exposure in Vietnam combat veterans with chronic Posttraumatic Stress Disorder: Relationship to combat exposure, symptom severity, guilt, and interpersonal violence. *Journal of Traumatic Stress, 11,* 777–784.

Bezwinska, J., & Czech, D. (Eds.). (1972). *KL Auschwitz seen by SS: Hoess, Broad, Kremer*. Panstwowe Muzeum w Osweicimiu, Poland.

Blass, T. (2000). *Obedience to authority: Current perspectives on the Milgram paradigm*. Mahwah, NJ: Lawrence Erlbaum Associates.

Bourke, J. (1999). *An intimate history of killing: Face-to-face killing in twentieth-century warfare*. Great Britain: Granta Books.

Bremner, J.D., Randall, P., Scott, T.M., Bronen, R.A., Seibyl, J.P., Southwick, S.M., Delaney, R.C., McCarthy, G., Gharney, D.S., & Innis, R.B. (1995). MRI-based measurement of hippocampal volume in patients with combat-related Posttraumatic Stress Disorder. *American Journal of Psychiatry, 152*, 973–981.

Brennan, W. (1995). *Dehumanizing the vulnerable: When word games take lives*. Chicago: Loyola University Press.

Breslau, N., & Davis, G.C. (1987). Posttraumatic Stress Disorder: The etiologic specificity of wartime stressors. *American Journal of Psychiatry, 144*, 578–583.

Breslau, N., Davis, G.C., Andreski, P., & Peterson, E. (1991). Traumatic events and Posttraumatic Stress Disorder in an urban population of young adults. *Archives of General Psychiatry, 48*, 216–222.

Briere, J. (1997). *Psychological assessment of adult posttraumatic states*. Washington, DC: American Psychological Association.

Browning, C.R. (1992). *Ordinary men: Reserve Police Battalion 101 and the Final Solution in Poland*. New York: HarperCollins.

Cabana, D.A. (1996). *Death at midnight: The confession of an executioner*. Boston: Northeastern University Press.

Carson, S. (1982). Post-shooting stress reaction. *The Police Chief*, October, 66–68.

Christie, R., & Geis, F. (1970). *Studies in Machiavellianism*. New York: Academic Press.

Collins, J.J., & Bailey, S.L. (1990). Traumatic stress disorder and violent behavior. *Journal of Traumatic Stress, 3*, 203–220.

Conway, L.G., Suedfeld, P., & Tetlock, P.E. (2001). Integrative complexity and political decisions that lead to war or peace. In D.J. Christie, R.V. Wagner, & D.D. Winter (Eds.), *Peace, conflict, and violence: Peace psychology for the 21st century*. Upper Saddle River, NJ: Prentice-Hall.

Dagan, Y., Lavie, P., & Bleich, A. (1991). Elevated awakening thresholds in sleep state 3–4 in war-related Post-traumatic Stress Disorder. *Biological Psychiatry, 30*, 618–622.

Dalton, J.E., Aubuchon, I., Agnes, T., & Pederson, S.L. (1993). MBTI profiles of Vietnam veterans with Post-traumatic Stress Disorder. *Journal of Psychological Type, 26*, 3–8.

Dateline NBC. (2000). *NYPD Blues* (transcript), December 26. Livingston, NJ: Burrelle's Information Services.

Davis, G.C., & Breslau, N. (1994). Post-traumatic Stress Disorder in victims of civilian trauma and criminal violence. *Psychiatric Clinics of North America, 17*, 289–299.

Domhoff, G.W. (1996). *Finding meaning in dreams: A quantitative approach*. New York: Plenum Press.

Dostoevsky, F. (n.d.). *Notes from the House of the Dead*, C. Garnett (Trans.). New York: Grove Press.

Durkheim, E. (1951). *Suicide: A study in sociology*. Glencoe, IL: Free Press.

Dutton, D.G. (1995). Trauma symptoms and PTSD-like profiles in perpetrators of intimate abuse. *Journal of Traumatic Stress, 8*, 299–316.

Esposito, K., Benitez, A., Barza, L., & Mellman, T. (1999). Evaluation of dream content in combat-related PTSD. *Journal of Traumatic Stress, 132*, 681–687.

Everett, C., & Shaw, J. (1992). *Blood money.* Oregon: Multnomah Press Books.

Fanon, F. (1968). *The wretched of the earth.* New York: Grove Press, Inc.

Foa, E.B., & Meadows, E.A. (1997). Psychosocial treatments for Posttraumatic Stress Disorder: A critical review. *Annual Review of Psychology, 48*, 449–480.

Foa, E.B., Riggs, D.S., & Gershuny, B.S. (1995). Arousal, numbing, and intrusion: Symptom structure of PTSD following assault. *American Journal of Psychiatry, 152*, 116–120.

Follette, V.M., Polusny, M.M., & Milbeck, K. (1994). Mental health and law enforcement professionals: Trauma history, psychological symptoms, and impact of providing services to child sexual abuse survivors. *Professional Psychology: Research and Practice, 3*, 275–282.

Fontana, A., & Rosenheck, R. (1995). Attempted suicide among Vietnam veterans: A model of etiology in a community sample. *American Journal of Psychiatry, 152*, 102–109.

———. (1999). A model of war zone stressors and Posttraumatic Stress Disorder. *Journal of Traumatic Stress, 12*, 111–126.

Frances, A., First, M.B., & Pincus, H.A. (1995). *DSM-IV Guidebook.* Washington, DC: American Psychiatric Press.

Freinkel, A., Koopman, C., & Spiegel, D. (1994). Dissociative symptoms in media eyewitnesses of an execution. *American Journal of Psychiatry, 151*, 1335–1339.

Funder, D.C. (1997). *The personality puzzle.* New York: W.W. Norton.

Gaudium et Spes [Constitution of the Church in the Modern World]. (1965). Rome: Second Vatican Council.

Gianelli, D.M. (1993). Abortion providers share inner conflicts. *American Medical News*, July 12.

Glover, H. (1985). Guilt and aggression in Vietnam veterans. *American Journal of Social Psychiatry, 1*, 15–18.

———. (1988). Four syndromes of Post-traumatic Stress Disorder: Stressors and conflicts of the traumatized with special focus on the Vietnam combat veteran. *Journal of Traumatic Stress, 1*, 57–78.

Goffman, E. (1963). *Stigma: Notes on the management of spoiled identity.* Englewood Cliffs, NJ: Prentice-Hall.

Goldsmith, S., Kaltreider, N.B., & Margolis, A.J. (1977). Second trimester abortion by dilation and extraction (D and E) surgical techniques and psychological reactions. Unpublished paper.

Green, B.L. (1990). Defining trauma: Terminology and generic stressor dimensions. *Journal of Applied Social Psychology, 20*, 1632–1642.

Greenberg, R., Pearlman, C.A., & Gampel, D. (1972). War neuroses and the adaptive function of REM sleep. *British Journal of Medical Psychology, 45*, 27–33.

Grossman, D. (1995). *On killing: The psychological cost of learning to kill in war and society.* Boston: Little, Brown and Company.

Haley, S.A. (1974). When the patient reports atrocities. *Archives of General Psychiatry, 30*, 191–196.

Hall, H.V., & Hall, F.L. (1987). Post-traumatic Stress Disorder as a legal defense in criminal trials. *American Journal of Forensic Psychology, 5*, 45–53.

Hallet, S.J. (1996). Trauma and coping in homicide and sexual abuse detectives. Dissertation, California School of Professional Psychology.

Hallock, D. (1998). *Hell, healing, and resistance*. Farmington, PA: The Plough Publishing House.

Hambridge, J.A. (1994). Treating mentally abnormal killers in a regional secure unit: Some suggested guidelines. *Medicine, Science and the Law, 34*, 237–241.

Haney, C. (2000). Reflections on the Stanford Prison experiment: Genesis, transformations, consequences. In T. Blass (Ed.), *Obedience to authority: Current perspectives on the Milgram paradigm* (pp. 193–237). Mahwah, NJ: Lawrence Erlbaum Associates.

Harrower, M. (1976). Rorschach records of the Nazi war criminals: An experimental study after thirty years. *Journal of Personality Assessment, 40*, 341–351.

Hartmann, E. (1996). Who develops PTSD nightmares and who doesn't. In D. Barrett (Ed.), *Trauma and dreams* (pp. 100–113). Cambridge, MA: Harvard University Press.

Hefez, A., Metz, L., & Lavie, P. (1987). Long-term effects of extreme situational stress on sleep and dreaming. *American Journal of Psychiatry, 144*, 344–347.

Hendin, H. (1997). *Seduced by death: Doctors, patients, and the Dutch cure*. New York: W.W. Norton.

Hendin, H., & Haas, A.P. (1984). *Wounds of war: The psychological aftermath of combat in Vietnam*. New York: Basic Books.

———. (1985). Posttraumatic Stress Disorders in veterans of early America. *Psychohistory Review, 12*, 25–30.

Herman, J.L. (1992). Complex PTSD: A syndrome in survivors of prolonged and repeated trauma. *Journal of Traumatic Stress, 5*, 377–391.

Hern, W.M., & Corrigan, B. (1978). What about us? Staff reactions to the D and E procedure. Presented at the 1978 meeting of the Association of Planned Parenthood Physicians, San Diego, October 26.

Herzog, H. (n.d.). Human morality and animal research: Confessions and quandaries. Unpublished paper. Cullowhee, NC: Western Carolina University.

Hilberg, R. (1961). *The destruction of European Jews*. Chicago: Quadrangle Books.

Hiley-Young, B., Blake, D.D., Abueg, F.R., Rozynko, V., & Dusman, F.D. (1995). War zone violence in Vietnam: An examination of premilitary, military, and postmilitary factors of PTSD in-patients. *Journal of Traumatic Stress, 8*, 125–140.

Hodge, J.E. (1997). Addiction to violence. In J.E. Hodge, M. McMurran, & C.R. Hollin (Eds.), *Addicted to crime?* New York: John Wiley & Sons.

Hoess, R. (1959). *Commandant of Auschwitz: The autobiography of Rudolf Hoess*, C. FitzGibbon (Trans.). London: Weidenfeld and Nicolson.

Hohne, H. (1969). *The order of death's hand: The story of Hitler's SS*, R. Barry (Trans.). Mcann, NY: Coward.

Hovens, J.E., Falger, P.R.J., Op De Velde, W., Meijer, P., De Groen, J.H.M., & Van Duijn, H. (1993). A self-rating scale for the assessment of Posttraumatic Stress Disorder in Dutch Resistance veterans of World War II. *Journal of Clinical Psychology, 49*, 196–203.

Hyer, L., Davis, H., Albrecht, W., Boudewyns, P., & Woods, G. (1994). Cluster analysis of MCMI and MCMI-II on chronic PTSD victims. *Journal of Clinical Psychology, 50*, 502–515.

Hyer, L., Davis, H., Woods, G., Albrecht, J.W., & Boudewyns, P. (1992). Relationship between the Millon Clinical Multiaxial Inventory and the Millon II value of scales for aggressive and self-defeating personalities in Posttraumatic Stress Disorder. *Psychological Reports, 71*, 867–879.

Hyer, L., Woods, G., & Boudewyns, P. (1991). A three-tier evaluation among chronic veterans. *Journal of Traumatic Stress, 4*, 165–194.

Jancin, B. (1981). Emotional turmoil of physicians, staff held biggest D and E problem. *ObGyn News, 16*, 15–31.

Janoff-Bulman, R. (1985). The aftermath of victimization: Rebuilding shattered assumptions. In C. Figley (Ed.), *Trauma and its wake: The study and treatment of Posttraumatic Stress Disorder* (pp. 14–35). New York: Brunner/Mazel.

Johnson, B. (1995). Narcissistic personality as a mediating variable in manifestations of Post-traumatic Stress Disorder. *Military Medicine, 160*, 40–41.

Johnson, E.C. (1960). *Jane Addams: A centennial reader*. New York: The Macmillan Company.

Johnson, R. (1998). *Death work: A study of the modern execution process*. Belmont, CA: Wadsworth.

Kaltreider, N.B., Goldsmith, S., & Margolis, A.J. (1979). The impact of midtrimester abortion techniques on patients and staff. *American Journal of Obstetrics and Gynecology, 135*, 235–238.

Keane, T.M., Caddell, J.M., & Taylor, K.L. (1988). Mississippi scale for combat-related Posttraumatic Stress Disorder: Three studies in reliability and validity. *Journal of Consulting and Clinical Psychology, 56*, 85–90.

Kibel, H.D. (1972). Editorial: Staff reactions to abortion. *Obstetrics and Gynecology, 39*, 1.

King, D.W., King, L.A., Gudanowski, D.M., & Vreven, D.L. (1995). Alternative representations of war zone stressors: Relationships to Posttraumatic Stress Disorder in male and female Vietnam veterans. *Journal of Abnormal Psychology, 104*, 184–196.

Koepp, M.J., Gunn, R.N., Lawrence, A.D., Cunningham, V.J., Dagher, A., Jones, T., Brooks, D.J., Bench, C.J., & Grasby, P.M. (1998). Evidence for striatal dopamine release during a video game. *Nature, 393*, 266–268.

Kruppa, I. (1991). The perpetrator suffers too. *The Psychologist, 4*, 401–403.

Kruppa, I., Hickey, N., & Hubbard, C. (1995). The prevalence of Post Traumatic Stress Disorder in a special hospital population of legal psychopaths. *Psychology, Crime & Law, 2*, 131–141.

Kulka, R.A., Schlenger, W.E., Fairbank, J.A., Hough, R.L., Jordan, B.K., Marmar, C.R., & Weiss, D.S. (1990). *Trauma and the Vietnam war generation: Report on the findings from the National Vietnam Veterans Readjustment Study*. New York: Brunner/Mazel.

Lansky, M.R. & Bley, C.R. (1995). *Posttraumatic nightmares: Psychodynamic explorations*. Hillsdale, NJ: The Analytic Press.

Lasko, N.B., Gurvits, T.V., Kuhne, A.A., Orr, S.P., & Pitman, R.K. (1994). Aggression and its correlates in Vietnam veterans with and without chronic Posttraumatic Stress Disorder. *Comprehensive Psychiatry, 35*, 373–381.

Laufer, R.S., Brett, E., & Gallops, M.S. (1985a). Symptom patterns associated with Posttraumatic Stress Disorder among Vietnam veterans exposed to war trauma. *American Journal of Psychiatry, 142*, 1304–1311.

————. (1985b). Dimensions of Posttraumatic Stress Disorder among Vietnam veterans. *Journal of Nervous and Mental Disease, 173*, 538–545.

Laufer, R.S., Gallops, M.S., & Frey-Wouters, E. (1984). War stress and trauma: The Vietnam veteran experience. *Journal of Health and Social Behavior, 25*, 65–85.

Lavie, P., Hefez, A., Halperin, G., & Enoch, D. (1979). Long-term effects of traumatic war-related events on sleep. *American Journal of Psychiatry, 236*, 175–178.

Lavie, P., & Hertz, G. (1979). Increased sleep motility and respiration rates in combat neurotic patients. *Biological Psychiatry, 14*, 983–987.

Lee, K.A., Vaillant, G.E., Torrey, W.C., & Elder, G.H. (1995). A 50-year prospective study of the psychological sequelae of World War II combat. *American Journal of Psychiatry, 152*, 516–522.

Leo, J. (2001). Kerrey Agonistes: Is the ex-senator baring his soul and spinning his story? *U. S. News & World Report*, May 7.

Levin, P. (1993). Assessing Posttraumatic Stress Disorder with the Rorschach projective technique. In J.P. Wilson, & B. Raphael (Eds.), *International handbook of traumatic stress syndromes* (pp. 189–200). New York: Plenum.

Lifton, R.J. (1986). *The Nazi doctors: Medical killing and the psychology of genocide.* New York: Basic Books.

————. (1990). Adult dreaming: Frontiers of form. In R.A. Neminoff, & C.A. Colarusso (Eds.), *New dimensions in adult development* (pp. 419–442). New York: Basic Books.

Lisak, D. (2000). Can murder traumatize the murderer? Answers from death row. Paper presented at the 108th Annual Convention of the American Psychological Association, Washington, DC.

Litz, B.T., Keane, T.M., Fisher, L., & Marx, B. (1992). Physical health complaints in combat-related Post-traumatic Stress Disorder: A preliminary report. *Journal of Traumatic Stress, 5*, 131–141.

Loo, R. (1986). Post-shooting stress reactions among police officers. *Journal of Human Stress, 12*, 27–31.

Lund, M., Foy, D., Sipprelle, C., & Strachan, A. (1984). The combat exposure scale: A systematic assessment of trauma in the Vietnam War. *Journal of Clinical Psychology, 40*, 1323–1328.

Lunnenborg, P. (1992). *Abortion, a positive decision.* New York: Bergin & Garvey.

MacNair, R.M. (1999). *Symptom pattern differences for Perpetration-Induced Traumatic Stress in veterans: Probing the National Vietnam Veterans Readjustment Study.* Doctoral dissertation, University of Kansas City, MO.

Mann, J.P., & Neece, J. (1990). Workers' compensation for law enforcement related Posttraumatic Stress Disorder. *Behavioral Sciences and the Law, 8*, 447–456.

Manolias, M.B., & Hyatt-Williams, A. (1993). Effects of postshooting experiences on police-authorized firearms officers in the United Kingdom. In J.P. Wilson, & B. Raphael (Eds.), *International handbook of traumatic stress syndromes* (pp. 386–394). New York: Plenum Press.

Marmar, C.R., Weiss, D.S., Metzler, T.J., & Delucchi, K. (1996). Characteristics of emergency services personnel related to peritraumatic dissociation during critical incident exposure. *American Journal of Psychiatry, 153*, 94–102.

Marmar, C.R., Weiss, D.S., Schlenger, W.E., Fairbank, J.A., Jordan, B.K., Kulka, R.A., & Hough, R.L. (1994). Peritraumatic dissociation and posttraumatic stress in male Vietnam theater veterans. *American Journal of Psychiatry, 151*, 902–907.

Marsella, A.J., Friedman, M.J., Gerrity, E.T., Scurfield, R.M. (1996). *Ethnocultural as-pects of Posttraumatic Stress Disorder*. Washington, DC: American Psychological Association.

Marshall, R.D., Olfson, M., Hellman, F., Blanco, C., Guardino, M., & Struening, E. (2001). Comorbidity, impairment, and suicidality in subthreshold PTSD. *American Journal of Psychiatry, 158*, 1467–1473.

Martin, C.A., McKean, H.E., & Vetkamp, L.J. (1986). Posttraumatic Stress Disorder in police and working with victims: A pilot study. *Journal of Police Science and Administration, 14*, 98–101.

Martin, G.N. (1993). A warden's reflections: Enforcing the death penalty with compe-tence, compassion. *Corrections Today,* July, 60, 62, 64.

McHoskey, J.W., Worzel, W., & Szyarto, C. (1998). Machiavellianism and psychopathy. *Journal of Personality and Social Psychology, 74*, 192–210.

Mead, G.H. (1967). *Mind, self, and society*. Chicago: University of Chicago Press.

Merton, R.K. (1996). Manifest and latent functions (1949). In P. Sztompka (Ed.), *On social structure and science*. Chicago: University of Chicago Press.

Miale, F.R., & Selzer, M. (1975). *The Nuremberg mind*. New York: Quadrangle.

Milgram, S. (1974). *Obedience to authority: An experimental view*. New York: Harper & Row.

Nadelson, T.N. (1992). Attachment to killing. *Journal of the American Academy of Psy-choanalysis, 20*, 130–141.

Nader, K.O., Pynoos, R.S., Fairbanks, L.A., Al-Ajeel, M., & Al-Asfour, A. (1993). A preliminary study of PTSD and grief among the children of Kuwait following the Gulf crisis. *British Journal of Clinical Psychology, 32*, 407–416.

Nathanson, B.N. (1979). *Aborting America*. Toronto: Life Cycle Books.

Neilson, E. (1981). The law enforcement officer's use of deadly force and post-shooting trauma. Dissertation, University of Utah.

Nietzsche, F. (1967). *Thus Spake Zarathustra*. New York: Heritage Press.

ObGyn News. (1986). Warns of negative psychological impact of sonography in abortion. February, 15–28.

Orr, S.P., Claiborn, J.M., Altman, B., Forgue, D.F., de Jong, J.B., & Pitman, R.K. (1990). Psychometric profile of Posttraumatic Stress Disorder, anxious and healthy Vi-etnam veterans: Correlations with psychophysiologic responses. *Journal of Con-sulting and Clinical Psychology, 3*, 329–335.

Orr, S.P., & Pitman R.K. (1993). Psychophysiologic assessment of attempts to simulate Posttraumatic Stress Disorder. *Biological Psychiatry, 33*, 127–129.

Owen, W. (1963). Insensibility. In C.D. Lewis (Ed.), *The Collected Poems of Wilfred Owen* (pp. 37–38). Great Britain: Chatto & Windus, Ltd.

Piekarski, A.M., & Sherwood, R. (1993). Personality subgroups in an inpatient Vietnam veteran treatment program. *Psychological Reports, 72*, 667–674.

Pitman, R.K., Altman, B., Greenwald, E., Longpre, R.E., Macklin, M.L., Poire, R.E., & Steketee, G.S. (1991). Psychiatric complications during flooding therapy for Post-traumatic Stress Disorder. *Journal of Clinical Psychiatry, 52*, 17–20.

Poe, E.A. (1845/1978). The imp of the perverse. In T.O. Mabbot (Ed.), *Collected works of Edgar Allen Poe and sketches 1843–1849, vol. 3* (pp. 1224–1226). Cambridge, MA: Belknap Press of Harvard University Press.

Pollock, P.H. (1999). When the killer suffers: Post-traumatic stress reactions following homicide. *Legal and Criminological Psychology, 4*, 185–202.

————. (2000). Eye movement desensitization and reprocessing (EMDR) for Post-traumatic Stress Disorder (PTSD) following homicide. *Journal of Forensic Psychiatry, 11*, 176–184.

Pro-Life Action League. (1989). [Videotape]. *Meet the abortion providers*. Chicago: Author.

————. (1993). [Audiotape]. *Meet the abortion providers III: The promoters*. Chicago: Author.

Reed, A.L. (2001). Bob Kerrey, an American shame. *The Progressive*, June 16.

Resnick, M.N., & Nunno, V.J. (1991). The Nuremberg mind redeemed: A comprehensive analysis of the Rorschachs of Nazi war criminals. *Journal of Personality Assessment, 57*, 19–29.

Ritzler, B.A. (1978). The Nuremberg mind revisited: A quantitative approach to Nazi Rorschachs. *Journal of Personality Assessment, 42*, 344–353.

Ritzler, B.A., Zillmer, E., & Belevich, A. (1993). Comprehensive system scoring discrepancies on Nazi Rorschachs: A comment. *Journal of Personality Assessment, 61*, 576–583.

Roe, K.M. (1989). Private troubles and public issues: Providing abortion amid competing definitions. *Social Science and Medicine, 29*, 1191–1198.

Rogers, P., Gray, N.S., Williams, T., & Kitchiner, N. (2000). Behavioral treatment of PTSD in a perpetrator of manslaughter: A single case study. *Journal of Traumatic Stress, 13*, 511–519.

Ross, R.J., Ball, W.A., Dinges, D.F., Kribbs, N.B., Norrison, A.R., Silver, S.M., & Mulvaney, F.D. (1994). Rapid eye movement sleep disturbance in Posttraumatic Stress Disorder. *Biological Psychiatry, 35*, 195–202.

Ross, R.J., Ball, W.A., Sullivan, K.A., & Caroff, S.N. (1989). Sleep disturbance as a hallmark of Posttraumatic Stress Disorder. *American Journal of Psychiatry, 146*, 697–707.

Rottman, L., Barry, J., & Paquet, B.T. (Eds.). (1972). *Winning hearts and minds: War poems by Vietnam veterans*. New York: McGraw-Hill.

Sapolsky, R.M. (1994). *Why zebras don't get ulcers: A guide to stress, stress-related diseases, and coping*. New York: W.H. Freeman and Company.

Schacter, D.L. (1986). Amnesia and crime: How much do we really know? *American Psychologist, 41*, 286–295.

Schnurr, P.P., Friedman, M.J., & Rosenberg, S.D. (1993). Preliminary MMPI scores as predictors of combat-related PTSD symptoms. *American Journal of Psychiatry, 150*, 479–483.

Shapiro, F. (1995). *Eye movement desensitization and reprocessing: Basic principles, protocols, and procedures*. London: Guilford Press.

Shatan, C. (1978). Stress disorders among Vietnam veterans: The emotional context of combat continues. In C.R. Figley (Ed.), *Stress disorders among Vietnam veterans: Theory, research, and treatment*. New York: Brunner/Mazel.

Shay, J. (1994). *Achilles in Vietnam: Combat trauma and the undoing of character*. Toronto: Maxwell MacMillan.

Sherwood, R., Funari, D.J., & Piekarski, A.M. (1990). Adapted character styles of Vietnam veterans with Posttraumatic Stress Disorder. *Psychological Reports, 66*, 623–631.

Silva, J.A., Derecho, D.V., Leong, G.B., Weinstock, R., & Ferrari, M.M. (2001). A classification of psychological factors leading to violent behavior in Posttraumatic Stress Disorder. *Journal of Forensic Sciences, 46*, 309–316.

Silver, S.M., & Iacono, C.U. (1984). Factor-analytic support for DSM-III's Posttraumatic Stress Disorder for Vietnam veterans. *Journal of Clinical Psychology, 40*, 5–14.

Silver, S.M., & Wilson, J.P. (1988). Native American healing and purification rituals for war stress. In J.P. Wilson, Z. Harl, & B. Kahana (Eds.), *Human adaptation to extreme stress: From the Holocaust to Vietnam*. New York: Plenum Press.

Simon, W.J. (1972). My country. In L. Rottman, J. Barry, & B.T. Paquet (Eds.), *Winning hearts and minds: War poems by Vietnam veterans* (p. 42). New York: McGraw-Hill.

Sleek, S. (1998). Older vets just now feeling pain of war. *APA Monitor, 29*, 1, 28.

Sloan, D., & Hartz, P. (1992). *Abortion: A doctor's perspective, a woman's dilemma*. New York: Donald I. Fine.

Solomon, Z. (1993). *Combat stress reaction: The enduring toll of war*. New York: Plenum Press.

Solursh, L. (1988). Combat addiction: Post-traumatic Stress Disorder re-explored. *Psychiatric Journal of the University of Ottawa, 13*, 17–20.

———. (1989). Combat addiction: Overview of implications in symptom maintenance and treatment planning. *Journal of Traumatic Stress, 2*, 451–462.

Southwick, S.M., Yehuda, R., & Morgan, C.A. (1995). Clinical studies of neurotransmitter alterations in Post-traumatic Stress Disorder. In M.J. Friedman, D.S. Charney, & A.Y. Deutch (Eds.), *Neurobiological and clinical consequences of stress* (pp. 335–350). Philadelphia: Lippincott-Raven.

Steiner, H., Garcia, I.G., & Matthews, Z. (1997). Post-traumatic Stress Disorder in incarcerated juvenile delinquents. *Journal of the American Academy of Child and Adolescent Psychiatry, 36*, 357–365.

Steiner, J. (1967). *Treblinka*. New York: Simon and Schuster.

Stratton, J.G., Parker, D.A., & Snibbe, J.R. (1984). Post-traumatic stress: Study of police officers involved in shootings. *Psychological Reports, 55*, 127–131.

Strayer, R., & Ellenhorn, L. (1975). Vietnam veterans: A study exploring adjustment patterns and attitudes. *Journal of Social Issues, 31*, 81–93.

Such-Baer, M. (1974). Professional staff reaction to abortion work. *Social Casework*, July, 435–441.

Taylor, S., Koch, W.J., Kuch, K., Crockett, D.J., & Passey, G. (1998). The structure of posttraumatic stress symptoms. *Journal of Abnormal Psychology, 107*, 154–160.

Thigpen, M.L. (1993). A tough assignment. *Corrections Today*, July, 56, 58.

Tisdale, S. (1987). We do abortions here. *Harper's*, October, 66–70.

Trombley, S. (1992). *The execution protocol: Inside America's capital punishment industry*. New York: Crown Publishers.

van der Kolk, B.A., Blitz, R., Burr, W., Sherry, S., & Hartmann, E. (1984). Nightmares and trauma: A comparison of nightmares after combat with lifelong nightmares in veterans. *American Journal of Psychiatry, 141*, 187–190.

van der Kolk, B.A., & Ducey, C.P. (1989). The psychological processing of traumatic experience: Rorschach patterns in PTSD. *Journal of Traumatic Stress, 2*, 259–274.

van der Kolk, B.A., & Fisler, R. (1995). Dissociation and the fragmentary nature of traumatic memories: Overview and exploratory study. *Journal of Traumatic Stress, 8*, 505–525.

van der Kolk, B.A., Greenberg, M., Boyd, H., & Krystal, J. (1985). Inescapable shock, neurotransmitters, and addiction to trauma: Toward a psychobiology of posttraumatic stress. *Biological Psychiatry, 20,* 314–325.

van der Kolk, B.A., McFarlane, A.C., & Weisaeth, L. (Eds.). (1996). *Traumatic stress: The effects of overwhelming experience on mind, body, and society.* New York: Guilford Press.

Van Wyk Smith, M. (1978). *Drummer Hodge: The poetry of the Anglo-Boer War, 1988–1902.* Oxford: Clarendon Press.

Varela, R.E., & Matchinsky, D.J. (1995). Posttraumatic Stress Disorder: Physiological vulnerability and temperament. Unpublished manuscript, Emporia State University, Kansas.

Vasquez, D.B. (1993). Helping prison staff handle the stress of an execution. *Corrections Today,* July, 70, 72.

Vistica, G.L. (2001). What happened in Thanh Phong. *New York Times Magazine,* April 29, 50–57, 66, 68, 133.

Wang, S., Wilson, J.P., & Mason, J.W. (1996). Stages of decompensation in combat-related Posttraumatic Stress Disorder: A new conceptual model. *Integrative Physiological and Behavioral Science, 31,* 237–253.

Weber, M. (1971). *The interpretation of social reality.* New York: Scribner.

Weigl, B. (1985). *The monkey wars.* Atlanta: University of Georgia Press.

White, D. (1998). It's a dog's life. *Psychology Today,* November/December, 10.

Wikler, N. (1980). Hidden injuries of war. In C.R. Figley, & S. Leventman, *Strangers at home: Vietnam veterans since the war* (pp. 87–106). Philadelphia: Brunner/Mazel.

Wilson, J.P., & Zigelbam, S.D. (1983). The Vietnam veteran on trial: The relation of Post-traumatic Stress Disorder to criminal behavior. *Behavioral Sciences and the Law, 1,* 69–82.

World Health Organization. (1992). *International statistical classification of diseases and related health problems* (10th revision). Geneva, Switzerland.

Yager, T., Laufer, R., & Gallops, M. (1984). Some problems associated with war experience in men of the Vietnam generation. *Archives of General Psychiatry, 41,* 327–333.

Young, A. (1995). *The harmony of illusions: Inventing Posttraumatic Stress Disorder.* Princeton: Princeton University Press.

Zillmer, E.A., Archer, R.P., & Castino, R. (1989). Rorschach records of Nazi war criminals: A reanalysis using current scoring and interpretation practices. *Journal of Personality Assessment, 53,* 85–99.

Zillmer, E.A., Harrower, M., Ritzler, B.A., & Archer, R.P. (1995). *The quest for the Nazi personality: A psychological investigation of Nazi war criminals.* Hillsdale, NJ: Lawrence Erlbaum Associates.

Index

About the Author

RACHEL M. MacNAIR is Director of the Institute for Integrated Social Analysis, a research organization specializing in the connections between various social issues of violence.